A major contribution to our knowledge of black politics in South Africa, this book describes the emergence of the first African political organisations and traces their development until 1912 when they merged into a national body — the present-day African National Congress.

The hitherto neglected early history of the black man's struggle for political equality in South Africa is here brought to life. By using untapped archival sources and vernacular newspapers, the author has succeeded in tracing and following some very obscure political movements. He has brought the story to the point at which these organisations can be related to each other, and has demonstrated connections between them which previous scholars like Walshe, Roux, Benson, and Karis and Carter were unable to make. Apart from this bridge-building, the book establishes that it was the National Convention which consolidated black opposition politics and provided the thrust from which the ANC emerged.

At the same time the author presents the essential background to our understanding of contemporary African nationalism. Many of the leaders dealt with — John Dube, S. M. Makgatho, Pixley Seme, T. M. Mapikela and Selope Thema — and many of the prototype movements, were to influence profoundly the course of African politics until well after World War Two.

This study fills an important gap in the political history of South Africa, and will become the standard work of reference for the early history of African political life.

*Jacket and cover illustration: John L. Dube (photo: T. D. Mweli Skota); John Tengo Jabavu and his son, D. D. T.*

# André Odendaal

# Black Protest Politics
# in South Africa to 1912

**BARNES & NOBLE BOOKS**
TOTOWA, NEW JERSEY

Boards edition under the title *Black Protest Politics in South Africa to 1912,* first published in Southern Africa 1984 by David Philip, Publisher (Pty) Ltd, 217 Werdmuller Centre, Claremont, 7700, South Africa; and in the U.S.A. 1984 by Barnes & Noble Books, 81 Adams Drive, Totowa, New Jersey, 07512

Paperback edition under the title *Vukani Bantu!: The Beginnings of Black Protest Politics in South Africa to 1912* first published in Southern Africa 1984 by David Philip, Publisher (Pty) Ltd

ISBN 0-86486-009-9 (David Philip, boards)
ISBN 0-389-20480-3 (Barnes & Noble, boards)
ISBN 0-908396-73-2 (David Philip, paper)

Library of Congress Cataloging in Publication Data

Odendaal, André.
  Black Protest Politics in South Africa to 1912.

  Bibliography: p.
  Includes index.
  1. Blacks—South Africa—Politics and government.
2. South Africa—Politics and government—1836–1909.
3. South Africa—Politics and government—1909–48.
4. Blacks—South Africa—Race identity.   5. Civil
rights movements — South Africa.   I. Title.
DT763.6.O33   1984        323.1'196'068        84-4304
ISBN 0-389-20480-3

Printed by Printpak (Cape) Ltd, Dacres Avenue, Epping, Cape Province, South Africa

# Contents

# Illustrations

# Abbreviations

| | |
|---|---|
| AME | African Methodist Episcopal. |
| ANC | African National Congress. |
| ANPU | African National Political Union. |
| APO | African Political Organisation. |
| BMIA | Becoana Mutual Improvement Association. |
| BPA | Basutoland Progressive Association. |
| CPNA | Cape Peninsula Native Association. |
| NEA | Native Educational Association. |
| NNC | Natal Native Congress. |
| ORCNC | Orange River Colony Native Congress. |
| ORCNTA | Orange River Colony Native Teachers Association. |
| ORCNVA | Orange River Colony Native Vigilance Association. |
| PAC | Pan Africanist Congress. |
| SAAA | South African Aborigines Association. |
| SANAC | South African Native Affairs Commission. |
| SANC* | South African Native Congress. |
| SANC* | South African Native Convention. |
| SANNC | South African Native National Congress. |
| SANPA | South African Native Political Association. |
| SAP | South African Party. |
| TNC | Transvaal Native Congress. |
| TNNU | Transvaal National Natives Union. |
| TNO | Transvaal Native Organisation. |
| TNU | Transvaal Native Union. |
| TNVA* | Transvaal Native Vigilance Association. |
| TNVA* | Transkei Native Vigilance Association. |
| TTGC | Transkeian Territories General Council. |

*These abbreviations are nowhere used where there can be doubt as to which of the organisations is being referred to.

# Notes on terminology

The phrase *'Vukani Bantu!'*, meaning 'Rise up you people!' in Zulu
or Xhosa, was used by members of the early educated African class
in Natal in efforts to galvanise the people into becoming politically
aware and active. Regarded by the Natal government as a dangerous
and seditious invitation to rebellion, the term came to assume an
emotive connotation. Its use contributed in 1903 to the govern-
ment-instigated closure of the first African-controlled newspaper
in Natal, the *Ipepa lo Hlanga*, and three years later the government
threatened to ban its successor, the *Ilanga lase Natal*, for the same
reason. The *Ilanga* again made the *'Vukani Bantu!'* call at the time
of the protests against the draft South Africa Act in 1909. Throughout the period of this study, the African political élite in other
areas of South Africa repeatedly made similar calls to arouse African public opinion and promote organisation. One such example
was the Xhosa expression *'Zemk' Inkomo Magwalandini!'*, meaning
'There go your cattle [i.e. rights], you cowards!', and implying
that Africans should stand together to guard their rights.

Every work on South Africa has to contend with the problem of
terminology. In this book words that have acquired a negative
racial connotation are avoided as far as possible. 'African' is used
as both a noun and an adjective, and refers to the country's
indigenous Bantu-language-speaking inhabitants. The word 'Coloured', referring to people of mixed race, is decapitalised and used
only as an adjective, as in 'coloured population' or 'coloured
people'. The word 'black' is used to describe African, Asiatic and
coloured people collectively. Words that now give offence—non-
European, non-white, kaffir, native, Bantu, Boer, Coloured—
appear in the text only in direct quotations (for example from the
period when Africans themselves spoke of 'non-whites' and had
organisations called 'Native Congresses'), or where the word has
become part of a standard term, as in 'native policy' or 'Anglo–
Boer War'.

Terms such as 'political élite' and 'political consciousness' are used with reference to politics and politicians of the western model. This does not mean that the writer does not recognise the existence of political consciousness among non-literate, tribal Africans, and also what has been called their 'spontaneous contribution to nationalism'. These terms are used merely to describe a different kind of politician and a different form of political consciousness. The new group of educated, westernised Africans was a separate class within a larger racial category, with its own particular interests and ideological forms functional to these interests.

# Preface

This book is intended as a contribution to the still largely unwritten 'African history' of South Africa. It focuses on the new forms of African political consciousness and response that emerged after the incorporation of previously independent, pre-colonial African societies into South African colonial systems in the nineteenth century. Convinced of the futility of traditional methods of resistance to white expansion, some Africans began to adapt to the ways of the conqueror and started to make use of European constitutional methods to protect African interests. The book looks at these beginnings of modern African politics in South Africa; it describes the emergence and development of the first black political organisations and independent newspapers, and shows how these regional interest groups gradually developed common aims and eventually united to form the first national organisation.

To date insufficient detailed research has been done on African organisational politics in the period before the establishment of the Union of South Africa. Scholars in the field, inspired often by events in the ages of decolonisation and apartheid, have been inclined to use the founding of the South African Native National Congress (later simply the African National Congress) in 1912 as the starting point in a description of African nationalist or protest politics in South Africa. This book takes one to that point from the beginning.

The study is mainly about African politics in the former Republics and British colonies that comprise the modern South African state, but at various stages the interests of the African people in these areas became tied up with those of other black groups. Periodically therefore there are fairly lengthy accounts of the political activities of Africans in the Protectorates—present-day Swaziland, Lesotho and Botswana—and those of the coloured and Indian people in South Africa as well.

Among the issues raised by the book I should like to comment on four in particular.

1 There is a long tradition of African political activity in South Africa. A century ago, within a few years of the launching of the *Die Patriot* newspaper and the formation of the Afrikaner Bond, both landmark events in the history of Afrikaner nationalism, Africans too had formed a Bond or *Imbumba* of their own and started an organ for 'Native Opinion'. Thousands also possessed the vote and participated enthusiastically in electoral politics, holding the balance of power in several frontier constituencies. In the South Africa of today many of the rights Africans enjoyed then are circumscribed or have been taken away completely.

2 The changing forms of white political control during the first decade of this century had a marked effect on African politics and significantly influenced its direction. The Anglo–Boer War and the process of South African unification stimulated and consolidated African political organisation, providing the thrust that caused the emergence of a broad African national consciousness and political unity. In this way black unity took shape alongside white unity.

3 The so-called 'school people' or educated élite who participated in the new western forms of politics described here were much more closely tied to their own communities, and much more concerned with traditional matters, than has been realised. They have also been described as naive, unrealistic, timid and conservative, and their strategies as inappropriate and short-sighted, by people writing from a later perspective, but of course their actions should be seen in the context of their time. Their aspirations were valid for their time and place, but their moderate political strategy—informed by a value-system based on pre-industrial African society, the Christian faith and mid-Victorian political liberalism—was overtaken by the great changes that took place in their lifetimes. The fundamental shift to an industrial society, and the failure of political liberalism as reflected in the Union of South Africa, led to changed material conditions—such as urbanisation—and forged new psychological and ideological constructs with which their ideology and strategy could no longer cope.

4 There is a line of continuity between this early period in African politics and modern-day African nationalism. For several generations the early political élite and its prototype organisations and strategies were to influence the direction of African politics in South Africa. Indeed, some of the early leaders—Dube, Makgatho, Gumede, Seme, Mapikela and Selope Thema—whose entries into

politics are described in this book, were active and influential until as late as after the Second World War. Later leaders, like J. S. Moroka, Albert Luthuli, D. D. T. Jabavu and Z. K. Matthews, were often closely related to the early leaders, and generally retained the latter's basic commitment to democratic non-racialism, although they adopted different strategies in line with changed circumstances.

This book is based on a dissertation submitted to the University of Stellenbosch in March 1981, and is part of a continuing study of early African politics in South Africa. Except for the addition of the final chapter and some minor revisions, the study is published in its original form. Archival and newspaper sources formed the bulk of the research material for the book. The African newspapers, particularly, were vital sources of information. They are essential reading for the student of early African political activity. The vernacular columns contain treasures still waiting to be exploited by Xhosa-, Zulu- or Tswana-speaking historians. Supplementing my own modest knowledge of Xhosa, Mr Richard Malinga and Mr Gordon Maputa, my former lecturers in the Department of African Languages at Stellenbosch, Mr David Gxilishe of the Institute for Language Teaching at the same university and Mr Clyde Daniel of Queenstown helped me with the Xhosa and Zulu translations. I also drew on translations in the Natal Native Affairs Department files and Ephes Mamkeli's dissertation on 'African Public Opinion and the Unification of South Africa' (University of Cape Town, 1954). Mr T. D. M. Mosomathane, also of the Department of African Languages at Stellenbosch, was responsible for the Sotho translations from the few extant issues of the newspaper *Naledi ea Lesotho* I was able to consult.

The bulk of my research was conducted in the Cape Archives Depot and the South African Library in Cape Town. I also made use of the facilities at the Special Collections Department of the University of Cape Town Library, the Library of Parliament in Cape Town, the Carnegie Library in Stellenbosch, the Cory Library at Rhodes University in Grahamstown, the Department of Historical Studies at the Witwatersrand University Library, the Johannesburg Public Library, the Documentation Centre for African Studies at the University of South Africa in Pretoria, as well as the Transvaal and Central Archives Depots in Pretoria, the Natal Archives Depot in Pietermaritzburg and the Orange Free State Archives Depot in Bloemfontein. The staff at the various libraries and archives were always most helpful. I owe the many friendly people who helped me at the two first-mentioned places a special word of thanks.

Except for a handful of items under the literature heading, only sources actually used in this book have been listed in the source list. These naturally form only part of all the sources consulted in the course of my research. In the case of the archival material, for example, important series, such as the Native Affairs Department files in the Cape, Natal and Transvaal Archives Depots and the Colonial Secretary's material in the Orange Free State Archives, were thoroughly and systematically researched, although only those files that were used are listed. Likewise, the computer lists of series detailed in the source list under that heading were checked from beginning to end and many files other than those listed were consulted.

As anyone with the experience will testify, a work of this nature is not possible without the support of friends, colleagues and professional assistants. I have been especially fortunate in this respect. There were numerous people besides those in the various depositories who gladly helped and encouraged me in one way or another. I am grateful to them all. My deepest debt is to my dissertation supervisor, Dr Hermann Giliomee. All along he has been a valued friend, advisor and critic. His guidance and incisive reading and criticism improved the standard of my work immeasurably.

Then I would like to thank Dr Christopher Saunders, who set the publication ball rolling, as well as Russell Martin, Felicia Stoch, Colin Bundy, Tim and Margy Keegan, Wayne Hendricks, Bill Nasson, William Beinart, David Brink, David Botha, Chris Aucamp and, not least of all, Cheryl Kingwill, Laureen Simpson and my parents for their support and encouragement.

I am also grateful to Professor T. R. H. Davenport of Rhodes University for providing me with material and recommending my work for publication; Professor Leonard Thompson for reading and commenting on some of my earliest draft chapters; Professors Thomas Karis and Peter Walshe and Drs Shula Marks, Richard Ralston and Brian Willan for responding to letters from me; and the co-examiners of my dissertation, Professors D. J. van Zyl and D. J. Kotzé, for their advice. The latter suggested important structural changes to original drafts. In addition, Karel Schoeman, the Afrikaans author, provided me with valuable material on early African political activity in the Orange Free State. His empathy with the subject was a source of inspiration to me.

I must also acknowledge assistance received from various bodies.

The Human Sciences Research Council provided me with a grant for my studies and the Centre for African Studies at the University of Cape Town made it possible for this work to be published by awarding a grant while I was a teaching Assistant in the Department of History at the University of Cape Town. I owe the convener of the Centre's publication committee, Dr Andy Smith, and Professor Colin Webb a special word of thanks. However, the two above-mentioned bodies are in no way responsible for any views expressed in this book. Finally, I wish to thank the publisher, David Philip, and his editor Jonathan Price for their co-operation and advice.

This book is dedicated to the kind of tolerant, non-racial South African society envisaged by the people whose activities are chronicled in the pages that follow.

1 *Mafukuzela*, 'the one who struggles against obstacles': John L. Dube of Natal.

2 Elijah Makiwane, John Tengo Jabavu and Isaac Wauchope, three of
the outstanding figures of the first generation of westernised African
political leaders, pictured on a 'Native Voters' Deputation' in 1888.

3 John Tengo Jabavu of *Imvo Zabantsundu.*
4 His rival newspaper editor, Alan Kirkland Soga of *Izwi Labantu.*
5 Sol Plaatje, his wife Elizabeth and Silas Molema with other staff
members of the *Becoana ea Koranta* outside the newspaper's printing
office in Mafeking.

6 The delegates from the South African colonies to the National Convention in Durban, 1908–9.

7 The South African Coloured and Native Delegation to Britain, 1909.

8 'The "Humming" Birds', a newspaper cartoon illustrating white South African cynicism towards W. P. Schreiner's mission to Britain with the South African Coloured and Native Delegation.

9 The executive committee of the Inter-State Native College Scheme included several well-known African political leaders: from left to right, Enoch Mamba, Scanlen Lehana, Simon P. Gasa, Isaiah Bud Mbelle, John Tengo Jabavu, John Knox Bokwe, Isaac Wauchope, Thomas Mtobi Mapikela.

10 Pixley Ka Isaka Seme, convener of the South African Native National Congress, 1912.

11 S. M. Makgatho, president successively of the African National Political Union, the Transvaal Native Organisation, the Transvaal Native Congress and, in succession to John Dube, the South African Native National Congress.

12 Alfred Mangena, the first African to practise as an attorney in South Africa, and one of the founders of the SANNC.

13 Dinizulu ka Cetshwayo, the symbolic head of the African people in South Africa in the early years of the twentieth century.

14 The three central figures, from right to left: Pixley Seme, the Swazi Queen Regent Labotsibeni and Crown Prince (later King) Sobhuza. The Swazi monarchy financed the *Abantu Batho* newspaper of the SANNC, thereby putting into effect the aim of its founder, of forming a political alliance between the educated élite and traditional leaders.

15 The link between early leaders and later African nationlists: John Tengo Jabavu and his son, D.D.T., later president of the All-African Convention.

16 The link between early leaders and later African nationalists: Dr J. S. Moroka and Albert Luthuli, the two ANC presidents in the 1950s, who were closely related to John Mokitlane Nyokong and Martin Lutuli, early leaders of the Becoana Mutual Improvement Association and the Natal Native Congress respectively.

# 1 African politics from the earliest years to 1899

The beginnings of present-day African protest politics in South Africa date back to the nineteenth century when previously independent African chiefdoms were incorporated into expanding colonial political structures. White expansion was accompanied by a European system of administration and preceded or followed by agents of imperialism such as missionaries, teachers, traders and farmers who brought the indigenous groups into contact with alien European political, religious, cultural and economic systems, institutions and norms. The effect was to undermine traditional relations within African societies. New forms of politics emerged.

Magistrates who assumed administrative control of newly created districts in the conquered territories undermined the authority of the chiefs by transforming them into minor officials with limited powers. Traders, selling commodities such as sugar, tea, blankets and iron pots that Africans came to regard as essentials, created a chain of trading stations throughout the districts, drawing Africans into the western cash economy. Christian missionaries established a similar network of mission stations and schools where Africans were given a basic western education, taught Christian doctrine in combination with British cultural values, and encouraged to denounce 'uncivilised' local customs, such as initiation, polygamy and *lobola* (the transfer of cattle on marriage), that were fundamental to African social solidarity. Each magistracy, each trading station and each mission became the nucleus of a new social grouping of Africans who detached themselves from traditional society and adapted to the European presence. In time all these points were physically linked by a communications network of road, railway and telegraph that opened up the African territories and facilitated further European penetration.

The process of incorporation began in the early nineteenth century in the Xhosa-populated frontier region of what is today the eastern Cape, the area with the longest tradition of interaction between Africans and whites, and then moved northwards as the African chiefdoms were subjugated one by one, until by the second half of the nineteenth century traditional political structures throughout South Africa had been weakened considerably.

The Xhosa lost their economic independence, and much of their political and military power, when thousands of destitute and starving people streamed into the Cape Colony during the Nongquase cattle-killing episode of 1856. With hardly any bargaining power left, they were increasingly integrated into the colonial economy on the terms set by the colonists. (1) The Xhosa were finally subjugated militarily in the ninth and last frontier war in 1878. This was followed by the annexation to the Cape of all the Transkeian territories as far north as the Mtavuma River, a process completed by 1894.

In 1868 Great Britain annexed Basutoland. Both the Zulu and the Pedi were subjugated by British forces in 1879. In the following year Griqualand West was incorporated in the Cape Colony. In 1884 Germany proclaimed a Protectorate over South West Africa. In 1885 the Tswana-inhabited areas south and north of the Molopo River were proclaimed by the British a Crown Colony and a Protectorate respectively. In 1895 the South African Republic annexed Swaziland, and in 1898 subjugated the Venda. (2)

The vigorous economic development which followed the discovery of diamonds and gold in the last decades of the century accelerated and intensified the process of tribal disintegration. Through pressures such as taxation and land alienation, Africans were pushed into the labour market in very high numbers. A large African urban proletariat and a tiny petty bourgeois class emerged on the Witwatersrand and the other smaller new industrial centres. (3) On the Rand mines alone, the African employment figure was 14 000 in 1890, rising to 88 000 by 1897. (4) This economic integration naturally had a marked effect on the traditional pre-colonial economic systems.

African responses to the imposed system of domination ranged from its rejection by traditionalists to active participation within its structures by people responding to the impulse of modernisation and change. The latter approach is of special relevance here. It manifested itself in the efforts by an emerging class of Africans to grope for involvement in the new economic and social order, rejecting war as a means of political contest and articulating its demands in terms of western constitutional political values. Unlike the traditionalists who preferred to live within tribal traditions and structures, this new class entered the cash economy, underwent a formal education, were Christians, and generally came to assimilate other prominent aspects of European culture.

Tribal authority began to become redundant and hence to disintegrate as traditional ideals were revolutionised and Africans were equipped to take their places in the new capitalist and western political order. Cleavages developed in African societies between the modernists and the traditionalists as a result. The conservative traditionalists in the Cape referred to educated and christianised Africans as *amagqoboka* ('people having a hole'). This was because the *amagqoboka* were said to have opened a hole in the Xhosa nation which had allowed the white man to gain a foothold. The modernists in Natal were known as *amakolwa* or 'believers'. (5) The decline in tribal authority also involved a shift of leadership away from the traditional authorities to the new educated élite.

The political awareness of this new class was shaped by three main factors: the influence of Christian missions, the development of a non-racial constitution at the Cape, and economic integration.

Of these factors the missionary stimulus was undoubtedly the strongest. By the 1860s the number of African converts throughout Southern Africa had risen to approximately 500 000. (6) The number of people receiving an elementary mission education rose from 9 000 in the 1850s to 100 000 by the end of the century. (7) Most of these people were in the Cape Colony.

Missionary education received government backing for the first time when Sir George Grey became Governor of the Cape in 1854. As a result, educational opportunities increased: new schools were opened at Healdtown, St Matthew's, St Mark's, Salem, Peelton, Mount Coke, and in Grahamstown, Cape Town and other centres. Existing facilities such as those at Lovedale were improved. (8) The African enrolment in government-aided schools in the Cape Colony rose to 49 555 in 1887. The numbers of Africans passing into secondary and tertiary occupations also showed a steady increase. For example, in just over three decades after 1874, 1 502 teachers were trained at the various institutions in the Cape Colony, (9) and by 1887 more than 2 000 Africans had received a secondary education at Lovedale alone. They became teachers, ministers, law agents, magistrate's clerks, interpreters, carpenters, storemen, transport riders, blacksmiths, telegraph operators, printers, clerks, journalists, etc. (10) Socially and economically equipped to fit into western society, and eager to advance within the new colonial structures, these people naturally began to aspire to a share of the political power in the Colony.

The non-racial political system of the Cape Colony provided an outlet for these aspirations and, in turn, stimulated African political consciousness still further. In time this system, though not free from criticism, was widely accepted by Africans as making reasonable provision for the expression of their political aspirations and was regarded as being a model for African participation in multiracial societies. (11)

The non-racial constitutional tradition of the Cape Colony had its foundation in Ordinance 50 of 1828, which abolished all existing restrictions applying to Khoikhoi and other free men of colour. This was followed by the emancipation of the slaves in 1834. Other measures which established equality before the law ensued. As early as 1836, blacks participated in Cape municipal elections, (12) and the constitution of the Colony, which was promulgated in 1853, secured the non-racial franchise. This constitution made no colour distinction. Every male citizen over the age of 21 years who either owned property worth £25, received a salary of £50 per annum or received a salary of £25 and free board and lodging was entitled to be a voter. (13)

The members of the new educated class of Africans which emerged in consequence of these developments soon became aware of the overall discrepancy between Christian doctrine and western political ideals on the one hand and the realities of white conquest on the other. In theory Africans in the Cape were equal to all other citizens, but in practice white colonists were 'more equal' than they were. (14) In the north there was no question of equality for educated or other Christian Africans. Prompted by unfulfilled expectations, the new class began to pose new challenges to the system of white control. Instead of trying to assert African independence as the chiefs had done, they accepted the new order and tried to change it. They mobilised themselves into societies and to voice their demands they made use of newspaper columns, electioneering, pamphleteering, petitioning, lobbying and pressure groups. Unlike the traditionalists they did not want to opt out of the system and did not reject European culture. They wanted to share political power with whites, they demanded to be allowed greater opportunities to assimilate European culture, they desired to advance economically, and most of all, perhaps, they wished to be recognised as a new class which had broken away from traditionalism. (15) They hoped that the evolving political institutions would ultimately make full and fair provision for the incorporation of a moderate African middle class; they believed in evolutionary change through constitutional means.

## The Cape Colony

The first Africans to become active in the Cape political system, and to be enfranchised, were the Mfengu (Fingo), originally refugees from scattered chiefdoms in Natal. After the Mfengu had sided with the colonial forces during the Sixth Frontier War, they were settled in the Victoria East district where they served as a buffer between the Xhosa and colonists. (16) They adapted willingly to the modern economy, soon becoming a progressive peasant community and serving as important agents of change amongst tribal Africans. (17)

As early as 1860, the return of William Stanton to the House of Assembly was attributed to the fact that 'all the black voters deserted the old missionary interest and one and all voted for him'. Nine years later the support of the Mfengu voters in Fort Beaufort enabled George Wood to win the Legislative Council seat for that constituency. The first attempt to have Africans enfranchised on a large scale occurred when Mfengu chiefs applied unsuccessfully to have 600 of their followers registered in 1866. Nevertheless, despite these early examples of political involvement, Africans as a general rule still did not avail themselves of their constitutionally guaranteed political rights, although many possessed the necessary qualifications. The establishment of responsible government in 1872 and the subsequent emergence of political parties, however, led to Africans showing an increased interest in politics and in gaining the vote. (18) In 1872, for example, more than 100 Mfengu were registered as new voters at Oxkraal near Queenstown. The local minister asked the Secretary for Native Affairs to make special provision for a polling station to be set up in the area. (19) Political candidates began to seek the favour of these qualified voters.

The small missionary-educated class of Africans which had emerged by the 1870s was by now thoroughly convinced of the futility of continuing to oppose white expansion through war. It therefore led the way in seeking new means of protecting African interests. Besides the ballot box, the press provided Africans with another channel to political expression. Consequently Africans began to use newspaper columns to debate new options and strategies. This approach is well reflected in a poem published by one of the early Xhosa poets, I. W. W. Citashe.

Your cattle are gone, my countrymen!
Go rescue them! Go rescue them!
Leave the breechloader alone
And turn to the pen.
Take paper and ink,
For that is your shield.
Your rights are going!
So pick up your pen.
Load it, load it with ink.
Sit on a chair.
Repair not to Hoho
But fire with your pen. (20)

Citashe's poem appeared in the Lovedale-based missionary newspaper, *Isigidimi Sama Xhosa*, which was the first significant forum
for African opinion. Started in 1870 as the *Kaffir Express*, the
newspaper underwent a change of name and acquired its first African editor, Elijah Makiwane, in 1876. In its columns the early
views of the new class of literate Africans were articulated. The
main topics discussed in the *Isigidimi* concerned religion and education, touching the heart of the whole issue of modernisation. *Isigidimi*, and Lovedale, provided an important base for political action. Some of the first large scale attempts at the registration of
voters emanated from Lovedale, and many of the political leaders
who were subsequently to emerge were educated there. (21)

The ninth (and last) frontier war of 1877–78 marked a turning
point in the development of African politics in South Africa. In
the 1880s, a time which roughly coincided with the passing of the
phase of military resistance, a considerable upsurge took place in
African political activity. The registration of voters snowballed,
Africans began to form political and other voluntary organisations,
an African-run newspaper was started and the first generation of
extra-tribal African political leaders came to the fore. The numbers
of the new educated class had also by now swelled to the extent
that these Africans were identifiable as a distinct, well-established
stratum of society.

The increasing electoral significance of the African population
was most impressively reflected in the figures for the six frontier
constituencies of the Cape—Aliwal North, Fort Beaufort, King
William's Town, Queenstown, Victoria East and Wodehouse—
where the number of African voters increased six-fold from 1 150
in 1882 to 6 045 in 1886 while the number of white voters in these
constituencies rose by only 914 to 8 077 in the same period. (22)

Clearly the African vote had assumed considerable importance in these areas.

At the same time the first African political associations were emerging. The first known association was the semi-political Native Educational Association (NEA) which was founded in 1879. (23) The NEA began to grow in strength from 1882 when it adopted an elaborate constitution and started to publicise its activities in the press. Its guiding principles, as enunciated in its constitution, were 'to take a special interest in all educational matters, in schools, in teachers and all others engaged in similar work, the aim of which is the improvement and elevation of the native races; to promote social morality and the general welfare of the natives'. (24)

The Association held regular meetings at places such as King William's Town, Grahamstown and the Macfarlane and Peelton mission stations, which delegates from throughout the eastern Cape attended. Occasional reports show that it discussed such questions as African progress after leaving school, the diffusion of African literature, the charge that Africans were not grateful for what the missionaries had done for them and matters of an explicitly political nature such as the pass laws, issues arising from the Transkeian annexation and liquor prohibition. (25) The Association aired its feelings in the form of resolutions and deputations and petitions to the authorities. Its leaders encouraged politically conscious Africans to do likewise: 'Memorials from all our people ... should be poured into the ears of members [of Parliament] without stint.' (26)

The membership of the NEA included a number of the most prominent members of the new class of eastern Cape Africans. Among them were Jesse Shaw, Elijah Makiwane, P. J. Mzimba, William Kobe Ntsikana and J. S. Dlakiya, the five presidents in the first 15 years of the organisation's existence, as well as W. B. Rubusana, J. T. Jabavu, Paul Xiniwe, W. Z. Soga, A. H. Maci and William Gqoba. Churchmen and teachers figured prominently among the members (Makiwane and Mzimba were the first African ministers to have graduated from Lovedale) but there were also tradesmen, businessmen, interpreters, wagon-makers and labour agents. (27)

Certain missionaries, perhaps feeling that their paternalistic control was slipping, criticised the movement for its political involvement. However, the NEA could hardly be considered radical. On the contrary, whites were asked to address meetings and the tone of the leaders was marked by moderation. In fact, one of the

NEA's early presidents, Elijah Makiwane, who had earlier become the first African editor when he took over the editorship of the *Isigidimi Sama Xhosa* in 1876, stated in a presidential address that Africans at that stage were still inferior to Europeans. He dwelt at length on the problem of young men, 'and more particularly those connected with the Association', who claimed to be equal to Europeans. 'The rising generation forgets', he said, 'that the natives are an inferior race.' It was foolish for a people who had just recently come into contact with 'civilisation' to compare themselves with a nation which had produced a Shakespeare, Bacon and Milton and which had the knowledge to build railways and make wire fences. (28) Makiwane's ideas reflect the extent to which the Victorians' selfconception of themselves as the leaders of civilisation and as pioneers of industry and progress moulded the ideas of the new class of Africans they had largely helped create in Britain's South African colonies. (29)

Unlike other contemporary associations, which soon became defunct, the NEA was still in existence at the turn of the century, although not in an active political role. (30)

The next association to emerge was the *Imbumba Yama Nyama*, which was formed at a meeting in Port Elizabeth in September 1882. The *Imbumba* was an explicitly political organisation which aimed to unite Africans in political matters so that they could band together 'in fighting for national rights'. The name of the organisation was taken from the words of the first African convert to Christianity, Ntsikana, who had warned Africans to be *imbumba yamanyama* (literally 'hard, solid sinew'), in other words, an inseparable group or union. (31) It was formed largely in response to the growth of the *Afrikaner Bond* which many Africans perceived to be a threat to their interests. After a branch of the *Afrikaner Bond* had been established in Cradock, moves were initiated to start a similar organisation for Africans and committees from Port Elizabeth and Graaff-Reinet met to finalise arrangements for the inaugural meeting and establishment of the *Imbumba*. (32) *Imbumba* members claimed that their organisation was the true *Afrikaner Bond*, while the organisation of the Afrikaners was merely the *Boeren Bond*. (33)

Several prominent Africans were involved with the new body. They included the Revd Simon P. Sihlali, the president, Isaac Wauchope, the secretary, Mesach Pelem, Paul Xiniwe and S. N. Mvambo. Sihlali was the first African to pass the Cape University Matriculation examination and Wauchope was an interpreter in the court in Port Elizabeth. He had earlier been a well-known pupil and missionary at Lovedale. Mesach Pelem was later to establish himself as one of the leading Africans in Cape politics. The name of the Revd James Dwane was also linked to the organisation. The *Imbumba* drew its support from centres such as Port Elizabeth, Cradock, Graaff-Reinet and Colesberg. In 1883 the branches in the last two towns claimed to have as many as 140 and 60 members respectively. Efforts were also made to extend the activities of the *Imbumba* to places such as Grahamstown, Queenstown, King William's Town and the Transkei, but these plans do not seem to have materialised, as the organisation survived for only a few years. (34)

One of the main concerns of the founders of the *Imbumba* was to counter the deleterious effects of the interdenominational church conflict. They considered this as the main reason for the disunity in African ranks and pointed out that, while the whites belonged to different churches, they were politically united. In articulating this concern S. N. Mvambo stated that 'the Black man makes the fatal mistake of thinking that if he is an Anglican, he has nothing to do with anything suggested by a Wesleyan, and the Wesleyan also thinks so, and so does the Presbyterian, . . . and in that way we lose our political rights'. (35) To bring about unity, conferences were to be held where all groups were represented. Reports of a conference held in 1883 show that the *Imbumba* was also concerned about matters such as the registration of voters, township grievances and education. Committees were formed to attend to these matters. The meeting also passed resolutions for submission to Parliament. In one of these it was requested that 'the franchise should be as it is at present and not be raised, so that browns [Africans] may always have the right to voting'. (36) In addition the association called for the closing of canteens to all Africans and protested against the proposed extension of magisterial authority to field cornets in the adjudication of cases between masters and servants.

The *Imbumba* was appreciative of the work of its counterpart, the Native Educational Association, and there were even unsuccessful attempts to unite the two bodies. One of the obstacles in the way of amalgamation from the *Imbumba*'s viewpoint was that the NEA was not open to all Africans. The *Imbumba* seems to have folded up soon after its 1884 annual conference in Cradock, as newspaper reports of its activities after that dry up. It was reported in 1886 that its first president, Simon Sihlali, who was then living in Cala, was trying to start another organisation based on the constitution of the now defunct *Imbumba*. (37)

Two other organisations to emerge at around this time were the South African Native Association and the Thembu Association. Both were based in the Glen Grey district where the Thembus were resisting attempts to have them settled in the Transkei. David Malasi was the president of the SANA, and Richard Kawa the vice-president. The leaders of the Thembu Association included James Pelem, a prominent spokesman who addressed several petitions to the government as secretary of Thembu mass meetings, Thomas Zwedala, Samuel Sigenu and Henry Vanqa. In May 1884 committees from the two organisations met for joint discussions on matters such as the forced disarmament of blacks, tax grievances, the importance of getting Africans registered as voters and the need for blacks on juries. The organisations also aimed to co-operate with bodies in other areas. Malasi and Kawa wrote to both the NEA and the *Imbumba* supporting the idea of national unity and enquiring about the possibilities of amalgamation. (38)

An organisation called the Gcuwa (later Transkeian) Mutual Improvement Society emerged in the Fingoland and Idutywa districts of the Transkei. It held regular quarterly meetings, with the proceedings being conducted in English, and sought closer ties with its counterparts. Its president, George Pamla, was a teacher in Butterworth, and a member of a prominent 'school' family. Other members included Patrick Xabanisa, Enoch Mamba, Joel Madubela, Solomon Maqina, M. N. Galela and Charles Veldtman. The 'educated' nature of the organisation was reflected in some of the topics that were discussed at meetings: 'Is it right for educated young men to marry uneducated girls?', and 'Which work is more prosperous for a man to do, agency or clerkship?' (39)

Local groups were also springing up in areas such as Kentani, King William's Town, Peddie and Victoria East in the early 1880s. In the 1884 elections a Native Electoral Association concerned with 'electoral politics and larger issues affecting the African population' played an active part in getting James Rose Innes, who was sympathetic to African interests, elected to Parliament in Victoria East. (40)

In the following year a prominent Mfengu headman from Tyumie near Alice, Mbovane Mabandla, was dismissed from his post by the government for meddling in politics after organising two large and what were described as 'thoroughly representative' meetings to discuss the formation of an African branch of the

Empire League. (41) The League had been established by Cecil John Rhodes to mobilise support for British intervention in the South African Republic. Many Africans supported it as they wished Britain to assume responsibility for 'native affairs' throughout southern Africa. (42) The meetings were attended by people from several districts. Newspaper reports also mention the formation in 1884 of a Stockenström Original Afrikander Association, which was also started in response to the growth of the Afrikaner Bond and which intended to establish branches elsewhere in the eastern Cape, the Transkei, Kimberley, Kokstad and 'Lusutu'. (43)

Though all these organisations helped to develop political awareness amongst Africans, and aimed to promote a broad African unity, they were generally unsuccessful in mobilising and representing African opinion. They were usually local groups that lacked the means and the organisation to spread their ideas. It was around a newspaper editor, John Tengo Jabavu, that African political activity began to coalesce during the last two decades of the nineteenth century. Jabavu was the outstanding political figure of his place and time. He tirelessly projected African aspirations and his views were carefully noted in England and by Cape newspapers and politicians.

Jabavu was born at Healdtown in 1859 of Mfengu parents. After attending school there, he became a teacher at the age of 17 years in Somerset East. In his spare time he apprenticed himself to the local newspaper and also studied further under Professor Kyd of Gill College. (44) His interest in politics at an early age is reflected in the letters he wrote as a teenager to Cape newspapers. Although some paternalistic missionaries threatened him with church censure if he persisted with his political activities, the young Jabavu soon became totally embroiled in politics. (45)

Jabavu took over the editorship of the *Isigidimi Sama Xhosa* in 1881 and became prominent in the Native Educational Association, of which he was Vice-president. From these platforms he protested against discriminatory practices. In 1884 he entered the arena of electoral politics when he acted as James Rose Innes's election agent in the Victoria East constituency. Helped by the Native Electoral Association, Jabavu actively canvassed African support for Rose Innes, one of a group of Independents with liberal views standing outside the two main political groupings. As a result of the determining vote of the Africans, Rose Innes was elected to parliament, to the alarm of the other parties. (46) After this Rose Innes's brother and James Weir, described as 'a friend of the African cause', set Jabavu up with his own newspaper, the *Imvo Zabantsundu* ('Native Opinion'), the forerunner of a number of political newspapers controlled by Africans which were launched throughout southern Africa around the turn of the century. Rose Innes and Weir provided the financial backing, but the initiative and planning had come from Jabavu himself. (47)

The aim of the newspaper, according to Jabavu, was to give untrammelled expression to African views and to help bring about closer bonds between blacks and between blacks and whites. (48) African grievances on a wide range of subjects were ventilated in *Imvo*. These included the pass laws, 'location' regulations, liquor laws, the maladministration of justice in the courts and 'anti-Native' legislation emanating from Parliament.

Using *Imvo* as a platform, Jabavu established himself as the leader and spokesman of African opinion. He launched a widespread registration campaign aimed at mobilising the African vote, and in 1887 he led the African protests against the Parliamentary Voter's Registration Act which curtailed the African vote after the incorporation of the Transkeian Territories into the Cape Colony. (49) This Act of 1887 extended the franchise over the newly acquired Transkeian Territories, but departed from previous practice by nullifying tribal tenure as a basis for property qualifications. (50) Africans protested against the legislation. Meetings were held throughout the eastern Cape to protest against the Act, which was considered a threat to African rights. (51) Jabavu sought without much success the aid of the Aborigines Protection Society, British Members of Parliament and other 'friends of the natives' in Britain. The Native Educational Association made representations to the Cape Government and set up a 'Native Committee' to keep the British Colonial Office informed of developments and to organise a deputation to Britain in the event of the Africans' failing to have their grievances redressed by the Cape authorities. And, finally, in October 1887 a conference of representatives from at least thirteen eastern Cape districts was held in King William's Town. Here criticism was levelled at the attack on the African franchise. This was seen merely as the beginning of a wider attack on African rights and privileges. (52) To protect African rights, an *Imbumba Eliliso Lomzi Ontsundu* (Union of Native Vigilance Associations) was formed. Many Africans hoped that this *Imbumba* would supersede the various existing political groups and that it would develop into a strong national organisation, along the same lines as the *Afrikaner Bond*, to protect African interests. Representatives from the various districts were to form local vigilance associations and meet again annually under the auspices of the *Imbumba*. The main aim of the organisation was to oversee the registration of African voters and to organise test cases in the Supreme Court to challenge disputed registration disqualifications. (53)

As a result of the Parliamentary Voter's Registration Act the names of 20 000 people were struck from the 1886 voter's roll. The overwhelming majority were blacks. Despite this the black vote still affected the results in a number of constituencies. By 1891 blacks comprised 30 per cent of the electorate in 12 constituencies and in a further 10 constituencies they accounted for between 20 and 29 per cent of the vote. Consequently renewed calls were made in Parliament for new legislation to curtail the number of black voters. (54) These calls culminated in the Franchise and Ballot Act in 1892 which raised the property qualifications and introduced a literacy test. (55)

Once again Africans opposed the Act, but this time Jabavu took up a reserved position. By now he was becoming increasingly involved in party politics through his close connections with Rose Innes and the latter's 'liberal' Independent political associates, J. W. Sauer and J. X. Merriman. All three men were members of the *Afrikaner Bond*-backed Rhodes cabinet at the time. But they resigned in 1893 because they refused to accept the grant of a lengthy catering monopoly on the Cape railways to a personal friend of the Commissioner of Public Works. When a political realignment took place in Cape politics after the Jameson Raid of 1896, which shattered the Rhodes–*Afrikaner Bond* alliance, Sauer and Merriman joined forces with the *Bond* against Rhodes and the pro-British Progressives. (56) Jabavu was now faced with a problem of loyalty towards his friends, who had joined forces with his erstwhile political enemies. This contradiction resolved itself for Jabavu when the *Bond* for the first time purposefully tried to woo black voters in the 1898 elections because Sauer and Merriman were dependent on African support in the frontier constituencies. When the *Bond* leader, J. H. Hofmeyr, made a speech in support of African franchise rights in March 1898, Jabavu took it at face value, described it as an 'epoch-making address in the politics of the country' and offered Hofmeyr electoral support in the constituencies fought by his liberal friends. (57)

Jabavu's action estranged him from large sections of evolving African opinion. For the first time now the African political class

in the Cape was divided along party political lines. His co-operation with the *Bond* also opened up other cleavages in African
ranks. For many years there had been simmering tensions between
the Mfengu and Xhosa groups, but as African voters had traditionally sided firmly with the English parties and uniformly opposed
the rise of Afrikaner political power, which they felt would be
detrimental to African interests, there was a degree of political
cohesion in the ranks of the new class that diffused these tensions. (58) However, when Jabavu, followed by most Mfengus,
changed his allegiance to the *Bond* the cleavages asserted themselves and African politics in the Cape came to acquire a strong
ethnic dimension. The struggles which ensued were to polarise
politically conscious Africans for many years.

Antipathy between the Mfengu and other Xhosa-speaking
groups had existed ever since the former, who in the past had
been servants of the Xhosa and Thembu, had fled into the Cape
as refugees from Natal and had received favoured treatment because of their relationships with the colonists. Subsequently the
Xhosa were subjugated with the help of the Mfengu and many of
them ended up in the employ of their former servants, some of
whom had become farmers. The Mfengu, who had been the first
Africans to participate in electoral politics, resented the younger
Xhosa politicians who began to emerge towards the end of the
century. These people—traders, clerks, interpreters, teachers and
Christian ministers—had become eligible to vote at a stage when
more stringent franchise qualifications had come into force and
were therefore often better educated and more 'progressive' than
many of the Mfengu voters who had qualified under the more re-
laxed electoral laws which had previously applied. As the transition
to modernisation gathered momentum these groups, which were
also numerically more powerful, gained in stature at the expense
of the more tradition-bound Mfengu. (59)

In addition to the party-political and ethnic factors, there was
also another reason for the estrangement which occurred in the
1890s between Jabavu, who for years had been the acknowledged
spokesman for Africans, and a group of emerging Xhosa politicians
who would eventually, in 1898, form the *Izwi Labantu* newspaper
and the South African Native Congress in opposition to him. Some
people wished to form a strong African political organisation to
protect African interests, but Jabavu was opposed to this. Although
the large African conference called to protest against the Parliamentary Voter's Registration Act in 1887 had empowered Jabavu

'to summon the Congress when occasion required', (60) he never did so. For several reasons, he wished to prevent a broad-based movement from developing. Partly this was because it would have threatened his prominent personal position in African politics, and partly because he wished to see Africans participating with whites in a single non-racial political party instead of forming an assertive African organisation. Jabavu felt that such a move would be seen as a threat by whites and stimulate racial distinctions instead of promoting practical non-racialism. (61) He believed that by working hand in hand with whites Africans would come to hold the balance of parliamentary power and influence the evolution of contitutional government. (62)

It was for these reasons that Jabavu opposed the attempts by Jonathan Tunyiswa in 1891 to weld the Native Vigilance Associations which had been formed in the various districts after the 1887 conference into a colony-wide organisation. Tunyiswa was a young schoolteacher from Mount Coke near King William's Town, who became one of the most respected African politicians. His view was that Africans should become organised now and not wait until a 'heavy calamity or cyclone' befell them before getting together. However Tunyiswa's plans for local and central organisations, embodied in a manifesto, were of no avail. At that stage it was virtually impossible to form a strong African political party without Jabavu's patronage. His hostility to the idea delayed such a development by a decade. Only when a rival newspaper, the *Izwi Labantu*, was formed in 1898 could this be done. (63)

The *Izwi Labantu* ('Voice of the People') was based in East London. Prominent in its foundation were men like Thomas Mqanda, R. R. Mantsayi, A. K. and W. D. Soga, A. H. Maci, N. C. Umhalla and Walter Benson Rubusana. (64)

Rubusana and A. K. Soga were the leading spokesmen for the *Izwi* group. Rubusana, a Congregational minister, in time eclipsed Jabavu as the leading Cape African politician, (65) while Soga, a member of a remarkable family, was for many years the editor of the *Izwi Labantu*. His father, Tiyo Soga, was the first ordained African minister in South Africa and the most prominent member of the earliest group of educated Africans. While studying in Scotland, Tiyo Soga married a Scotswoman, then returned to the Cape to do mission work amongst his people. His children, most of whom also achieved prominence in life, were educated in Scotland as well. (66)

The *Izwi Labantu* was backed by Cecil John Rhodes. He had

helped get the newspaper off the ground after failing to get Jabavu's support in the 1898 elections. Rhodes assumed financial responsibility for the *Izwi* and put a Member of the Legislative Assembly, C. P. Crewe, in charge of its financial affairs. Crewe clashed
with the African directors who reported him to Rhodes for being
arrogant and attempting to assume functions not concerned with
finance. (67)

With a newspaper to publicise their activities the *Izwi* group
immediately set about reviving the vigilance associations with a
view to forming a colony-wide organisation. In 1898 they organised an electoral convention where it was decided to support
the Progressive Party in the forthcoming elections. This was the
first significant political gathering of Africans in which Jabavu did
not take part. (68) Calling itself the South African Native Congress
(SANC), the body forwarded resolutions to the government. (69)
It was to be some years, however, before the SANC finally established itself as a fully-fledged political organisation.

Thus by the end of the nineteenth century there was a sizeable
class of politically conscious Africans in the Cape. The members of
this class were drawn mainly from the constantly growing numbers
of educated Africans in the colony, with the nucleus being formed
by the 8 000-odd registered African voters. (70) This new class
had also begun gradually to supersede traditional authority in political influence on both a local and wider level. Its members were
usually organised into local voters' and district committees and
they exerted considerable electoral influence in several frontier
constituencies. However, they had not yet organised themselves
into effective ethnic umbrella organisations to protest against political, economic and social inequalities. To a large extent this was
indicative of their political moderation, thought to be necessary if
their hopes of ultimately being accepted fully into the Cape political system were to be realised. Subsequent events were to dent
these hopes and stimulate Africans into articulating themselves
more forcefully through their own political organisations.

## Natal

In Natal a system of segregation and racial differentiation was implemented after the region came under British control in 1842. As
far as possible, the government maintained the tribal identity of
the indigenous groups. Tribal Africans were governed by Native
Law. They were not eligible for the franchise. (71)

Theoretically, acculturated, mission-educated Africans with the necessary qualifications could participate in colonial politics, and their rights were constitutionally entrenched, but in practice they were excluded from effective participation in the social and political structures of Natal society. Because traditionalism formed the cornerstone of the Natal government's policy, the authorities disapproved of the egalitarian teachings of the missionaries and were distinctly hostile to the mission-educated Christian Africans who rejected traditionalism and began to seek assimilation into colonial society. (72)

According to the provisions of the 1856 constitution, Africans who attained the necessary qualifications could be voters for or members of the Legislative Council. All men above the age of 21 years, who possessed any immovable property worth £50 or who rented property to the yearly value of £10, and who were not aliens or criminals, were eligible for the vote. (73) However, steps were soon taken to restrict the African franchise.

The most important measures in this respect were Acts 11 of 1864 and 1865. They effectively excluded Africans from the franchise. The former stipulated the conditions under which Africans could be exempted from the operation of Native Law and become subject to the general laws in Natal, while the latter laid down the new conditions for Africans to become enfranchised. An African wishing to be exempted from Native Law had to petition the Governor, giving particulars about his family, property, chief, etc., and furnishing proof of his ability to read and write. An unmarried woman needed a European of good standing to support her exemption application as well. The applicant was then required to take the oath of allegiance. Letters of exemption were not automatically acquired once these stipulations had been properly followed. It was in the Governor's discretion to grant or refuse the application. (74) If exemption was granted, qualified Africans had (under Act 11 of 1865) to wait for a further period of seven years, and show that they had resided in Natal for 12 years, before they could petition the Governor for the franchise. Petitions for the franchise had to be accompanied by a certificate signed by three registered European voters and endorsed by a Justice of the Peace or Resident Magistrate. Once again, it was in the Governor's discretion to grant or refuse the application. (75)

In fact such franchise applications usually proved to be a futile exercise. The South African Native Affairs Commission found in 1903 (76) that in the 38 intervening years only two Africans out of a total estimated Natal African population of 904 041 (77) had the vote. In contrast the system of exemption was working, though exemptions were only sparingly granted. By 1904 an estimated 5 000 people, including the progeny of exempted men, were living under the exemption law. (78) However, the authorities remained hostile to the exemption measures, which they saw as undermining the traditionalism which formed the basis of native policy in the colony.

The government tried to avoid treating exempted Africans as a special category of people and spoke of Africans in blanket terms. Exemption was defined in the narrowest terms. Exempted Africans were freed from customary law only, and not from many of the discriminatory restrictions applying to Africans in general. (79) Therefore this class of Africans found themselves in the unenviable position of being regarded as outsiders by both the tribal Africans, whose way of life no longer satisfied them, and the colonists, whose way of life they wished to imitate. To them this was a painful and frustrating situation. (80) Johannes Kumalo, the head of the Driefontein Mission, reflected this frustration when he said he felt there was a desire to push him back into the heathen state from which he had hoped to escape. (81)

Despite government hostility, the mission-educated Christian Africans, known as *kolwa* ('believers'), and including both exempted and non-exempted Africans, began to assert themselves and articulate their feelings in a distinct way by the turn of the century. At this time the *kolwa* element consisted of 40 000 communicants and 100 000 adherents to Christianity. They were mainly peasant farmers congregated around mission stations. There were also professional people such as ministers, teachers and lawyer's clerks, and traders, labour agents and skilled or semi-skilled urban workers. The political awakening of this class manifested itself in the development of European-type political organisations and the establishment of independent African churches. These movements were shaped by resentment caused by the colour bar and stimulated by political developments like the subjugation of Zululand and the visit of the missionary Joseph Booth to Natal in the 1890s. Booth's visit caused widespread reaction in the colony and had a marked stimulatory effect on African political activity. (82)

The first European-style African political organisation in Natal, and the only one to emerge there in the nineteenth century, was the *Funamalungelo* (literally 'demand civic rights') Society (83) which was started in 1888 by John Kumalo. Kumalo was an 'exempted' African from Estcourt. His main aim was to provide the means for exempted Africans to 'get to know and understand one another; as well as learn something of their position as exempted Natives; and above all to improve themselves so as to attain the highest state of civilisation'. (84) From Estcourt the *Funamalungelo* branched out to the Driefontein Mission in the Klip River division and then to Edendale near Pietermaritzburg. Later reports in the vernacular newspaper, *Inkanyiso lase Natal*, stated that the exempted Africans were growing attached to the Society and that it was proving a success. (85) A notice of a meeting in Edendale in 1894 gives an indication of the subjects discussed at *Funamalungelo* meetings. On that occasion they discussed their 'elevation to a proper state of civilisation and the best means of arriving at it'.(86) It was also reported that 'white friends who had studied the Native interest and bore it at heart attended a meeting of the society and took part in the discussions'. (87)

The *Funamalungelo* petitioned government for clarification of the status of exempted Africans, (88) and also begged relief from discriminatory laws affecting them. However, the petitions brought no relief. Exempted Africans continued to be dissatisfied with the treatment meted out to them.

Towards the end of the century attempts were made to extend the scope of the *Funamalungelo* into a more representative African organisation on the lines of the white Farmers' Congress and Gandhi's Indian Congress, but these plans had not materialised by the end of 1899. The reason, according to one of the principal participants, was that some individuals were pushing their own interests instead of merging them with those of the whole. (89)

## The South African Republic and the Orange Free State

The pattern of race relations in the South African Republic and the Orange Free State differed fundamentally from that in the Cape Colony and Natal. In the Afrikaner Republics there were no pretensions about political, economic and social equality.

In the Transvaal the underlying principle, entrenched in the constitution of state, was that there would be *'geene gelijkstelling van gekleurden met blanke ingezetening . . . noch in Kerk noch in Staat'*. (90) Similarly, in the Orange Free State relations between whites and blacks were conducted on a level of *'bazen tegenover dienstknechten'*. (91) Only whites could become citizens of the country. (92) Rigid social segregation was maintained. (93)

The indigenous groups had no political rights, and no claims to economic and social equality. Their main function was to provide labour—a position supported by the considerable British-controlled mercantile and mining interests, situated mainly on the Rand. Government policy was that those Africans who were not used for labour in towns or on farms were to be segregated in reserves. (94) As the Republican administrations did not wish to encourage acculturation and assimilation, they did not encourage education for Africans, which was left in the hands of missionaries. In the Transvaal missionary education was unaided by the state, (95) but in the Orange Free State the state accepted the principle of providing education for Africans and a small grant was made annually. However, in terms of numbers matters were only marginally better there. The class of school-going Africans numbered 4 210 in 1887, compared to 3 720 in the Transvaal. (96)

As a result of the restrictive policies of the two Republics, the size of the educated class of Africans remained low and the emergence of African political associations and mouthpieces in the form of independent vernacular newspapers was retarded. The developments which had occurred along these lines in the Cape, and to a lesser extent in Natal, were not paralleled until the demise of the Republics after the second Anglo-Boer War. However, that is not to say there was an absence of African political awareness. Although Africans in the Republics only organised themselves into formal political associations after the war, they showed themselves to be politically conscious years before. In many cases people who were to emerge later as leaders of the first political organisations had established themselves at an early stage as leading men in the townships and reserves.

There are several examples in the case of the Orange Free State to substantiate this point. In May 1882 the inhabitants of the Waaihoek township in Bloemfontein chose Jacob Lavers, a later President of the Orange River Colony Native Vigilance Association, as a field cornet. For some reason, Lavers was dismissed from his post in October 1884, upon which the inhabitants of the township drew up a letter to the Town Council asking for his reinstatement. The letter was removed from the minutes when a councillor complained that it was beneath the dignity of the Council even to receive such a representation. (97) Subsequently, Jan Mocher, another long-serving leader of the same organisation, was elected to the field cornetcy in Waaihoek in 1891. (98)

With the aim of facilitating the administration of Africans in townships, the government appointed certain Africans to act as intermediaries between the authorities and the residents. In the

Waaihoek township in Bloemfontein these people were known as
'block men'. Each of these 'block men' represented a block of
buildings in the township. Matters affecting the inhabitants were
referred to them. (99) After a visit to Bloemfontein in 1894, John
Tengo Jabavu wrote approvingly of this sytem of local government,
and noted that Waaihoek had its own 'town hall and a council of
its own composed of Natives, which is presided over by the
Mayor'. He said the benefits of the system could be seen in the
'good and decent buildings' in the township. (100) These block
men or councillors were in the vanguard when African political
organisations emerged under British rule. Existing relationships
were merely formalised when the first political organisations were
started. (101)

In other examples of political activity in Waaihoek before the
war, African residents petitioned the Bloemfontein municipality
to apply the pass laws less stringently and complained about police
action in this regard, (102) and the wives of the householders in
the township presented an illuminated 'address' to President Steyn.
One of the signatories to the address was a lady bearing the sur-
name Mocher. (103)

In Thaba Nchu, further to the east, Joel Goronyane, who was
later to lead the Becoana Mutual Improvement Association, had
already established himself as one of the *'voormannen der Baralong
natie'* by 1899. In that year Goronyane, Moses Masisi and John
Mokitlane Nyokong petitioned the State President about land
rights in the Moroka (Thaba Nchu) district. (104). The latter two
men were prominent for years in Baralong affairs, and were to
become members of the executive of the Becoana Mutual Improvement Association under Goronyane.

The political ideals of these early politically conscious Africans
in the Orange Free State were influenced largely by the egalitarian
principles which were disseminated in certain churches and church-
controlled educational institutions in the country. Despite opposition from local white church members, the Anglican Church, for
example, challenged the policy of the state by largely ignoring
racial divisions, especially with regard to funerals and the administration of sacraments. (105) The church thus served as a breeding
ground for new non-racial ideas and in time these values spread
amongst the small class of educated, Christian Africans. This class
was generally at the helm of the African political organisations
which were later formed, and which all put a high premium on the
principle of political equality regardless of colour. The first

Presidents of the two African political associations to emerge later in the Orange River Colony were both Christian ministers.

Another important stimulus to politicisation was the link with Cape society. African Cape leaders visited Bloemfontein for reasons such as church conferences, while many of the educated Africans in the Orange Free State had studied at institutions such as Lovedale and Healdtown in the Cape or, indeed, had been born and brought up there. (106) These people maintained their links and kept abreast with developments in the eastern Cape. The newspaper *Imvo Zabantsundu*, for instance, was circulated in the Orange Free State and Africans from there reported regularly about conditions in the country in the *Imvo*'s columns. One such correspondent was W. N. Somngesi of Rouxville, who, in 1891, described the Free State as a slave state. (107) In the following year Somngesi entered the broader political arena by writing a letter to the *Cape Mercury* in which he rebutted points made by the President of the Orange Free State in an article on 'The Native Question'. The letter was reprinted in the Bloemfontein newspaper, *De Express*. Repeating his *Imvo* theme in the main point of his argument, Somngesi declared:

His Honor the President says: 'The days of slavery are gone, and let us be thankful that it is so.' I may ask first, what is a slave? A slave is any one in bondage. Are the natives free in the Free State? Are the native ministers and other respectable people not bound to carry passes, which they are bound to pay for? Are the natives free to go and see their friends who are living on farms close by? I say no. It does not matter whether your friend was dying on a farm, you dare not pass the boundaries of the town commonage without a sixpenny pass. Native preachers dare not forget their passes on Saturdays if they have to go out preaching on Sundays—*pas op*, for a fine of £3 or one month's imprisonment with hard labour. Do they not pay a poll tax, and [get] nothing in return done for them; whilst the white man is free from the tax, and his children's schooling supported by Government?

Secondly, a slave means one wholly under the will of another. Now, Mr Editor, a native has no voice in politics here—not even in things concerning themselves. They have to do the will of a white man, and the will they must do; and what return to they get for their servitude? *Nil*.

Thirdly and lastly, a slave means one who has lost all power of resistance. What I have said on the first and second points will explain the third, and I will, therefore, dwell no longer on this painful subject of 'The Native Question', with the prayers and hopes that the Lord will hasten the time when all nations will be entirely freed from bondage. (108)

Besides church and educational links, contacts with the Cape also took place on a social level. Reports in the *Imvo* give details of cricket matches between sides from the Cape and centres such as Rouxville and Bloemfontein. (109) The fact that Africans were playing a traditional Englishman's game in this Afrikaner-dominated country is in itself a commentary on the influence of British missionaries and the acceptance by Africans of British values, including, of course, idealised non-racial political values.

In the Transvaal too there were similar politicising influences at work, and early indications of African political activity. As we have seen, after the discovery of gold in 1886 hundreds of thousands of Africans from throughout the sub-continent converged on the Witwatersrand. A number of these people were educated ministers, teachers, contractors, tradesmen, etc, who had lived in the Cape or had been educated there. They became keenly aware of the disabilities suffered by Africans and emerged as spokesmen for local communities. In 1898, for example, several petitions complaining of 'the ill-treatment we have suffered from time to time under the laws and officials of the Transvaal Government' were sent to the Cape Government Labour Agent in Johannesburg by stand-holders in the 'Kaffir Location' there. (110) Another major indication of African political awareness was the emergence of the separatist or so-called Ethiopian Church movement in the Transvaal during the 1890s under the leadership of people such as Mangena Mokone and Edward Tsewu, who were from other colonies and who were to be prominent in organised politics in the early twentieth century.

## 'Ethiopianism'
The philosophy of religious independence, which manifested itself in the rise of African separatist churches that broke away from the paternalistic control of white missionaries, was another form of response by Africans towards growing white domination in South Africa. It was commonly known as 'Ethiopianism' and differed fundamentally from the modern participatory approach of the political organisations and newspapers described above. Unlike those who believed in evolutionary change through constitutional means, the separatists were impatient with white control and pessimistic about the prospects for evolutionary change. Disillusioned by the imperfections of colonial society, they withdrew from white-dominated structures and formed exclusively African organisations, through which they sought to gain fulfilment and self-advancement. Their policy was to throw off the shackles of

white domination and reassert their former independence, while at
the same time retaining what they considered to be the best
elements of European civilisation.

Although religious in nature, and not specifically political, the
Ethiopian movement had broad political implications. The assertion of African independence and the separatists' rallying cry of
'Africa for the Africans' posed explicit challenges to white domination. The fundamental principle, adopted by later generations of
African nationalists in South Africa, was that white power should
be opposed by black unity.

Although they differed fundamentally from each other, neither
the integrationist nor the separatist approach was totally exclusive
of the other. In fact they complemented each other. In so far as
they sought to protect and further black interests, their aims were
identical. (111)

The first African separatist church, the Thembu Church, was established in Thembuland in the Transkei in 1884 by the Wesleyan
minister, Nehemiah Tile. Tile, a fervent Thembu nationalist, left
the Wesleyan church in 1882 after clashing with his white supe-
riors because of his participation in political matters. His Thembu
Church was adapted to the African heritage of the tribe. The Paramount Chief, Ngangelizwe (later succeeded by Dalindyebo), was
set up as its head, following the precedent of the English sovereign
as head of the Church of England. (112) A new edition of the
prayer book was arranged in which the Queen's name was to be replaced by that of Chief Dalindyebo. (113)

At a time when the Thembu tribal independency was fast being
eroded after a decade of increasing white control, Tile became one
of the closest advisers to the Thembu Paramount Chiefs. He
spearheaded the development of more subtle forms of Thembu
protest—through the church and in petitions to the Cape Government—which became necessary after the failure of military resistance. In this way new channels were created whereby the deep-
felt grievances of the Thembu could be expressed, both in religious
and political terms. The aim of this protest was to unite all Thembuland, with a maximum degree of tribal autonomy under indirect
imperial rather than direct colonial control. To counter the
administrative fragmentation of Thembuland, he demanded the
removal of the various magistrates and the appointment of a single
resident official instead. These protests were unsuccessful. In 1885
Thembuland was formally annexed to the Cape. (114)

Tile soon landed in trouble with the authorities. After being arrested for inciting the chiefs to refuse to pay the hut tax to the magistrates, he declared that the fear of banishment, imprisonment or death would not deter him from doing what he considered to be his duty to his Chief and people. (115)

When Dalindyebo got into difficulties with the colonial authorities because of Tile's church, he withdrew support and returned to the mission fold. Tile nevertheless continued with his work and before his death in 1892 he had reasserted his influence on Dalindyebo. The chief magistrate described him as the initiator of all the 'agitations' at Dalindyebo's Great Place. (116)

Subsequent secession movements from various Christian denominations led to the establishment of the Native Independent Congregational Church in British Bechuanaland in 1885 and the Lutheran Bapedi Church and the Africa Church in the South African Republic in 1889. (117)

But the secession movement really took off when the separatist ideas spread to the Witwatersrand where thousands of African labourers and many African ministers from several tribes congregated after the discovery of gold in 1886. The influx of diverse ethnic groups provided the foundation for the first African mass movement on truly 'national' lines. This was the Ethiopian Church, which was established in Pretoria in 1892 by Mangena Mokone. Mokone and a number of indignant fellow ministers formed the church after having been excluded from a meeting of their white Wesleyan colleagues. They called themselves Ethiopians in reference to biblical texts such as Psalm 68:31, 'Ethiopia shall soon stretch out her hands unto God', and Acts 8:27, which they interpreted as a promise of the evangelisation of Africa. The church was to be open to all Africans and it was to be run by African leaders. (118)

The Ethiopian movement soon spread beyond Pretoria, incorporating more and more secessionists from the white-controlled churches. Plans were made for co-operating with other dissident church bodies. Mokone travelled to Thembuland to discuss closer links with the African Native Mission Church of Jonas Goduka, who had succeeded Nehemiah Tile as leader of the Thembu Church, and had changed the name of the church in the process. He also began corresponding with the African Methodist Episcopal (AME) Church in the United States with a view to closer co-operation. (119) This church, founded by a former slave in reaction to colour discrimination in the Methodist Episcopal Church in the United States, had a membership of about 400 000. Its policy was to encourage black assertiveness. (120)

In 1896 the Ethiopian Church decided to seek affiliation to the AME Church. James Dwane, another well-known separatist from the Wesleyan Church who had been recruited into the Ethiopian Church by a special delegation sent from Pretoria to Queenstown to interview him, (121) was deputed to go to America for this purpose. Dwane received a cordial welcome in America and it was agreed that the two churches should amalgamate. Pending the arrival of an accredited Bishop, Dwane was appointed General Superintendent of the AME Church in South Africa. By virtue of this appointment he now took over from Mokone as head of the church. (122)

On Dwane's return the newly-designed AME Church began to make itself felt throughout the Cape, Natal, the Orange Free State and the South African Republic. Serious upheavals occurred in the work of the mission societies. Church and school disputes resulted as the Ethiopians proselytised members of the established churches and undermined their influence. Secessions affected all denominations. (123) By acquiring property the separatist churches set the framework for permanent organisations. (124)

Significantly, the Ethiopian Church succeeded in gaining recognition from the government of the South African Republic. (125) It also approached Cecil John Rhodes for permission to extend the activities of the church to the north of the Limpopo and Dwane communicated with King Menelik of Abyssinia in order to extend mission work to the Sudan and Egypt. In doing so he reflected the broad aims of the movement. Africa must not be evangelised by Europeans, not even by American blacks, but by real Africans, he said. (126)

In 1898 one of the leading dignatories of the AME Church in the United States, Bishop H. M. Turner, visited South Africa to consolidate the position of the South African branch. Bishop Turner received a triumphant welcome and achieved some startling results in his visit of five weeks. He succeeded largely in welding the scattered groups who went widely under the Ethiopian title into a stronger unit. Two large conferences were held in Pretoria and Queenstown. In Queenstown a site was bought for a future centre for higher learning. More than 6 000 new members joined the Church, pushing the total membership past 10 000 people gathered in 73 congregations, 65 new ministers were ordained and, finally, at the request of both conferences Bishop Turner consecrated Dwane as Mission Bishop of South Africa.

When Bishop Turner returned to the United States he reported enthusiastically about his visit, but Dwane's consecration as bishop found no general sanction there. Dwane also waited in vain for the promised money for the erection of a college. In order to clear the impasse Dwane travelled to the United States for a second time in 1899. However, he failed to gain the desired financial support, and to have his consecration as bishop confirmed. Strains also developed over differences in church policy and administration. (127)

Dissatisfied with the results of his visit to the United States and attracted by the prospect, held out to him by Julius Gordon, a white minister with whom he had struck up a relationship, of occupying high office in the Anglican Church, Dwane seceded from the AME Church in 1899 to join the Anglican Church in a semi-independent body, the Order of Ethiopia. Dwane took over with him an estimated 5 000 members of the AME Church. However, Mangena Mokone and most of the members in the Orange Free State and South African Republic refused to follow Dwane. In time the Order of Ethiopia became an almost exclusively Xhosa body.

The marriage with the Anglican Church was attended for several years by disagreement and friction. It took almost a decade before the compact in terms of which Dwane and his followers joined the Anglicans was finally endorsed by the Anglican Church as a whole. Dwane never received the bishopric he had hoped for and the Order of Ethiopia subsequently declined in influence. (128)

On the other hand, after initially losing some ground, the AME Church became firmly established. Today it is one of the largest and most influential churches working amongst blacks in South Africa.

Standing apart from the above groups were two other separatist churches, the Negro Missionary Society and the Presbyterian Church of Africa. The former represented the Negro Baptist Churches of America and was accepted for a time as a branch of the local Baptist Church before recognition was withdrawn. This church was stationed in Cape Town with the Revd Jackson as its head. (129)

Of greater significance was the secession of the Presbyterian Church of Africa led by Pambami J. Mzimba from the United Free Churches of Scotland in 1897. This secession came as a particular shock to the Presbyterians because Mzimba was a widely respected minister in the missionary and educational town of Lovedale and had been connected with Lovedale for more than

thirty-five years. (130) He was the first African minister to be ordained by the Free Church of Scotland in South Africa. (131)
He may have been prompted to secede by James Dwane who
was his house guest a short while before he led one thousand members of his congregation, all Mfengus, away from Dr James Stewart's
mission. (132)

Mzimba worked energetically to further his movement. Soon
after its foundation, he visited the United States, taking with him
eight African youths to study at Lincoln University. He was also
granted an interview at the Colonial Office in London. Within five
years his adherents were conservatively estimated at 17 000. They
were spread throughout the Cape Colony, including Bechuanaland.
(133) By 1910 Mzimba claimed the total had risen to 39 017.
This total included approximately 9 500 followers in Natal and
Zululand, 1 100 in the Ermelo and Johannesburg districts in the
Transvaal and 1 360 in the Orange River Colony. (134)

In Natal, in the meantime, several independent African religious movements had also emerged. (135) The most important of
these was the Zulu Congregational Church founded in 1896 by
Samungu Shibe. Of note also was the Cushite movement started in
southern Natal in 1899 by the American Negro Baptists. The AME
Church was banned in Natal. (136)

The separatist movement in Natal was given a big boost by the
visit of the turbulent American missionary Joseph Booth in 1896.
Booth was one of the earliest and most forceful proponents of the
idea of 'Africa for the Africans'. He demanded equal rights and the
restoration of the land to Africans. Furthermore the blacks of the
United States and the West Indies should return to Africa 'like the
Israelites of the Exodus'. He proposed the formation of an African
Christian Union to collect funds for the establishment of industrial
mission stations where, under the tutelage of the more advanced
Negroes, Africans would be taught how to become self-sufficient.
Amongst other things they would be shown how to start mining
and other industries so that they could tap the rich natural resources of Africa to uplift all Africans. They would be trained also in
commercial, engineering, nautical, medical and other professional
skills. (137)

Booth's scheme caused widespread reaction. Although it was
eventually rejected at a twenty-six hour meeting of more than a
hundred educated Africans, his meetings on the whole were attended by large crowds and his general utterances fell on ready ears.
His visit increased white suspicions of African intentions. (138)

Booth subsequently went to Nyasaland where he had a more sympathetic response to his plans. (139) However, he landed in trouble with the authorities and fled the protectorate after a warrant for his arrest and deportation for seditious conduct had been issued. Later he returned to South Africa and was active in the Cape and Transvaal still preaching 'Africa for the Africans', predicting that soon they would be freed from the hardships of British rule and rule themselves with their own laws and rights in a new heavenly millenium. (140)

By the end of the nineteenth century the Ethiopian movement had gained thousands of adherents and spread throughout South Africa. Implicitly political in nature, it indirectly complemented the formal activities of the political élite by politicising Africans, articulating dissatisfaction with the inequalities of white rule and propagating African assertiveness.

It is against the background of events outlined in this chapter that developments in African organisational politics in South Africa in the first decade of the twentieth century must be seen.

# 2 The Anglo–Boer War, 1899–1902: African attitudes, involvement and disenchantment

The new century dawned with South Africa in the grip of the Anglo-Boer War, an event which was to have a profound effect on African, quite as much as white, politics in the region. When hostilities broke out on 11 October 1899, politically conscious Africans generally supported Britain in the struggle against the South African Republic and the Orange Free State. They hoped that a British victory would result in the extension of idealised British non-racial ideals over the Afrikaner Republics. Applied to South Africa, these ideals were best exemplified by Cecil John Rhodes's dictum of 'equal rights for all civilised men south of the Zambesi'(1) —words used in the 1898 election campaign for political gain rather than out of conviction—and in the non-racial constitution of the Cape Colony.

## Imperial assurances

The pronouncements of Imperial officials before and during the conflict gave strength to the hope that a new political dispensation was in the offing for Africans in South Africa in the event of a British victory. In October 1899 the Colonial Secretary, Joseph Chamberlain, declared, 'The treatment of the Natives [in the Transvaal] has been disgraceful; it has been brutal; it has been unworthy of a civilised Power.' (2) A few months later Lord Salisbury, the British Prime Minister, said there must be no doubt that, following victory, 'due precaution will be taken for the philanthropic and kindly and improving treatment of these countless indigenous races of whose destiny I fear we have been too forgetful'. (3) The British High Commissioner in South Africa, Lord Milner, similarly assured a coloured deputation, 'It is not race or colour but civilisation which is the test of a man's capacity for political rights.' (4) Milner, in fact, used the ill-treatment of black people in the South African Republic as one of the reasons for intervening in affairs there. (5)

## African attitudes

The Imperial pronouncements undoubtedly gave rise to expectations amongst politically conscious Africans, and encouraged
support for the British war effort. This point was well illustrated
by the resolutions passed by a meeting of 'leading Africans',
chaired by Alfred Mangena, who was later to become prominent
on a national level in African politics, in Cape Town in October
1899. The resolutions expressed loyalty to Britain and gratitude
that 'the Chief Minister of the Queen has mentioned the welfare
of the Native people as one of the things he is bearing in mind'. (6)
In a similar vein, the Rhodes-backed, pro-Progessive *Izwi Labantu*
newspaper in the eastern Cape also repeatedly praised imperial
officials like Chamberlain and Milner (7) and vigorously endorsed
imperial intervention in South Africa on the basis that it would
reverse increasingly reactionary trends in colonial attitudes towards
Africans. (8) According to the *Izwi* only the triumph of British
democratic ideals would ensure lasting progress, prosperity and
peace for South Africa. (9) The newspaper envisaged that after
victory had been achieved the British government would 'purify
our Courts and Temples, and that an era of peace and good government will be established for all time'. (10) The so-called native
question would finally be disposed of. (11) For these reasons, the
*Izwi* wholeheartedly backed Britain in the war. Its condemnation
of Republican attitudes and activities was as wholehearted as its
support for Britain. The newspaper repeatedly listed 'Boer atrocities' on Africans (12) and wrote of the 'narrow, prejudiced and
inhuman tyranny of Boer Republicanism'. The Afrikaner was
said to be a natural savage. (13) The editor of the *Izwi*, A. K.
Soga, demonstrated his loyalty by actually serving as a trooper
in Brabant's Horse for several months before returning to resume
his duties on the newspaper. He saw action on the front at Storm-
berg and Dordrecht. (14)

The *Izwi* also used the war issue to score party political points.
It attacked 'mugwumps' like Merriman in the South African Party
who were critical of Imperial intentions, and cast doubts upon
their patriotism. (15) Inevitably this criticism brought the people
grouped around the *Izwi* into conflict with John Tengo Jabavu
and his group, who supported the South African Party, especially
'liberals' in the SAP like Merriman and Sauer. These people regarded the war as unjust and preferred to align themselves with
the *Afrikaner Bond*, rather than compromise with the Milner-
Rhodes-Progressive axis, whose policies were geared to promoting

capitalist interests and Imperial intervention. Merriman and Sauer undoubtedly influenced Jabavu's attitude to the war as well. (16)

To the dismay of many people Jabavu adopted an independent pacifist approach to the war in his *Imvo Zabantsundu* newspaper. Although expressly loyal to Britain and 'wishing for the triumph of British arms', Jabavu disagreed with the necessity of war and criticised the 'war party' which had eagerly sought the 'war remedy' rather than attempting to avoid conflict through diplomacy which, he felt, was possible. By the war party, he meant the Milner-Rhodes-Progressive axis, which Jabavu declared had precipitated the war to further its own ends. (17)

Despite his pro-SAP loyalties, very few had expected Jabavu and his newspaper to adopt an independent stance in a war between Boer and Briton. His stand held serious implications for him. Although he emphasised that his criticism of the war did not affect his loyalty to Britain or mean that he sided with the Afrikaner Republics, Jabavu's antagonists accused him of behaving in a disloyal, if not treasonable, manner. He was subjected to virulent attacks by the *Izwi Labantu* and other newspapers of the Argus group, which supported the Progressive viewpoints. Moreover, his stand lost him substantial support amongst Africans, most of whom saw the issue only in terms of loyalty or disloyalty to the Crown. It also caused his old friends, R. W. Rose Innes and James Weir, whose financial support was instrumental in founding the newspaper, publicly to withdraw their subscriptions and general support for the *Imvo*. In a sequel to this action, the Mercury Printing Press terminated its contract to print the *Imvo*. Worst of all, despite a more cautious and guarded approach after the promulgation of Martial Law, the *Imvo* was banned by the military authorities in August 1901. (18)

The banning of the *Imvo* was greeted with unmitigated approval by the *Izwi Labantu*. The *Izwi* said the action was long overdue, and that the *Imvo* had brought humiliation on to the native press and placed Africans on the side of the enemy. 'Nemesis–which punishes the arrogant and tyrannical abuse of prosperity has found out our native contemporary at last', the newspaper declared with obvious satisfaction. (19) The *Imvo* did not reappear for more than a year.

Africans in Natal also came out firmly in support of the Imperial forces, although the *Ipepa lo Hlanga*, the first African-owned newspaper in Natal, soberly noted the discrepancy between the liberal promises made by Britain and the actual discrimination suffered by Africans in the British colony of Natal. (20)

During the war, a Natal Native Congress was formed with the aim of extending the scope of the existing *Funamalungelo* and representing African interests in the same way as Indian and far-mers' interests were served by the Natal Indian Congress and the Farmers' Congress. (21) From the start, this body supported Britain in the war. At the inaugural meeting in June 1900—attended by 57 delegates representing local associations in various parts of the colony—a great deal of attention was paid to the war and sev-eral resolutions pledging loyalty to Great Britain were adopted. The first—to 'our beloved Queen'—was carried by members standing and singing *God Save the Queen*, and then followed by three cheers. The resolutions expressed mistrust of 'Boer designs' and the policies of the two Republics. Chamberlain and Milner were thanked for their firm stand on Transvaal affairs, especially regarding the liberty and rights of Africans, and the British govern-ment was asked to safeguard such rights in regard to educa-tion, to provide a degree of direct African representation in the legislatures of the different states, and to grant Africans the freedom to trade and to acquire land. Finally, the hope was expressed that steps would speedily be taken to bring about a confederation of the South African states after the annexation of the Afrikaner Republics, whose existence was described as making lasting peace and prosperity impossible. (22)

There were no newspapers and no formal organisations to ex-press the attitudes of the African urban bourgeoisie and working class in the Republics, but there were a number of incidents which clearly reflected the pro-British sympathies of these groups. The British troops who occupied Bloemfontein during the war were greeted with enthusiasm by Africans parading in the streets. (23) A house servant proudly announced, 'Now I am an Englishman.' (24) Similarly, when the British troops occupied Johannesburg, many Africans destroyed their passes as they believed, wrongly, that the Republican pass laws had become obsolete. They expected immediate equal treatment, and those in public employment sought an increase in wages to the pre-war level, with arrears. When it became clear that their expectations would not be met, some showed 'such a mutinous spirit' that the assistance of troops was necessary to arrest them. (25)

## African participation

Officially, the Anglo-Boer war was a white man's war. It was the policy of the Imperial, Colonial and Republican governments to limit, as far as possible, African participation. Neither had any intention of endangering white control over Africans. (26)

The Cape government maintained that the arming of Africans would have an unfavourable influence on the African mind in the future. They declared that Africans should not be used for any offensive purposes whatever, but Africans could be used for defence purposes where the conditions required. (27) The British government, which did not wish to offend colonial opinion, endorsed this policy. (28) Similarly, even after the fall of the major centres in the Republics, the Republican armies declined to arm potential African allies at the risk of undermining the security of whites in South Africa. (29) How much such arming was against the principles of the Republican leaders is clear from the reaction of General Cronje to the arming of Africans by the British in the besieged town of Mafeking. General Cronje wrote as follows to Colonel Baden-Powell:

It is understood that you have armed Bastards, Fingoes and Baralong against us—in this you have committed an enormous act of wickedness . . . reconsider the matter, even if it costs you the loss of Mafeking . . . disarm your blacks and thereby act the part of a white man in a white man's war. (30)

Recent studies have shown, however, that although the war was officially white, tens of thousands of Africans were involved in not only non-combatant but also combatant roles, and as suffering bystanders, sucked into the vortex of war. The most significant African contribution to the war was in the non-combatant field. Thousands of Africans were used by both sides in non-combatant capacities such as scouts, guides, runners, drivers, despatch riders, grooms, cattle herders and trench diggers. This form of African collaboration was more often than not motivated by economic considerations or attained through coercion rather than political loyalty. A substantial proportion of the black British military labour force defined their relationship in strictly contractual terms. (31) High wages and high commodity prices provided an attractive economic incentive for collaboration. (32) Some African labourers earned three or four shillings a day, as opposed to the modest one shilling of the average British soldier. (33) The military also used coercion to get hold of labour. People such as pass offenders, vagrants and suspected deserters were detained involuntarily in British labour depots. (34)

Africans also participated actively in the war although this was officially frowned upon. African troopers in the Cape Mounted Riflemen and Cape Police carried out arduous and dangerous duties in the field. (35) In the Transkei, African contingents were enrolled. A force of 500 Zulu police was recruited to protect the Zululand border and other tribes, such as Linchwe's in the Transvaal, were also armed to protect themselves against possible Republican agression. Africans fought on the British side at Dordrecht and Sterkstroom, and at Mafeking (36) where 300 Africans were formed into the 'Black Watch'.

The Africans of Mafeking were amongst the people hardest hit by the war. In the seven-month period from 12 October 1899 to 17 May 1900, 557 Africans died in the beleaguered town. No less than 117 of these people were killed in action or died as a result of their wounds. (37) Many of the other fatalities were the result of starvation and related diseases. In the most recent history of the war, Thomas Pakenham has revealed how Colonel Baden-Powell, the renowned Commander of the British garrison in Mafeking, was able to withstand the siege on the town by the republican forces by cutting back on the Africans' meagre rations to bolster the already superior rations of the whites. In the end Baden-Powell gave the Africans the choice of starvation or of expulsion from the town and running the gauntlet of the enemy. (38)

The most serious incident involving armed Africans occurred at Qulusi in Zululand where 56 of the 70 Afrikaners in an encampment were surprised and killed by a Zulu impi which itself suffered 52 dead and wounded. (39)

Official statistics are difficult to come by, but Lord Kitchener admitted in March 1902 that over 7 000 armed Africans were employed at that stage. Some estimates put the number at 30 000. After the war, when Africans were ordered to hand in all firearms, they handed in 50 488 in the Transvaal alone. (40)

The Republican forces did not arm Africans except in isolated cases. General Smuts testified that Africans fought on the side of the Afrikaners at Mafeking, but they were armed without official knowledge. (41) Generals Buller and French also reported occasional cases of armed African participation on the side of the enemy forces. (42)

The third category of Africans involved was the passive bulk of the African population, situated mostly in the rural areas, which found itself unwittingly embroiled in the war, and significantly affected by its course.

Kitchener's 'scorched earth' policy of devastating land which could be useful to the enemy and clearing affected areas of inhabitants had serious consequences for Africans in these areas. Thousands of Africans on Afrikaner farms (and in many cases those in separate African villages) had their huts burnt and were removed from the land. Most of the African males so affected were pressed into service in army departments, while the women and children were sent to concentration camps. By July 1901 there were 37 472 Africans in concentration camps in the South African Republic and the Orange Free State. More than 30 000 of these people were women and children. Ten months later the total had risen to a massive 107 344. (43)

Republican incursions and military overrule had a similarly disruptive effect on African communities and bit deep into the social and political fabric of these groups. Provisions and labour were commandeered and, in areas where firm control was established, Republican 'native law' was declared. For example, when in 1899 Republican forces occupied Jamestown in the Cape, Commandant Olivier announced that African suffrage rights would immediately be revoked. Registered African voters were ordered to report to a landdrost where their hands were specially stamped and they were issued with a pass. In this way Africans were deprived of their civil liberties and assimilated into a cheap or unpaid labour force, just at the time when thousands of Africans were being attracted by high wages to work in the British military sector. (44)

The above evidence clearly confirms the significant involvement of Africans in the Anglo-Boer War. In fact, African activities raised on both sides the spectre of a 'Native uprising'. The threat posed by Africans was a major consideration in the decision by the Republican representatives to surrender. In stating the reasons for their surrender in the discussions that preceded the Treaty of Vereeniging in May 1902, the Afrikaner leaders gave as a third reason the fact that 'the Kaffir Tribes' inside and outside the Republics had almost all been armed and were fighting against them, and that this had 'brought about an impossible state of affairs in many districts'. (45) A fortnight before the Republican surrender, General Botha had declared, 'The Kaffir question is becoming daily more serious.' (46)

The concern of the ministers of the Cape government at the arming of Africans by the military authorities (47) and the careful reading of intercepted African letters by the military censors, (48) to name just two cases in point, indicate that the 'native threat' was also never far from the surface in colonial thinking.

Against this background of Imperial guarantees and African loyalty, involvement and sacrifice in the war, Africans had hopes of a post-war dispensation in which black political rights would occupy a more prominent position in colonial politics. They hoped at least that the Cape franchise system would be extended to the Transvaal and Orange River Colony.

### The settlement

At an early stage during the war the Imperial authorities had moved to extricate themselves from the statements of Lord Salisbury and Chamberlain. By March 1901 there was no longer any doubt as to what stance the British government had adopted. In that month, Lord Kitchener, the supreme commander of the British forces, informed the Republican governments that in the event of peace it was not the intention of the British government to grant the franchise to Africans in the two Afrikaner territories before representative government was granted. And if it was given, it would be limited 'to secure the just predominance of the white races'. The legal position of coloured persons would, however, be similar to that which they held in the Cape Colony. (49)

Kitchener's statement formed the basis of the clause relating to the African franchise which was inserted in the peace treaty. Clause 8 stated simply, 'The question of granting the Franchise to natives will not be decided until after the introduction of self-government.' (50) No mention was made of Kitchener's promise to put coloured people on a level of equality with whites. The stipulations in the peace treaty were arrived at without pressure from the Afrikaners. Milner told Hertzog and Smuts, 'On this question I am at one with you.' (51)

### African post-war disenchantment

The treaty of Vereeniging came as a rude shock to Africans. Instead of alleviating their position, the status quo was maintained. They were aggrieved that the Afrikaners, who had been 'enemies of the King and British principles' in a war, were favourably treated, while the interests of Africans who had shown their loyalty by 'heart and deeds' were ignored. (52)

Why did Britain spurn an alliance with Africans during the war? As Denoon has pointed out, despite the rhetoric of Imperial paternalism, the interests of Africans were incompatible with British interests. Britain needed the Afrikaners as a collaborating group in

South Africa. Therefore, even while it was engaged in a homicidal struggle with them, Britain did not want to close the avenues to future co-operation. Africans were powerless and of little real use as a political and economic collaborating group at that stage. To promote African interests would have been to alienate even further the white communities of South Africa. To quote Denoon again, the task of the Imperial officials was to manipulate South African affairs, not to precipitate social change. This approach explains the conciliatory terms of the peace treaty. (53)

Thus it was made clear to Africans that the continuity of political life in the defeated Republics would not be disrupted by the advent of British rule. The political colour bar was retained and the position of Africans remained fundamentally the same. Measures such as the Republican pass laws continued to be applied, (54) and neither the franchise, which many desired, (55) nor the widely envisaged transfer of Afrikaner lands to Africans, (56) nor better economic opportunities, materialised. Africans soon realised that no major changes would be effected.

Sir Godfrey Lagden, who became the Commissioner for Native Affairs in the Transvaal, was forcibly struck by the false hopes held by the Africans and instructed his officers to impress on the African mind that the Afrikaners would not be deprived of their land and that the Africans should be respectful to the whites. (57) According to the testimony of General Louis Botha, before this position had been brought home to them, the 'Kaffirs looked down upon the [conquered] Boers' and regarded themselves as equals under British rule. (58)

In some cases there was an actual deterioration in the position of certain African groups after the advent of British rule, a fact which has been overlooked by many historians whose views are based on the simplified assumptions that a repressive Republican administration was replaced by a more enlightened British control. According to a Wesleyan minister in Pretoria, some 'civil, self-respecting' Africans who spoke the Dutch language fluently and had seen the 'best side of the patriarchal government', now found themselves bound by such hindrances as the pass laws from which they had been practically exempt before. (59) According to Lagden the pass laws were applied more vigorously than formerly, and defaulters in matters such as taxation were now also more speedily and effectively brought to book. He conceded that this had given rise to African discontent. (60) Africans in the Transvaal also complained that land which had previously been their inalienable property was now being appropriated by whites. (61) There was also considerable dissatisfaction in the field of labour. Africans on the Witwatersrand felt that after the war working conditions on the mines had deteriorated alarmingly. (62) Having anticipated substantial social and economic reforms, the workers were faced instead with a drastic reduction of wages, with forced labour, and with the prospect that there would be little chance of their position improving. This was brought about as a result of the massive expansion of industry planned by the Imperial government as the main component of its policy of post-war reconstruction in the Transvaal.

Thus, as Denoon points out in his provocative analysis of the Transvaal labour question, there was a clash of interests. While the capitalist mine managers expected a great volume of cheap labour, the African proletariat expected an improvement in their working conditions. The outcome was that Africans withheld their labour, giving rise to an acute shortage on the mines. According to Denoon this response to the situation by Africans was deliberate. The African labour supply was not, as might have been supposed, an inert mass there to be manipulated and exploited at will. (63)

In the rural areas too there was economic dissatisfaction and hardship after the war. Most Africans in the Republics emerged from the conflict poorer. The British scorched-earth campaign led to a large scale impoverishment. (64) The problem was exacerbated by slow and insufficient compensation payments. In 1905 there were still 5 692 claims by Africans outstanding. Africans were also disgruntled by the low rate of payment. The figures for 1904–05 show that out of a total amount of £657 003 claimed in the Transvaal only £87 517 had been paid out. The rate of seventeen per cent was lower than that which applied to the Afrikaners. (65)

Therefore, with 12 000 fatalities, their political and economic aspirations unfulfilled, unsatisfactory compensation payments and massive impoverishment in the wake of the hostilities, Africans had clearly paid a heavy price in the white man's war. (66)

# 3 African political organisations emergent, 1900–05

It was against the background of hope and disillusionment described in the previous chapter that African political activity burgeoned in the first few years of the twentieth century. A network of political organisations and newspapers, stretching through all the colonies, emerged.

## The Cape Colony

In the Cape, the group around the South African Native Congress (SANC), formed in 1898, had set out to establish the body during the war years, (1) and by 1902 it had become an organisation which the Civil Commissioner of King William's Town described as being 'influential' and representing the 'best elements of Native society'. (2) Thereafter, although handicapped like all African ventures of that time by a lack of funds, the SANC grew in importance.

Regular meetings were held at central and branch levels. From 1902 an annual SANC conference was convened at venues like King William's Town, Grahamstown and Queenstown. It was attended by delegates representing the various area branches known as the *Iliso Lomzi* (Vigilance Association). (3) At these conferences wide-ranging social and political matters were discussed. The best methods of protecting African rights and their liberties as British subjects usually formed the main topics of discussion. (4) The issues discussed and decisions taken there were fully ventilated in the columns of the SANC's organ, the newspaper *Izwi Labantu*. SANC grievances were submitted to the Cape and British governments in the form of resolutions and petitions. In a lengthy petition to the Secretary of State in 1903, for example, it raised the questions of religion, education, administration of justice, civil service appointments, labour, the franchise, polygamy, locations, liquor and 'native government', and said it viewed with concern the closing of ranks between Boer and Briton against the 'alleged black menace'. (5) In 1906, it complained about the 'apparent decline' in once proud British standards in the treatment of the African population. (6)

The SANC claimed to have branches in twenty-five districts by 1903. Many of these were active. The East London Native Vigilance Association, for example, held monthly meetings that were attended by up to 400 people of all classes. Wide-ranging issues were discussed and the grievances of the local community were forwarded to the Town Council and other local bodies. Social functions were arranged to raise funds to cover expenses and send delegates to the SANC congresses. (7) The branches were mainly in the eastern Cape and the Transkeian territories, but were also to be found in labour centres like Port Elizabeth, Cape Town, Kimberley and, significantly, Johannesburg (8) and other centres in the Transvaal. Members of the SANC formed the Transvaal Native Congress in 1903, which was affiliated to the SANC (9), and people from the Transvaal attended SANC meetings. Thus the aims of the SANC were not merely limited to the Cape. 'Native affairs' were considered from a South African perspective. In its resolutions and petitions, the SANC often raised matters affecting Africans in other colonies. Its broad aims were also reflected in the fact that the *Izwi Labantu* had Sotho columns until 1905. It claimed the right to speak on behalf of all Africans, the 'whole nation', (10) and the government was asked to leave it to the SANC to select representatives and witnesses to appear before commissions, as local officials often put forward 'irresponsible witnesses' (11) and 'ignorant chiefs and headmen' (12). But despite its aims the SANC lacked the resources, the organisation and the following to make it a truly representative mass movement.

SANC activities revolved mainly around a coterie of officials headed by Thomas Mqanda and Jonathan Tunyiswa, the President and Secretary for many years, and executive committee members such as Walter Rubusana, Charles Madosi, Robert Mantsayi, W. D. Soga, Peter Kawa, Attwell Maci, Chalmers Nyombolo, S. E. Mqhayi, the renowned Xhosa writer, and the successive Vice-presidents, Nathaniel Umhalla and Mesach Pelem. Mqanda was a farmer and headman in Peddie, and Tunyiswa a teacher based at Mount Coke near King William's Town. Mesach Pelem, who had been involved in the founding of the pioneering *Imbumba Yamanyama* in 1882, was a successful labour agent and businessman in Queenstown. The others were also prominent in their communities.

As editor of the *Izwi Labantu*, A. K. Soga was another important

SANC figure. Although not of pure African descent—he had a
Scottish mother—he always regarded himself first and foremost as
an African and worked in the interests of the African people. This
was in accordance with the wishes of his father. In a tract entitled
*The Inheritance of my Children*, Tiyo Soga left his children sixty-
two guidelines to help them through the difficulties of life in general and of racial prejudice in particular. In the first of these he
wrote:

Among some white men there is a prejudice against black men; the prejudice
is simply and solely on account of colour. For your own sakes never appear
ashamed that your father was a Kafir, and that you inherit some African
blood. It is every whit as good and pure as that which flows in the veins of
my fairer brethren. . . . I want you for your own future comfort to be very
careful on this point. You will ever cherish the memory of your mother as
that of an upright, conscientious, thrifty, Christian Scotchwoman. You will
ever be thoughtful of this tie with the white race. But if you wish to gain
credit for yourselves—if you do not wish to feel the taunt of men, which you
sometimes may be made to feel—take your place in the world as coloured, not
as white; as Kafirs, not as Englishmen. (13)

From his writings in the *Izwi Labantu*, and his activities in the
SANC, it is clear that this was a maxim that A. K. Soga accepted
and followed.

The Cape government was tolerant of the SANC. In a cabinet
minute, ministers regretted the apparent want of moderation in
the tone of the SANC, but entertained no suspicions about its loyal
intentions and recognised that it consisted of men who had
attained some prominence in their respective spheres. These
included newspaper editors, clergymen, law agents, government
headmen, traders and labour agents. The Government regarded the
public expression of the organisation's views as preferable to a dis-
contented silence. It was recognised as constituting as fairly representative a political body of advanced Africans as would be found
in any organised form, apart from in the Transkeian Territories
where the General Council system, which the government regarded
as being a model for African political participation, was in operation. (14)

The antecedents of the SANC can be traced back to the very
beginnings of African political activity in the Cape. Scholars like
Walshe and Karis and Carter describe the early organisations as
scattered and uncoordinated groups which soon expired. To some
extent this is true, but there is also no doubt that a measure of
continuity existed between some of the earlier associations and

the SANC. A distinct thread runs from the initial organisational developments of the 1880s through to the activities of the SANC. Prominent members like Rubusana, (15) A. K. Soga (16) and Mesach Pelem (17) in fact claimed that the SANC was established in the 1880s, differing on whether the year was 1884 or 1887. Jonathan Tunyiswa and N. C. Umhalla, two of the people known to have been involved in 1891 in the unsuccessful plans for a colony-wide organisation of the native vigilance associations, (18) also featured prominently in the consolidation of the SANC. (19) Clearly, in these cases, there were continuing interactions between people representing like-thinking interest groups. In 1895, Pelem wrote to Rhodes saying many opposed *Imvo*'s (Jabavu's) policy, but they had no paper to express their opposition. (20) Walter Rubusana gave an indication of the extent of the informal inter-action which took place in a letter to J. Wardlaw Thompson of the South African Native Races Committee in March 1900. Writing about the position of Africans in South Africa, he stated that his replies had been drawn up in conjunction 'with several of my educated native friends', no doubt referring to his *Izwi* and SANC confidants, who had formed their views after 'frequent travelling and coming into contact with native chiefs and leading men, both in the Colony proper and the Transkeian Territories as well as Basutoland'. (21) In a later communication he said that the as yet imperfectly organised South African Native Vigilance Association (i.e. the SANC) would in time 'undoubtedly assume the position of the representative native association'. (22) Within a few years the Congress had undoubtedly gone some way in realising this aim.

Unlike his opponents in the SANC, John Tengo Jabavu did not attempt to mobilise his supporters into a strong organisation after the war. He continued with his gradualist approach to Cape politics. Rather than form an assertive all-African body, he maintained his close co-operation with white Cape politicians and, when the *Imvo Zabantsundu* reappeared in October 1902, he continued to influence his significant informal following through the columns of his newspaper in the long-term hope that Africans would ultimately be allowed an extended role within the Cape political system. An assertive ethnic body, he felt, would stress the racial distinctions he wanted to see diminished. It would not fit with his eventual aim of a fully non-racial system. (23)

Jabavu continued to play an active and influential role in Cape electoral politics. He was actually asked by the *Afrikaner Bond* to stand for parliament in the Fort Beaufort constituency in the

1904 elections. While Jabavu saw the offer as 'at once unique and epoch-making', he turned it down on the grounds that he had already committed himself to a candidate in the field. The Progressives tried to play down the significance of the offer by claiming that it was contrived and that Jabavu was never meant to accept it, but there is no doubt that they respected Jabavu's political influence. (24)

Relations between Jabavu and his pro-Progressive SANC political opponents remained strained throughout the early years of the century. The *Imvo Zabantsundu* and the *Izwi Labantu* continued to refer to each other in unflattering terms. This enmity helped perpetuate the ideological, generational and ethnic split which had surfaced in African politics in the 1890s.

The only other active African political organisations in the Cape at the time besides the SANC were the Transkei Native Vigilance Association (TNVA) and the Transkeian Territories African Union (TTAU).

The driving force behind the TNVA was Enoch Mamba, a man who featured prominently in African politics in the eastern Cape in the first decade of the century. Educated at Healdtown, Mamba moved to Idutywa in *c*. 1878. After teaching for a few years, he became Interpreter and Assistant Clerk in the Magistrate's Office, and later headman of the local Lota location. In 1896 he was dismissed as a headman after a row with the magistrate, W. T. Brownlee. He then set himself up as a licensed labour agent. (25)

In October 1901 Mamba notified the authorities of the formation of a Native Vigilance Association (*Iliso Lomzi*), based in Idutywa, and said that it intended 'looking after the educational and local interest of the Transkeian natives generally'. (26) Initially, the association would not discuss 'higher politics' due to the prevailing war conditions in the country. (27) Mamba then set about broadening the base of the organisation. Early in 1902 he and another member of the *Iliso Lomzi* made a tour of the various districts in the Transkei to ascertain public opinion (28) and consolidate 'other organisations' which had begun to function in some districts. It is clear that some of these local vigilance groups had been functioning, even if intermittently and haphazardly, in certain areas for several years. (29) As a result of Mamba's efforts, branches were formed in Butterworth, Nqamakwe, Tsomo and Kentani. (30)

The TNVA emerged in reaction to the council system which was in operation in Idutywa and the abovementioned four districts (until 1903, when the council was enlarged to include more districts). It consisted of educated, Christian Africans who were dissatisfied with the powers exercised by traditional leaders in the District and General Councils. They said these people were unrepresentative, self-interested, illiterate 'red heathens' (31) who were averse to all civilisation. (32)

The Council system provided for partial local self-government. In each district there was a District Council, composed predominantly of local headmen chosen from amongst their own numbers or appointed by the government, which exercised some degree of local authority. Representatives of these District Councils in their turn met annually at meetings of the Transkeian Territories General Council, which discussed a broad range of subjects concerning local matters (for example, roads, education, health, agriculture) as well as general issues affecting Transkeian Africans. (33)

On behalf of the TNVA, Mamba now lobbied the General Council (34) and government officials such as the Chief Magistrate, Sir Henry Elliot. (35) On a local level, the TNVA groups in the various districts made representations to the District Councils. (36) Mamba explained the objectives of the TNVA as follows:

We found that the country was ruled by the unenlightened Natives. I mean Chiefs and Headmen. Most of the Headmen were less enlightened than the ordinary man.

At any rate, in almost every location you will find a man who is more intelligent than the Headman, who has been better educated; and the interests of education and general progress have been neglected because these Headmen are not able to give us assistance in that direction. And so we found that we should establish an Association which would both help the Natives in the district, and teach the Natives a little more of politics, a little more of agriculture, a little more of farming; instruct them in better ideas of farming and education. (37)

As many headmen in the Councils could not read or write or count money, the TNVA aimed to articulate local grievances which could then be properly submitted to the General Council for consideration. (38)

Although Mamba tried hard to gain official recognition and emphasised that the organisation was not 'antagonistic' to the government, (39) the TNVA met with official hostility from the start. The Idutywa Magistrate said it was inadvisable to recognise the body, as Mamba was an agitator who might do much harm if he succeeded in leading African opinion in the area. (40) His sentiments were echoed by the Chief Magistrate who felt that the existence of the TNVA was inimicable to the interests of the government. According to Elliot, 'The notorious and discredited Enoch Mamba was a fairly well educated, wholly unprincipled native whose education and the position he formerly held in the Government service have acquired for him much influence over the less astute natives.' (41) The government accepted these judgements. Consequently it did not encourage the TNVA or in any way recognise it. The view of the government was that the General Council and District Councils afforded Africans ample means of voicing their opinions and safeguarding their interests. (42)

To counter Mamba's influence, a meeting of headmen in the Butterworth district in 1903 decided, subject to government approval, to form a rival *Iliso Lomzi*. Its aims would be to consider and discuss all matters connected with the public welfare of the district (43) and to dissociate the district from the TNVA. (44) Both the resident magistrate, W. T. Brownlee, (45) whose involvement was perhaps not coincidental in the light of previous events, and the chief magistrate (46) saw no objection to the formation of the proposed association, but the government opposed it on the same grounds as it opposed the TNVA. (47)

The branches of the TNVA went by the same name, *Iliso Lomzi*, as those of the SANC, but the two bodies had no ties. This was simply a common designation for local vigilance associations. The two organisations in fact were involved in a dispute at one stage. In 1903, the SANC criticised the fitness of Mamba and Chief Veldtman Bikitsha to represent African interests before the Glen Grey Committee. (48) Mamba, in his turn, declared that the urban-based SANC could not understand or represent the grievances of the Transkei. (49) Differences were later smoothed over and Mamba took part in the activities of the SANC, (50) probably taking his supporters with him.

Against this background, and in the light of Mamba's reinstatement as a headman in 1904 and his subsequent participation as a leading member of the Transkeian Territories General Council, (51) it is no surprise that the TNVA had disappeared from public notice by the second half of the decade.

In 1905 another organisation, the Transkeian Territories African Union, emerged in the Transkei. Little is known about it besides the fact that it registered a strong protest against the report of the South African Native Affairs Commission in that year, and that it was active in at least four districts, Tsomo, Mount Frere, Mount Fletcher and Matatiele. The Secretary of the Union was a Mr Ntloko, probably S. Milton Ntloko, a well-known Tsomo-based member of the Transkeian Territories General Council and an ally of John Tengo Jabavu in Cape politics. (52)

In British Bechuanaland, which had the largest concentration of Africans in the Cape Colony outside the Transkeian Territories and the eastern Cape, (53) no European-style political organisations sprang up after the Anglo-Boer War as they did in other parts of British South Africa. Participation in electoral or protest politics took place under the guidance of the traditional and still widely prevalent tribal authority. This was the result of imperial policy in the region, which had the effect of bolstering rather than weakening the power of the chiefs.

When British Bechuanaland was transferred to the Cape in 1895 the status of these chiefs was left virtually untouched. Their interests were protected by the Bechuanaland Annexation Act. For all practical purposes they continued to fulfil the executive functions of administration. To remove this anomaly in the Cape system of native administration, (54) in the first decade of the century the Cape authorities attempted to weaken the powers of the Tswana chiefs and gradually to subordinate them to local administration. This gave rise to considerable dissatisfaction, at the centre of which was Paramount Chief Badirile Montsioa. He strenuously resisted the encroachment of white authority and consequently his relationship with the government was a stormy one. (55)

Representatives of the emerging educated class acted in liaison with these chiefs rather than form separate political organisations. This is corroborated by the statement of Solomon Plaatje, one of the leading members of this class, to the South African Native Affairs Commission that there were no native vigilance associations in Bechuanaland, but that whenever anything affecting Africans arose they immediately advised the Chief about the matter and asked him to take steps. The chiefs would carefully consider this counsel. Chief Badirile Montsioa explained that

The older headmen of the tribe are a number of primitive men who know nothing about South African politics, which appear to be difficult to be understood by the white people themselves. If anything affecting the welfare of the nation is under consideration, we have enlightened men among ourselves whom we consult under such circumstances, and their counsel may be relied upon to be better than that of a solicitor, as their interests will be at stake. (56)

There was, therefore, close co-operation between the tribal and educated élites to preserve from further encroachment the rights and independence the Baralong still possessed. To a greater or lesser degree, this applied elsewhere in South Africa as well.

There was little scope for an alternative approach in this isolated

and traditional society. The extent to which traditionalism dominated in Bechuanaland can be gauged from the fact that there
were only about a hundred Africans on the voters' roll there in
1904. Plaatje stated that this was an accurate assessment of the
number of people capable of exercising the vote intelligently.
(57) These figures remained constant for several years. (58)

Bechuanaland too was served by a newspaper controlled by
Africans. This was the *Koranta ea Becoana* (Bechuana Gazette)
which was published in Tswana and English. It was started in
April 1901 by Nathaniel Henry Whales who was also the proprie-
tor of the *Mafeking Mail and Protectorate Guardian*. After twelve
numbers had been published it was purchased in August or September of that year by Chief Silas Molema, a member of the royal
family of the Baralong tribe, and secretary and chief adviser to
Paramount Chief Montsioa. (59) The *Koranta* was the first Tswana-
owned newspaper. The shareholders included chiefs such as Israel
Moiloa and Bathoen (60) and also, in all likelihood, members of
the Montsioa family.

Solomon Tshekisho Plaatje, regarded as a son by Chief Molema,
became editor of the newspaper. Although he had received little
formal schooling, Plaatje was to achieve considerable political and
literary renown. Besides his journalistic achievements—he later edited another paper, *Tsala ea Batho*—Plaatje distinguished himself as
a leading African National Congress politician; as a political writer
(whose classic work *Native Life in South Africa* is an indictment
of the 1913 Native Land Act); and as a diarist, linguist, interpreter
and social worker. Amongst other things, he helped produce the
first Tswana phonetic reader and translated several of Shakespeare's works into Tswana. Several years of travel abroad added
to his varied experiences, making him one of the most remarkable
South Africans of his time. (61)

Like its counterparts, the *Koranta* had circulation problems (62)
and consequently was dogged throughout by financial difficulties,
which resulted in its appearing irregularly. Eventually these problems were to force Chief Molema into liquidation. At the end of
1906 control of the newspaper passed back into white hands. (63)

Towards the end of 1900, a fourth African-controlled newspaper
in the Cape Colony, the *South African Spectator*, was launched in
Cape Town. The editor was West African-born F. Z. S. Peregrino,
who became a well-known and colourful figure in Cape politics.
After leaving West Africa, Peregrino studied in Britain, where he
lived for twenty-three years before moving to the United States.

He stayed there for a short while and then settled in South Africa in November 1900. Within weeks of his arrival the first issue of the *Spectator* appeared. (64)

Peregrino made it clear that the aim of the *Spectator* was to advocate the cause of all sections of the black population. He said it was an organ for all 'the people who are not white' and it was published by one 'who aspires not to be white'. (65) Based as it was in Cape Town, it catered mainly for coloured readers, but Xhosa columns aimed at an African audience also appeared. Because Peregrino could not understand Xhosa he was dependent upon others for the tone and accuracy of the reports. (66)

Peregrino wished to see the African press co-operating more closely than it did. He succeeded in establishing close relations with the editor of the *Izwi Labantu*, A. K. Soga, whom he met in Cape Town in March 1902. He saw the *Spectator* as playing a complementary role to the African newspapers appearing elsewhere in South Africa. His paper adopted a high moral tone, carrying no advertisements for alcohol, fortune telling or other activities that he thought undermined the morals of the populace. He made it clear that he would not use the *Spectator* to provoke quarrels or denigrate others. Much information about American blacks appeared in the *Spectator*, particularly the activities of the African Methodist Episcopal Church. To instil race pride in blacks, articles were published on their world-wide advancements and achievements. The *Spectator* also frequently complained about cases of colour discrimination in the Cape. However, Peregrino, who was socially conservative, cautioned blacks to seek redress for their grievances by working with rather than against the relevant authorities.

Besides his newspaper activities, Peregrino founded the Cape People's Vigilance Society, which again was open to 'all people in South Africa who are not known as white'. The Society survived for a decade, but it was never a large organisation. (67) It was later described derisively, but not wholly inaptly, by Peregrino's opponents as having consisted of only him and his office boy. (68) Peregrino also acted as an agent for African tribes and interest groups, amongst others the South African Native Congress. (69) The extent of his activities can be gauged from his voluminous correspondence with government officials of all four South African colonies.

## The Transvaal

Under the new post-war British administration, educated Africans in the Transvaal began to organise themselves into formal political associations to protect their interests and articulate their views for the first time. Within a few years more organisations had emerged in the Transvaal than in any other colony. This was probably because of the diverse composition of the African labour force in the mining industry. Following the pattern of the Cape and Natal, an independent African newspaper was started.

The first organisation to come to the notice of the authorities was the Zoutpansberg Native Vigilance Association. It soon broadened its activities and developed into the Transvaal Native Vigilance Association (TNVA). It was founded during the course of 1902 and applied for government recognition in December of that year. P. A. Masibi was the first chairman (70) and many of the principal chiefs of the Transvaal were members. The authorities were unwilling to allow the TNVA to call these chiefs together for meetings, as this would give the Association 'an undesirable importance in the minds of the natives'. (71) Nevertheless it is clear that the TNVA maintained contact with chiefs in the northern Transvaal and that they in turn co-operated with the TNVA and brought to its attention certain grievances. In reply to government queries the TNVA Secretary declared (according to still incomplete records) that 226 people had contributed to the Association's funds. The membership was much higher, however, as returns from outside branches were not available. (72)

The TNVA espoused the cause of political and civil rights for every civilised man irrespective of colour, and the full privileges of British citizenship for all. One of its objects was to educate Africans in their rights. In this respect significant success was achieved when representations regarding unsatisfactory railway transport and the over-charging of Africans on the railways led to government investigations which resulted in an improvement in the situation. (73) The TNVA also made representation to the government on behalf of African squatters who were being turned off land—sometimes with standing crops—as the new British administration began seriously to implement the 1895 Republican Squatters Law in order to promote 'closer settlement' and capital-intensive agriculture. (74)

With the idea of spreading the influence of the TNVA, it was decided at a meeting of the Association in July 1903 to start a newspaper. As a result, the first African-owned and -controlled newspaper in the Transvaal, the *Leihlo la Babathso* (the Native Eye) appeared with columns in Pedi, Sotho and English. (75) However, after a year it was discovered that the editor, Levi Khomo, had become mentally deranged and had squandered the Association's hard-earned finances. The paper was obliged to close down a few months later. (76)

When Simon Molisapoli, Khomo's successor as the Association's Secretary and editor of the newspaper, attempted to convene a meeting to investigate this state of affairs, Sir Godfrey Lagden, the Chief Commissioner for Native Affairs in the Transvaal, re- fused to sanction the gathering on the grounds that 'the public assembly of Africans from all parts of the colony was calculated to prejudice the peace, order and good government'. (77) The local *Zoutpansberg Review* criticised Lagden's refusal in the light of the findings of the South African Native Affairs Commission, which had approved of the principle of African political activities being conducted openly, and of which Lagden himself had been chair- man. (78) Eventually, almost a year later, permission was granted for the meeting after a petition had been sent directly to the Lieutenant-Governor through a local lawyer. At the meeting it was decided to raise the Association's subscription to one pound so that the *Leihlo* could be resuscitated and the Association be put on its legs again financially. (79)

Lagden's role in the affair hardly supports Eric Rosenthal's and Les and Donna Switzer's contention that he was a patron of the newspaper and encouraged its activities. Far from giving any real support Lagden detailed the Native Commisioner of the Northern District to be watchful of Khomo's political activities. He said further, 'The best way to deal with a mischievous man, if this man be so, is to employ him and I should be glad if you saw your way to give him some kind of work. If he is attached to Government his thoughts will have full play and the possibility of his making serious mischief will be curtailed.' (80) If in fact any assistance was provided, therefore, it was probably done with ulterior motives in mind.

In the meantime, members of the Cape-based South African Native Congress were active in the Transvaal. On 16 May 1903 a Transvaal branch was formed in Johannesburg and the General Secretary of the SANC mother body notified the Transvaal Native Affairs Department about its existence. Two SANC represen- tatives were also reported to have held meetings in the Waterberg Dis- trict and in Rustenburg, where they succeeded in forming another branch. (81) Later meetings of the Transvaal body were attended by delegates from throughout the colony stretching as far afield as Pietersburg. (82)

The Congress was multi-ethnic in composition. Members of the Xhosa-based SANC established the organisation and for a number of years its activities revolved around a Basotho tramming contractor, Jesse M. Makhothe, while a Zulu, Saul Msane, also featured prominently in Congress affairs. Msane, a compound manager for the Jubilee and Salisbury gold mining company, was a founder member of the Native Congress and later became Secretary-General of the African National Congress and editor of its newspaper *Abantu Batho*. (83) According to Makhothe's evidence the Congress was a society comprising educated Africans and some chiefs. (84) Its main aims, as set out in the constitution, were to protect and promote African rights with regard to the surveying of lands, education and religion, to lay grievances before the authorities, and to suggest alternatives to the Government. (85) The Congress became one of the two most influential African organisations in the Transvaal before Union.

The most important organisation next to the Congress was the Transvaal Basotho Committee. Its founding date is not certain, but in 1904 it was represented before the South African Native Affairs Commission by its chairman, Paulus Malatye, and eight others. On this occasion Malatye, who had been born in the Transvaal and grew up there, called for Africans to be permitted to own land and complained about the ill-treatment meted out to them in Johannesburg, and about the taxation and the curfew regulations imposed on them. His complaint that the curfew interfered with their church work and activities such as concerts indicates the involvement of westernised Africans in the organisation. (86) Moreover, the Basotho Committee took an active interest in education, being at one stage the only body recognised by the Government for the purpose of receiving contributions towards the Inter-Colonial Native College Scheme. (87) Like all its counterparts the Committee sought to protect African interests or, as it was put in the vernacular, to be 'the husband of the widows and the father of the blind'. (88)

The Basotho Committee emphasised that its concern was not limited to the position of Basothos only and in 1905 it approached the Secretary for Native Affairs with a view to bringing existing African organisations under the Committee. William Letseleba, the secretary, stated that on account of the many bodies in the Transvaal Africans 'are in great trouble'. The Basotho Committee wanted one body to co-ordinate the activities of all Africans. Enquiries by the Native Affairs Department showed that the Committee's request was motivated by the divisive activities of the *Iliso Lomzi* organisation, which appeared to have 'incurred the displeasure of the majority of the educated natives of Johannesburg'. (89) However, nothing came of the Committee's plan and the bodies continued to function independently of each other.

The *Iliso Lomzi Lo Notenga* (Transvaal Native Landowners' Association) (90) consisted, according to the evidence of a Native Commissioner, of Edward Tsewu, moderator of the Independent Presbyterian Church, and a number of his personal friends. (91) Other leading members were Tyesi Gunuza, D. H. Hlati and James Ngubane. (92)

Born and educated in the eastern Cape, Edward Tsewu was a typical representative of the new educated African class. A student contemporary of men like Elijah Makiwane and P. J. Mzimba at Lovedale, he obtained a teacher's certificate there in the late 1870s and was subsequently ordained as a minister there in 1883. After working for a while in the Transkei, he was sent to Johannesburg by the Presbyterian Free Church as a missionary to the rapidly expanding urban labour force on the Rand. In the 1890s he clashed with the church authorities and, following the example of Tile and Mokone, he established his own separatist church. (93)

Tsewu achieved prominence in 1905 when he successfully brought a court suit against the Registrar of Deeds on the question of African land rights. The exclusion of Africans from rights to acquire property in the Transvaal had for long been a constant and major source of irritation to them. They were dissatisfied with the continuation of prohibitive Republican land measures after the war, and with the abuses that resulted from the practice whereby Africans acquired land through sometimes unscrupulous white intermediaries.

Matters came to a head when Tsewu contested the refusal by the Registrar of Deeds to register land in his name. The judgement decided that the relevant Republican legislation was invalid and that there were no legal impediments to prevent the registration of property in the name of Africans in the Transvaal. (94)

While the court decision was a triumph for the Africans who wished to extend their rights and opportunities, it raised the fierce opprobrium of the white community which was united in its resolve to prevent this from happening. Sir George Farrar introduced a resolution in the Legislative Council aimed at reversing the court ruling. It was passed and embodied in a draft ordinance. (95) Africans protested to the Colonial Office against the proposed measure (96) and when it came before the new Liberal government in England, the Colonial Secretary Lord Elgin refused to sanction the ordinance. (97)

Tsewu later fell into disfavour with Africans from other organisations by claiming the 'entire credit' for the successful test case. They also accused him of attempting to interfere with associations like the Native Congress and the Basotho Committee. At one stage there was even talk of applying to the Native Affairs Department for Tsewu to be deported, but no such action materialised. (98) But around the time of Union, he was back in the forefront of African politics again.

In addition to the Native Vigilance Association, the Native Congress, the Basotho Committee and the *Iliso Lomzi*, there were also smaller organisations in the Transvaal, such as the Bapedi Union and the African Political Society in Pretoria, (99) of which little is known. All these bodies displayed a more or less common policy and approach. They all resented the inferior status of Africans in Transvaal society, and the Native Affairs Department files bear testimony to their persistent efforts to alleviate their position. They expressed grievances on such wide-ranging issues as taxation, passes, education, religion, trading rights, labour, land tenure, travelling on railways, ill-treatment in towns where they were prohibited to use pavements and tram cars, and the lack of protection against physical abuse. On the whole the government was tolerant towards the development of African associations. Often grievances submitted by these bodies were passed on to the relevant departments for consideration and representations were sometimes replied to in great detail. However, in the final analysis, although the organisations were tolerated their demands went largely unheeded.

## The Orange River Colony

As was the case in the Transvaal, a small group of Africans in the Orange River Colony began to organise themselves politically and to articulate their views after the imposition of British authority over the country.

In January 1901, within a few months of the occupation of Bloemfontein, a deputation headed by D. T. Matsepe, A. P. Pitso, J. B. Twayi, Jan Mocher and E. Slamat presented a 'loyal address' on behalf of 25 000 blacks living in the colony to the Military Governor. The address was signed by over 250 people including several Basotho, Baralong and other chiefs. The address stated that the British occupation 'brought with it relief and contentment in the hearts of many'. The British government, the signatories added, was 'the only government to which a native can look for his common rights'. Finally, 'We wish to assure Your Excellency . . . of our constant readiness to prepare the way for the introduction of Civil Government, and with it those changes in the constitution of the late Orange Free State to which we most humbly and anxiously look forward.' (100)

Clearly blacks envisaged greater freedom under British rule but, as we have seen, these illusions were soon dispelled. The status quo was retained and they remained excluded from rights which they desired. Almost a decade later there were still thirty-one laws which discriminated against blacks on the statute books of the Orange River Colony. (101) Frustrated, yet allowed more freedom of expression than previously, they began to articulate their feelings.

The first organisation to come to the notice of the authorities was the Native Committee of the Bloemfontein District in 1902.

The Committee was composed of pre-war leaders in the Waaihoek township who had gathered themselves into a formal organisation with the advent of British rule. Previously, they had been 'block men' appointed by the former government. These were people, each representing a block of buildings in Waaihoek, to whom any matter affecting the location could be referred. They had now formed themselves into a 'reflection committee' which discussed all questions of interest to blacks. (102)

In March 1902 the Committee presented an address to the Deputy Administrator, Sir Hamilton Goold-Adams. He was also handed two petitions for transmission to the High Commissioner and the Secretary of State. The one petition was signed by 1 479 blacks from the districts of Bloemfontein, Thaba Nchu, Kroonstad, Rouxville, Smithfield, Fauresmith and Zastron. The petition was not as extensively signed as the organisers had hoped because the war conditions had complicated the collection of signatures, particularly in the rural areas. The circulation of the petition in these areas and the issues raised by the Committee indicate that it was not merely concerned with local matters.

The petitioners requested the imperial government to grant blacks in the Orange River Colony the same political, land, educational and commercial rights as other British subjects. They

declared that there could be no liberty without representation. On
the local level the Deputy Administrator was asked to put a stop
to the shameful lashing of black offenders. The petitioners stated
that it was unbecoming of the British authorities who prided
themselves on their standard of civilisation to allow such a practice
to continue. (103)

The members of the Committee who composed the deputation
to Sir Hamilton Goold-Adams were A. P. Pitso, J. B. Twayi, E.
Shimmat, J. Lavers, A. Louw, P. Motsufi, I. Motshselella, A. Jordaan and P. Phatlane. (The first three had been in the 1901 deputation referred to above.) The deputation reflected the scattered
and diverse ethnic composition of the black population of the
colony outside the 'reserves'. Its members were drawn from the
Basotho, Baralong, Mfengu and Thembu groups, as well as from
the coloured population. (104) The Basotho formed by far the
largest group in the colony, followed by the Baralong, Zulu and
Mfengu. In 1904 these groups numbered 130 313, 37 998, 35 275
and 6 275 respectively. (105)

It is significant that a person of mixed parentage was a member
of the Native Committee. In the Orange River Colony all blacks
were defined as 'Coloureds'. No distinction was made between
Africans and people of mixed blood. (106) Because of this, and
the fact that locations were mixed, (107) and that the scattered
African population in the colony did not have a strong sense of
tribal identity, inter-African as well as African-'Coloured' co-
operation was facilitated. This was in contrast to what was happening in the other colonies.

Later this co-operation was affected by the formation of a separate organisation for coloured people, the Orange River Colony
affiliate of the Cape-based African Political Organisation, formed
in Cape Town in 1902. In the ensuing few years the APO formed
branches in Bloemfontein, Edenburg, Fauresmith, Jagersfontein
and Reddersburg. (108)

In May 1903 the Native Committee, now styled the Bloemfontein
Native Vigilance Committee, was officially recognised by the government. (109) By the following year an Orange River Colony
Native Vigilance Association was in existence. It appears to have
been a loose alliance of vigilance committees from various centres
in the colony. The leaders of the Bloemfontein committee were
the driving force behind the ORCNVA. When the Association appeared before the South African Native Affairs Commission in
September 1904 it was represented by names already familiar to

us: J. B. Twayi, J. Mocher, J. Lavers and A. Jordaan, in addition to B. Kumalo, E. T. Mpela and Peter Thaslane. (110)

Although the earlier petitions reflected the same desire, the ORCNVA was the first concrete attempt to unite Africans on a colony-wide basis. The idea behind the Association was to arrange meetings where common problems could be discussed by the various local committees. The Association also interviewed and petitioned the colonial and imperial authorities.

The leaders of the ORCNVA were representative of the emerging class of modernists. The group mentioned above which appeared before the South African Native Affairs Commission consisted of two ministers of religion, two cartage contractors, a mason, a brickmaker, and a dray-cart driver. (111) Although the Association represented the 'progressive, enlightened' Africans, it also sought to encourage those in a traditional state to become 'civilised'. This term was defined in a wide sense. Civilisation was reflected in the mode of living and 'progressiveness' of an individual. One did not have to be a Christian or be able to read or write to fall into this category. (112) The case of Jacob Lavers was given as an example. He could neither read nor write, but he lived like a civilised man at home, was a successful businessman, and had become a leader in his community. (113) The ORCNVA regarded most Africans in the colony as being civilised according to these standards. (114)

The Association felt that all Africans who had attained a certain level of progressiveness based on Cape standards should be allowed the franchise and the related privileges of civilisation. Failing this it wished Africans to be represented by special representatives elected by themselves. Although they wanted no colour differentiation, they were satisfied that these representatives should be white until such time as relations between the races improved. Tribal Africans should be governed by Native Law, but at the same time encouraged to become enlightened. When that stage was reached they should become subject to regulations applicable to civilised men. (115)

The Association was also dissatisfied that all Africans were treated the same regardless of class. Under Ordinance 2 of 1903 only ministers of recognised Christian denominations and teachers in recognised educational institutions holding higher education certificates were exempt from Native Law. (116) Ministers of African separatist churches were excluded from these provisions. (117)

The greatest grievances harboured by blacks were against the special oppressiveness of municipal laws which they felt infringed seriously on their rights and reduced them to a position of virtual slavery. Municipalities not only passed the most stringent laws without consulting them, but they also sometimes refused to entertain deputations sent to present grievances. (118) The Bloemfontein Native Vigilance Committee, for example, was not recognised by the Municipality. (119) It was told that grievances should be brought forward by the individuals directly concerned.

The Crown Colony government, on the other hand, recognised the need for African spokesmen, (120) and sometimes intervened on behalf of Africans in disputes with local authorities. For instance, on one occasion it approached the Bloemfontein Town Council in regard to grievances about compensation payments raised by Jacob Lavers and Peter Phatlane, Chairman and Secretary respectively of the local vigilance committee, which it felt were justified, (121) although strictly the government had no right to interfere in this entirely municipal matter. (122)

Unlike the Town Council, the government also demonstrated its respect for the Native Vigilance Committee in Bloemfontein by asking for its advice and assistance. Government notices and laws were disseminated through the Secretary of the Committee, (123) advice was sought on suitable candidates for positions in government departments, (124) and the body was asked to help the authorities trace people. (125)

Another important African body was the Orange River Colony Native Teachers' Association (ORCNTA), which was formed in 1903. Although not a specifically political organisation it had clear political implications. Politically conscious Africans regarded education as the greatest instrument of enlightenment and progress. (126) Therefore the Native Teachers' Association had a valuable role to fulfil. The fact that at one stage the Secretary of this body was also the Secretary of the Orange River Colony Native Vigilance Association, and made representations on behalf of both bodies to the government, (127) reflects this. The aim of the ORCNTA was to make provision for 'the development of the Natives' within the Colony by means of a sound education. (128)

Unlike the other colonies, the Orange River Colony produced no African newspaper. However, a fortnightly African newspaper from neighbouring Basutoland, the *Naledi ea Lesotho* (*Star of Basutoland*), was circulated in the colony. The *Naledi* was launched in 1904 by Solomon Morine. (129) Articles were in Sotho and

English. Because óf Basutoland's close proximity to the other colonies, news from these areas appeared regularly in the *Naledi*. The newspaper was also circulated in the Transvaal and Bechuanaland. (130) Although it was no proper substitute for an organ presenting the views of local groups, the *Naledi* nevertheless kept Africans in the colony in touch with African opinion in the rest of South Africa. The few extant copies of the *Naledi*, and the references to it in the contemporary press, give an insight into its editorial policy. Broadly speaking, like the other African newspapers, the *Naledi* campaigned for African rights and was critical of the discriminatory treatment meted out to Africans throughout South Africa. (131)

## Natal
Meanwhile, the Natal Native Congress (NNC), founded during the war years, continued to grow. A few months after its inaugural meeting in June 1900, the Congress met again. (132) It now claimed to have twenty-three different branches scattered through Natal. (133)

The NNC was a more representative organisation than the *Funamalungelo* and was open to all Africans, exempted or not. (134) The aim of the NNC was to cultivate a political awareness amongst Africans by educating them about their rights under the prevailing system of government and laws and, most importantly, to act as a forum for ventilating grievances. As a result several petitions were sent to the colonial and Imperial authorities in the first years of the century.

Although the NNC was formed specifically to cater for all classes of Africans, it struggled to gain the support of traditional chiefs. Martin Lutuli, the chairman of the NNC for its first three years (and an uncle of Albert Luthuli, later leader of the African National Congress and winner of the Nobel Peace Prize), told the South African Native Affairs Commission in 1904 that the NNC was in touch with the chiefs, some of whom were in sympathy with it, but that they failed to send representatives to Congress meetings. Nevertheless they were as far as possible kept informed of developments. (136) Later in the decade, Lutuli and other Congress members were prominent in the formation of another political association, the *Iliso Lesizwe Esimnyama*, which was apparently formed with the aim of ensuring greater tribal participation in politics. (137)

The political demands of the NNC and the politically conscious class it represented were moderate compared to those in the other colonies. Instead of demanding full participation for 'progressive' Africans in the colonial political system, it asked only that they be represented in Parliament by sympathetic whites. (138) As Mark Radebe put it at the inaugural Congress meeting, 'The natives must not rely too much on themselves, but, where possible, must endeavour to enlist the sympathy of English gentlemen.' (139) At this stage, therefore, politically conscious Africans in Natal shared the paternalistic assumptions of the dominant group that Africans 'should not fancy themselves as equals of the white man and expect the same rights as him'. These words, used by a specially invited 'native sympathiser' at the same meeting, (140) give an idea of the extent to which the whites in Natal were imbued with conceptions of white exclusivity and superiority. Any attempts by Africans at political expression were viewed with the utmost hostility, particularly in view of the unrest which became prevalent after the Anglo–Boer War in Natal.

Against this background, the NNC was viewed with suspicion and disapproval by colonists and government alike. Although it was far from radical, the general feeling was that it was a mischievous body which should never have been allowed to meet at all. (141) The government did not attempt to interfere with the growth of the NNC, probably because any action of this nature would have been irregular in terms of the privileges granted to exempted Africans, (142) but a close watch was kept on its activities. The Criminal Investigation Department was detailed to keep a check on it, but was unable to gain admission to its meetings. African detectives reported that private meetings were held to which admission was reserved for holders of tickets issued by the Congress Secretary to people whose credentials had been established, and they were, therefore, unable to ascertain what had taken place. (143)

The NNC feared antagonising the touchy Natal government so it took pains to emphasise the moderate intentions of the organisation. (144) Irresponsible or unconstitutional actions could have had detrimental consequences, not only for the Congress, but also for individuals. Chiefs, for example, were servants of the state and could be removed from their positions on the grounds of their being 'unsuitable to fill a position of trust under the government'. (145) This action was contemplated against Stephen Mini, a prominent member and later President of the NNC. (145) His political activities probably also contributed to the rejection by the Natal

Cabinet of his application for the franchise in 1905. (147)

Although the NNC had been intended to supersede the *Funamalungelo* after the turn of the century, this latter organisation appears to have continued to exist, if quietly and precariously, or to
have been temporarily reformed. In 1905, it raised £25 to challenge
before the Supreme Court a Native High Court decision that children of exempted fathers were not themselves automatically
exempted because they had been born after exemption had been
gained. Its efforts, however, were in vain. The Supreme Court up-
held the decision of the Native High Court and nothing came of
the *Funamalungelo's* previously stated intention to take the matter
to the Privy Council. (148)

The first African-owned newspaper in Natal was the *Ipepa lo
Hlanga*, which was launched shortly before the NNC was founded
in 1900. It was sponsored by the Zulu Printing and Publishing
Company floated by Chiefs Isaac Mkize and James Majozi, who
also played a prominent role in the formation of the Congress;
Chief Mkize was its first President. (149) Mark Radebe, another
Lovedale graduate, was the editor of the *Ipepa*. Radebe described
the aims of the newspaper to the South African Native Affairs
Commission as 'speaking for the nation, . . . that is to say for the
Black people'. One of the Commissioners thereupon remarked,
'Your aspirations are rather national.' (150) Most of the *Ipepa*'s
contributors were members of the Congress. The newspaper
provided them with a vehicle to disseminate their ideas, as embodied
in NNC attitudes, at grassroots level.

The *Ipepa* met with white hostility from the start. It was regarded
generally as a seditious propaganda organ for the Ethiopian movement, an ominous and vague appellation under which all African
political aspirations were subsumed. (151) The newspaper followed a bold policy critical of white attitudes, which soon led to
its suppression by the Natal government. After several articles
seemingly seditious to whites, including one entitled '*Vukani
Bantu!*' (i.e. 'Rise up you people!'), had appeared in the *Ipepa*'s
columns, the directors were summoned before the Under–Secretary
for Native Affairs at the end of 1901. Chiefs Mkize and Majozi
were given a 'friendly warning' whereupon they 'voluntarily'
decided not to take out a licence for publication the following
year. At the time of its closure, the *Ipepa* had 550 subscribers and
had distributed 50 free copies. (152)

The *Ilanga lase Natal*, edited by John L. Dube, was the next
African newspaper to appear in Natal. Started in 1903, the *Ilanga*

was printed initially on the same press as the *Indian Opinion* at Gandhi's Phoenix Settlement. Later Dube acquired a separate press which was housed at his neighbouring Ohlange Institute, the first African-controlled industrial school in South Africa. Ohlange was run along the lines of Booker T. Washington's famous Tuskegee Institute in the United States, where his philosophy of race pride, industrial education and self-advancement was implemented. Dube's success with the Ohlange Institute and his editorship of the *Ilanga* helped him rise to an undisputed position of leadership in Natal African politics. By the time of Union he was to rival Jabavu and Rubusana in influence. He was reverently called *Mafukuzela*, 'the one who struggles against obstacles'. (153) Like the *Ipepa*, the *Ilanga* was also regarded with suspicion and kept under strict surveillance by the authorities. Regular translations of the newspaper's Zulu columns in the Native Affairs Department files testify to this.

* * *

Thus within a few years of the turn of the century the small politically conscious African educated class had everywhere mobilised themselves into political organisations, which, the South African Native Affairs Commission noted, 'were taking an active and intelligent interest in political affairs', (154) and had established newspapers to serve their general interests. In addition, in some areas, local political or semi-political associations which had no ties with any of these groups were formed to protect local interests. These included location committees and, in the Cape, local voters' organisations. To cite a few examples: in 1903 the Germiston and District Native Vigilance Association presented an address to the Colonial Secretary, Joseph Chamberlain, during his visit to South Africa; (155) in evidence before the South African Native Affairs Commission the existence of a 'Young Native Party' is mentioned but no further details are given; (156) the interests of Zulus working in Cape Town were protected by the Cape Town and District Zulu Association; (157) and John Tengo Jabavu led his local association in King William's Town.

These groups may have had irregular lifespans and received little exposure, but they were symptomatic of an ever-increasing African interest in political affairs and organisation at grassroots level. This also manifested itself in numerous African voluntary organisations such as teachers associations, social and sports clubs, temperance and debating societies, and organisations for the protection of African financial interests. (158) Although not explicitly political in nature, these bodies had the effect of heightening social and political awareness.

The activities of the various associations were reported in the vernacular newspapers, some of which were official mouthpieces for these groups. There was a broad tendency for African political organisations and political newspapers, working in tandem and fulfilling complementary roles, to emerge almost simultaneously. The political organisations enabled leading men to discuss strategies while the newspapers provided them with a vehicle to disseminate these ideas. The newspapers played an invaluable role in stimulating African political consciousness and publicising the activities of political groups.

With the aim of bringing about closer co-operation between these newspapers, a short-lived Native Press Association was inaugurated after a meeting in King William's Town in 1904. The initiative for the meeting came from F. Z. S. Peregrino, editor of the *South African Spectator*. This Association reflected a growing collective awareness amongst politically conscious Africans, a move in the direction of political unity, and a desire to represent and lead African opinion. In its way it was a forerunner of the national political organisations which later emerged. However lack of co-operation, notably on the part of John Tengo Jabavu of the *Imvo Zabantsundu*, soon caused the Association to collapse. (159) Attempts to resuscitate it in the second half of the decade failed. (160)

Although the circulation of these newspapers was never high, their impact was wide. Their influence extended to the most remote kraals and locations. Often eager groups of illiterate Africans would crowd around the local minister, school-teacher or other educated person whose task it was to read the latest news and the newest pronouncements of a *Mafukuzela* (John Dube) or an *into ka Jabavu* (son of Jabavu). Sol Plaatje recalled how as a boy he had frequently been called upon to 'read the news to groups of men sewing karosses under the shady trees outside the cattle fold'. (161) In this way interest in politics amongst Africans of all classes was stimulated and the political horizons of the audiences were broadened by discussions and comments on matters affecting them in the newspapers.

# 4 Towards African political unity

The emergence and growth of African political organisations and newspapers in all the colonies after the war went hand in hand with the development of more unified African responses to events, and with greater co-operation between these like-minded interest groups. They began gradually to develop a sense of mutual identification and to co-ordinate their activities across territorial boundaries and parochial barriers.

A growing, increasingly interdependent economy encouraged African mobility and integration, and the very fact that after the Anglo-Boer War Africans in all the South African colonies were for the first time under the control of Britain made it easier for them to set common goals and seek ways of co-operating. Despite colonial boundaries, there was now a common South African infrastructure.

Furthermore, the Treaty of Vereeniging, which perpetuated the Africans' status quo instead of heralding the beginning of a new political order for them, provided a political rallying point which should not be underestimated. Africans were aggrieved that the Boers, who had been 'enemies of the King and British principles' in the war, were now favourably treated, while the interests of Africans, who had shown their loyalty by 'heart and deeds', were ignored. (1) They were offended that 'the avowed cause of Justice, Freedom and Equal Rights, for which the war had been undertaken, should have been so easily abandoned'. (2) For many years African politicians in all the colonies would denounce Vereeniging as one of the greatest injustices that had been perpetrated against them. (3) To a great extent, these strong mutual feelings of outrage served to unify African political opinion throughout South Africa.

Within a few years after the war further major developments occurred which confirmed the trend towards greater white local political autonomy and power at the expense of African interests and the idealised democratic British non-racial principles which Africans wished to see implemented. Fully aware of the threat which the developments posed to these aims, African opinion became more vocal, organised and united in protest.

## The South African Native Affairs Commission

As one of the first steps in the direction of a federation of the British colonies in South Africa after the war, Lord Milner, the British High Commissioner for South Africa and the chief architect of the post-war policy of reconstruction, convened the South African Customs Conference in Bloemfontein in March 1903 for the purpose of discussing customs dues and other questions of common inter-colonial interest. The Conference issued a ten-point resolution, the last of which reads as follows:

That in view of the coming federation of the South African Colonies, it is desirable that a South African Commission be constituted to gather accurate information on affairs relating to the natives and native administration, and to offer recommendations to the several Governments concerned with the object of arriving at a common understanding on questions of native policy. (4)

As a result, the South African Native Affairs Commission (SANAC), under the chairmanship of Sir Godfrey Lagden, and consisting of representatives from the four colonies, came into being. The Commission travelled extensively throughout South Africa to collect evidence in the sixteen months it took before reporting in April 1905. In its report it rejected the principle of political equality between Africans and whites, thus reinforcing majority white opinion and setting important guidelines for future South African policy.

SANAC favoured a segregationist policy. It recommended separate voters' rolls for Africans and whites. Africans should vote for a fixed number of members to represent them in the various legislatures. While recommending an extension of political rights to Africans in the northern colonies, it wished to see these rights restricted in the Cape Colony. SANAC arrived at this decision after noting with alarm the growing influence exerted by African voters in the Cape. It concluded that the political system prevailing in that colony was 'sure to create an intolerable situation and is an unwise and dangerous thing . . . , pregnant with future danger'. While recognising that some form of representation was essential, it believed that this should be granted without conferring on Africans political power 'in any aggressive sense, or weakening in any way the unchallenged supremacy and authority of the ruling race'. (5)

From the start Africans reacted with scepticism to SANAC, fearing that it would make exactly the recommendations it eventually did, thus paving the way for the disenfranchisement of Cape Africans. (6) While it was collecting evidence, spokesmen from all the colonies in South Africa appeared before it to air African grievances and formulate their views on broad intercolonial matters. Mostly the demand was for the franchise and the extension of the Cape political system to the other colonies as well as for land rights and greater economic and educational opportunities. There was also widespread reaction in the wake of the SANAC report. Views were expressed in the columns of newspapers, in meetings and statements by political organisations and in petitions to the authorities. Among the organisations to discuss SANAC's findings were the Transvaal, Natal and South African (i.e. Cape) Native Congresses, (7) and the Transkeian Territories African Union. The Secretary of the latter body corresponded with other Cape leaders with a view to arranging a 'General Native Congress' to discuss the 'averse' report, but this did not materialise. (8)

The South African Native Congress was probably the most outspoken critic of SANAC, which had refused to accept a statement by the Congress on the grounds that it did not believe that 'the true expression of Native Opinion in South Africa is to be obtained either by Public Meetings or through the existing Associations'. (9) Both the Congress and its organ the *Izwi Labantu* newspaper, referred for a number of years in disparaging terms to SANAC. The recommendation that the Cape franchise should be altered was the chief source of hostility. The *Izwi*/Congress alliance considered that Lagden was merely a tool in the hands of the Rand mining magnates. (10)

There was another reason for the Congress's hostility towards SANAC. In its report, SANAC proposed a scheme for a central college for African higher education similar to the Queen Victoria Memorial Scheme started by the Congress in 1902 when it decided to collect funds for an African College to be built in memory of Queen Victoria. (11) The Inter-State Native College Scheme, which was started towards the end of 1905, a few months after SANAC had reported, soon overshadowed the Queen Victoria Memorial Scheme. Tensions arose as a result.

The Inter-State scheme enjoyed the patronage of influential whites and Africans in all the colonies, (12) while support for the

Queen Victoria scheme was restricted mainly to South African Native Congress supporters. Of course, the latter could not compete with their opponents in terms of organisation and resources. The Congress tried to counter the influence of the Inter-State scheme by expressing reservations about the religious denominational bias that it claimed the white-supported scheme would have, and by saying that it did not come from Africans, but was being imposed upon them. (13)

The competition between the two schemes also acquired a political dimension because John Tengo Jabavu, the political adversary of the *Izwi*/Congress group, was an enthusiastic supporter of the Inter-State scheme. He was not only a member of its executive committee but also its travelling Secretary. In this capacity, he travelled extensively to address meetings and bring the scheme before the people.

In contrast to the Queen Victoria scheme, which faded and quietly expired, the well-organised Inter-State scheme grew from strength to strength. Although it was directed mainly by whites, and backed by the Cape government, Africans from all the colonies enthusiastically supported the venture.

Many Africans served on local committees and attended the conventions held at Lovedale at the end of 1905 and in 1908 to dicuss the scheme. The first convention was attended by 160 prominent African delegates from the four colonies and the three protectorates in Southern Africa, and was the most representative gathering of Africans that had yet taken place anywhere. In less than two years, Africans had already guaranteed a total of £40 000, more than double the sum initially estimated from that source by the organisers. (14) Support was forthcoming from bodies such as the Basutoland National Council, the Transkeian Territories General Council, African political organisations such as the Transvaal Basotho Committee and the Transvaal and Orange River Colony Native Congresses, local African communities and African newspapers. (15) Later, prominent members of the South African Native Congress, including the Vice-president and Secretary, also joined the scheme. Even the convenor of the Queen Victoria Memorial Scheme, A. K. Soga, was tempted to join but refrained from doing so at the insistence of his supporters as this would have involved a loss of face. (16)

The Inter-State Native College Scheme eventually reached fruition when the South African Native College, the present-day University of Fort Hare, was founded in 1916. Many of the African political leaders of subsequent generations in sub-equatorial Africa were educated at Fort Hare. (17)

## The Bambatha rebellion in Natal

The SANAC report was followed closely by disturbances in Natal which culminated in the outbreak of the Bambatha rebellion in 1906, and by developments towards responsible government in the Transvaal and the Orange River Colony.

The Bambatha rebellion started in February 1906, when two white police officers were killed by a party of armed Africans in the Richmond area of Natal, and lasted for several months. Ever since the war there had been unrest, which was exacerbated by the imposition of a Poll Tax on all adult males in the colony at the end of 1905. When the disturbances broke out, martial law was proclaimed and the militia were sent in to quell the unrest in the disaffected areas. The dissident Chief Bambatha and his followers retreated to the dense Nkandla Forests where they engaged the troops in a guerrilla struggle for over a month. In June 1906 this resistance was crushed at Mome Gorge. Further outbreaks occurred in the Mapumulo division. These too, were soon put down, bringing active fighting to an end. However, unrest continued throughout 1907. The disturbances exacted a terrible toll. Between 3 500 and 4 000 Africans were killed, in contrast to some two dozen whites. (18) The Natal disturbances were a cogent factor in promoting the idea of inter-African political co-operation throughout South Africa. Dr Marks ends her superb work on the rebellion by declaring that its most important outcome was the national unity it engendered amongst Africans. (19) Most politically conscious Africans were outraged by the heavy-handed actions of the Natal government during the disturbances.

The *Izwi Labantu* condemned the actions of the Natal authorities in the strongest terms, and declared that Natal whites were unfit to rule themselves let alone a million Africans. *Izwi* also raised the question why Great Britain, with whom ultimate responsibility rested, had allowed this 'shameful' and 'monstrous' situation to develop. (20)

The editor of *Izwi Labantu* A. K. Soga, who was now pushing a socialist line in the newspaper, regarded the Rand mining magnates as one of the root causes of the harsh repression of Africans during the disturbances. He said this repression was aimed at impoverishing Africans and forcing them to the mines. According to Soga, the capitalist mining magnates ('plutocrats, moneyed interests, bloated millionaires, Randlords and their confederates') were at the bottom of the retrogression that was taking place in 'native policy' throughout South Africa. They were aided by the collaborating 'extremist Dutch anti-nigger type'. (21) At this stage Soga was also encouraging Vigilance Associations to begin to think about the question of strikes and labour disputes as this would be 'a phase of the coming struggle between capital and labour'. (22)

Another severe critic of the handling of the disturbances was Alfred Mangena, who adopted a legalistic view in contrast to Soga's class interpretation. Mangena, a South African studying law in London, drew up two petitions against the Natal government and laid a charge against the Governor of Natal for illegally declaring martial law. The Natal government attempted to discredit Mangena, but this led to law suits in which Mangena was awarded damages. (23) His stout resistance to the Natal government greatly enhanced his reputation, (24) and when he returned from Britain a few years later as the first African in South Africa to have qualified as a Barrister-at-Law, he immediately sprang to prominence for his defence of African interests. (25)

Jabavu's *Imvo Zabantsundu* was also vigorous in its condemnation of Natal's handling of the disturbances. The newspaper stated during the unrest that the fighting could be over in a few days if the Natal government changed its vindictive attitude to an approach more consonant with reason. Many Africans wished to stop fighting, but continued for fear of being 'butchered' like their compatriots at Richmond, *Imvo* added. (26)

The South African Native Congress placed the blame for the disturbances squarely on the Natal government and declared that the imposition of taxation without representation was a crime. (27) The Transvaal Native Congress adopted a similar line. It declared that the situation in Natal served as a warning of the dangers of granting responsible government without adequately providing for African representation. It recalled the words of Harry Escombe, one of the prominent Natal politicians of the time, who had warned that 'if it is right to tax people it is right to give them representatives to say whether the taxes should be lessened or made as light as possible', and said his standpoint had been vindicated by events. (28)

In Natal itself, the position of all Africans, particularly those who were politically active, was questioned by the colonists and authorities when the rebellion broke out. However, according to Marks and Welsh, the Natal Native Congress was at no stage

even remotely implicated in the rebellion. It was really a traditionalist or peasant rebellion. Although many members of the Congress were not without sympathy for the rebels, they realised the
futility of violent methods. Some *Kolwas*, mostly members of
independent African separatist churches, did take part in the rebellion, and others supported the government forces, but the majority
preserved a precarious neutrality. This gained for them the tag of
*amambuka*, 'traitors', from the rebels. (29)

As Marks has pointed out, there was a tendency on the part of
whites to see every educated African as a dangerous Ethiopian
ready to drive the white man into the sea. When it became known
that separatist preachers had accompanied Bambatha's forces into
the field, they regarded this fear as having been justified. A massive white backlash developed and the spectre of Ethiopianism
loomed larger than ever. The Ethiopian menace and other exter-
nal influences, rather than genuine grievances, were given as the
main reasons for the disturbances. (30)

Against this background, any agitation on the part of educated
Africans was treated with deep suspicion by the authorities. Africans were unable to speak their minds on the events without fear
of retribution. This was nowhere better illustrated than in the
controversy that developed around the *Ilanga lase Natal* newspaper. After John Dube had used the words *'Vukani Bantu!'*–they
had earlier led to the suppression of the *Ilanga's* predecessor, the
*Ipepa lo Hlanga*–in an editorial, (31) the *Ilanga* was branded as
dangerous, libellous, seditious and treasonable by the *Natal Witness*, (32) and Dube was summoned before the Governor. He was
given a severe reprimand and told that since even whites refrained
from discussing the situation openly it was out of the question
that Africans should do so. (33)

A belated apology in the *Ilanga* followed. Dube wrote that he
regretted having given the government cause to suspect his loyalty.
He added, 'There are grievances to be dealt with, but I can fully
realise that at a time like this we should all refrain from discussing them, and assist the government to suppress the rebellion.'
(34) Dube's retraction met with scathing criticism from the
*Izwi Labantu*: 'We would rather lose a thousand papers than our
self respect.' (35)

However, this was easier said from the calm atmosphere of the
Cape than done in the reality of rebellion-racked Natal. To sur-
vive Dube had to rely on a politically ambiguous strategy. Thus
while he strove for black unity and believed that 'justice would

be done only when the African ruled the country', a moderate approach was the only feasible means of obtaining political power for Africans. (36) To have reacted aggressively would have been to invite almost certain suppression. Even this moderate approach did not put the authorities at ease. In August the Minister of Native Affairs suggested the suppression of the newspaper, (37) but apparently Dube's status as an African exempted from Native Law prevented this. The Governor, Sir Henry McCallum, stated in the following month that if the *Ilanga* persisted in publishing mischievous and seditious articles, additional powers would have to be requested. (38)

Clearly, therefore, to speak out needed considerable courage, particularly in the case of Dube, who wished to gain white financial assistance for his industrial school, the Ohlange Institute, and ran the risk of alienating prospective backers. (39)

## Responsible government

At the same time that the disturbances in Natal were taking place, the Transvaal and the Orange River Colony were being led towards reponsible government by Sir Henry Campbell-Bannerman's Liberal government. (40) As early as 1904 Milner and Lyttleton had admitted the failure of Crown Colony government in the Transvaal. Accordingly the Unionist government in Britain looked for alternatives. The result was the promulgation of the Lyttleton Constitution in March 1905, which granted the Transvaal a representative constitution. (41)

However, this constitution never came into force. It was abrogated in February 1906 by the Liberal government which had come into power at the end of the previous year. A committee under the chairmanship of Sir J. West Ridgeway was sent to South Africa to investigate an electoral system suitable for the colonies. (42) During its stay of two months, the committee collected evidence from all interested parties. Its recommendations were accepted by the British government. With regard to the question of the African franchise, the committee recommended that the matter should be left to the new self-governing states themselves to decide. Any attempt to dictate policy to the colonies would be bitterly resented. The best policy would be 'to trust to their sense of justice'. The committee was convinced that sooner or later the new legislatures would deal with African representation in a liberal spirit. However, the report added, 'It cannot be reasonably expected that the native population will ever be placed on an equality with the white population in the matter of franchise.' (43)

On 6 December 1906 Letters Patent were issued by an order-in-council granting the Transvaal responsible government. (44) In June 1907 the Orange River Colony was given similar status. (45) With all four colonies now enjoying responsible government, the prospects for federation increased.

The issue of responsible government presented the fledging African political organisations with their first real opportunity to protest. They responded keenly to these developments. Africans realised that the inferior position they occupied in the ex-Republics would be permanently entrenched under responsible government unless adequate safeguards were adopted. As a result they appealed to the imperial government to protect their interests in the most concerted political action yet displayed on their part.

## African responses to responsible government
### The Transvaal

With constitutional change in the offing, a massive petition of Africans was forwarded to the British government by the United Native Political Associations of the Transvaal in April 1905. The petition referred to the deterioration in the position and status of Africans since the British occupation, and asked the imperial government to reserve for consideration all legislation affecting Africans under the new constitutional dispensation. It was signed by no less than 46 chiefs and 25 738 others. (46) Typically, Lagden played down the strength of feeling that existed. He said the petition 'was rapidly engineered by a few half-educated natives who are connected with native newspapers . . . [and] cannot be taken to have been understood by or to represent the natives in general'. (47)

The United Native Political Associations were probably, as the title suggests, a loose alliance of the main political organisations in the Transvaal, namely the Transvaal Native Congress, the Transvaal Native Vigilance Association, the Transvaal Basotho Committee and Edward Tsewu's *Iliso Lomzi*. Later in the same year, the leaders of these four organisations represented African grievances in a joint deputation to the Governor, Lord Selborne, and Lieutenant-Governor, Sir Arthur Lawley, on which occasion they again emphasised the great importance Africans attached to imperial protection. The Transvaal Native Congress appears to have played the leading part in the alliance. It drew up the address which was presented to Selborne and Lawley, while the other bodies then added insertions and signed the address. (48) The co-operation between these bodies, which was to be repeated the following year, was only a temporary arrangement and did not affect their independence. It seems to have been partially inspired by the government, which advised the different groups to work together. (49) For practical purposes, the government preferred to deal with them all at once, instead of one by one, when they requested interviews.

When the West Ridgeway committee was in the Transvaal in May 1906 to investigate attitudes towards responsible government, it heard representations from African representatives as well. On 19 May 1906 Mangena Mokone, founder of the separatist Ethiopian Church and later leader in South Africa of the African Methodist Episcopal Church, led a deputation that appeared before the committee in Pretoria. Three days later the Transvaal Native Congress testified in Johannesburg. (50)

During their visit to the Orange River Colony in June, the Commissioners also heard the views, amongst others, of a deputation from the 'Transvaal Basuto Political Association' in Bloemfontein. (51) Whether the deputation represented the Transvaal Basotho Committee, which had perhaps for some reason not given evidence while the West Ridgeway Committee was in the Transvaal, or whether it was an *ad hoc* local committee of Transvaal Basothos is uncertain.

The West Ridgeway Report does not detail the views of the various organisations. It mentions only that many associations and individuals pressed the claim for blacks to have the vote. These people were informed that according to the terms of the Vereeniging treaty, the committee was not in a position to deal with the question. (52)

However, around the same time, African views in the various colonies on the subject of responsible government were clearly enunciated in several petitions to the Imperial authorities. The timing of these petitions suggests that they were drawn up in response to the visit of the West Ridgeway committee.

On 5 June 1906, Jesse Makhothe, the Secretary of the Transvaal Native Congress, requested an interview for the Congress executive with Governor Selborne. (53) The purpose of the interview was to discuss matters which the Congress intended raising in a petition to the King. (54) One of the subjects they wished to raise at the interview was the reservation of Africans to the Crown if responsible government was granted. (55) The Congress subsequently withdrew the request (56) because Lord Selborne was away in the Orange River Colony, and would not have been able to meet the executive until after the petition had been finalised. (57)

In their fourteen-page petition to the House of Commons the executive asked for the protection of the Crown and the implementation of Rhodes's dictum of equal rights for all civilised men. The British government was urged 'not by any means to hand over Natives to the colonial legislators' as the trend in native legislation in recent years had been towards keeping Africans in a position of inferiority and perpetuating the stereotype image of Africans as 'hewers of wood and drawers of water'. Instead of promoting African interests, the Native Affairs Department was fulfilling a negative role. Moreover, there was no clear-cut native policy. Africans were governed neither by 'native law' nor by 'civilised law' and this had lead to great confusion. The Congress criticised British post-war policy and the records of British administrators, especially people like Milner and Lawley. It said that they had acted as 'disinterested spectators' while African interests came increasingly under pressure. The Congress was emphatic about its demand for representation and was equally insistent that it was the responsibility of Britain to see that this was granted. Besides the wider political issue, the Congress also listed a whole range of specific grievances such as pass laws, education, the labour question, war compensation and taxation in its petition. (58)

In a three-page petition to King Edward VII, attached to the one above, the United Native Political Associations of the Transvaal requested that African interests should be safeguarded under responsible government. Unless Africans were in some way protected in the framing of the Transvaal constitution, their position would be 'a degrading and humiliating one, and one on which your petitioners look with considerable alarm'. They asked that the Imperial government protect African interests either by assuming entire control and responsibility, through the High Commissioner, for Africans in the Transvaal, or by reserving an Imperial veto on legislation affecting Africans until such time as they were granted a franchise similar to that enjoyed by Africans in the Cape and Rhodesia. (59)

During this period of political excitement, yet another major African political organisation. emerged alongside the four existing groups in the Transvaal. This was the African National Political Union (ANPU), which was formed early in 1906. (60) The aims of the Union were 'to unite all the natives of Africa into one body socially and politically', to represent to the government any grievances which affected the African population and to secure for them the same liberties enjoyed by other British subjects. The Union was led by Sefaka Mapogo Makgatho (61) (who later became the President-General of the African National Congress from 1917 to 1924). (62) Initially he had sought to join the Basotho Committee, but on meeting with no response, he grouped his followers into a separate association. (63)

Although the ANPU was soon active throughout the Transvaal, its strongholds were at Mphahlele's Location near Pietersburg where Makgatho, the son of a chief, was born, and in Pretoria where he and the secretary of the ANPU, Phillip Maeta, were attached to the teaching staff of the Kilnerton Institution run by the Wesleyan Methodist Church. (64) Besides Mphahlele, many other chiefs in the northern Transvaal became members of the ANPU. These included Sekhukhuni, Matlala, C. J. L. Kekane, Dinkuanane and Phasuane. Records show that Makgatho and some of his followers were also involved at one stage or another in the activities of the Transvaal Native Vigilance Association, (65) the other political organisation with its stronghold in the northern Transvaal. In this region more than half the African locations in the Transvaal, and an almost proportionate figure of the African population, were situated. (66) The position here roughly paralleled that in British Bechuanaland where members of the educated class worked closely with the chiefs. The former kept the latter informed and also acted as spokesmen for them. (67)

Makgatho, who spent three years studying in England before teaching at Kilnerton between 1887 to 1906, was also the founder of the Transvaal African Teachers' Association which in time became one of the strongest African organisations in the country. (68)

## The Orange River Colony

In the Orange River Colony too the level of African political activity intensified with the approach of responsible government. In efforts to guard their interests, Africans made representations before the West Ridgeway Committee, approached the colonial authorities and petitioned the Crown.

During the fortnight the West Ridgeway Committee was in the Orange River Colony, several African interest groups appeared before it. On 7 June, deputations from the Native Vigilance Association and the AME Church testified in Bloemfontein, and on 19 June the Committee met a deputation of Baralongs at Thaba Nchu, as well as the aforementioned Transvaal Basuto Political Association in Bloemfontein. (69)

Also in that month the Orange River Colony Native Vigilance Association interviewed the Lieutenant-Governor, Sir Hamilton Goold-Adams, (70) and petitioned the King. The petition had much in common with those of the Transvaal Africans. The petitioners expressed confidence that the welfare of Africans in the colony would not be forgotten in the consultations leading to responsible government, and drew particular attention to the question of African representation:

Your petitioners earnestly deprecate the clause in the Vereeniging Peace Terms which compromised the claim of the Natives to what they feel is a legitimate franchise. Indeed, it seemed to them deplorable that before bloodshed ceased the avowed cause of Justice, Freedom, and Equal Rights, for which the war had been undertaken, should have been so easily abandoned.

Your petitioners believe that without some measure of representation in the legislatures of this Colony their interests will ever remain in jeopardy, and that however they may conform to the rules of civilised life they can never hope to enjoy those of its privileges as, for instance, liberty to trade and to own land, which are at present withheld from them. (71)

The petition went on to ask for some kind of representation or the retention of control over native affairs by the Imperial government until African enfranchisement was accomplished. It then highlighted the hardships caused by municipal laws in the colony.

In another significant development the various local vigilance associations decided at their annual meeting in Bloemfontein on 16 June to revise the constitution of the Vigilance Association and to form a permanent and more explicitly political organisation. As a result in the new body's title the designation 'Vigilance' was replaced by 'Political'. (72) The government refused to recognise the body unless it revised its title, regarding the use of the word 'Political' as 'injudicious and incorrect'. The Governor made several amendments to its constitution, which he stated were 'all in the direction of showing that the Natives wish to do everything in a constitutional manner'. (74) The Association was forced to comply. It dropped both words from the title and simply styled itself the Orange River Colony Native Association. The word 'Association' was gradually superseded by 'Congress'. Local vigilance committees were also reorganised to fall in line with the terms of the revised constitution.

Despite the change in name and the shift in emphasis from a largely defensive to a more active and agressive role, no major changes occurred. The composition of the organisation remained the same and it continued to pursue a moderate, strictly constitutional path in attempting to achieve its aims. Established figures like Kumalo, Lavers, Mocher, Phatlane and Twayi, together with emerging leaders like Elijah Tshongwana and Thomas Mtobi Mapikela, continued to play a prominent part in its activities.

The official aims of the Congress were to further the material, social, political and religious welfare of Africans in the Orange River Colony. Branches were to gauge local opinion, present grievances to the local authorities and keep themselves informed about any new regulations. If the regulations were detrimental to the interests of the people, it was the duty of the branches to offer alternative suggestions to the local authorities. Matters that went beyond the jurisdiction of the local authorities had to be submitted to the annual congress of the organisation, which would approach the government in a 'fit and proper manner', after due consideration of the subject. Urgent matters could be submitted direct to the Executive Committee. The constitution emphasised the fact that the members should act in a responsible manner so that 'the bonds of friendly relations between His Majesty's European and Native subjects' would not be jeopardised. All activities were to be in complete accordance with statute law, local municipal regulations and the consent of the local authorities. (75)

*The Cape Colony*

Africans in the Cape Colony whole-heartedly supported the appeals for the protection of African interests in the ex-Republics. With their long record of participation in electoral and organisational politics in the relatively liberal political system of the Cape, they naturally assumed the responsibility of acting as spokesmen for the subordinated Africans in the other colonies. This was borne out when the South African Native Congress decided at its annual conference in April 1906 to send a cable to the British Secretary of State for the Colonies, Lord Elgin, asking to be represented before the West Ridgeway Committee. (76) The SANC was advised to apply direct to the Committee itself. (77) However, as the West Ridgeway Committee did not take evidence in the Cape Colony, the SANC did not have the opportunity of presenting its views. This concern nevertheless demonstrated that the people in the Cape wished to see their fellow Africans freed from their subservient status. They also were reacting to the approach of a broader South African unity, dominated by the principles of the white colonists and threatening existing African rights.

In July 1906 John Tengo Jabavu and thirteen others presented a petition to the House of Commons. In it they not only demonstrated their opposition to a colour bar in the constitutions of the Transvaal and the Orange River Colony, but also foresaw that precedents were being set for the restriction of the political rights of Africans in the Cape. The petitioners declared that the exclusion of African British subjects from the franchise would be 'an unmerited degradation of all natives', would establish a new departure in South African British colonies, and would give weight to attempts to deprive blacks 'not only of a privilege due to them in the Federal Union which is much sought after, but of these which they hold in the Cape Colony itself'. (78)

A lengthy petition to the Commons printed in the *Izwi Labantu* in June 1906 on behalf of the African and coloured people of South Africa had similar aims to Jabavu's. It sought assurances against any tampering with the traditional Cape political system and wished to see the principle of equality before the law, 'which is a basic tenet of all civilised governments', extended to the ex-Republics. That Africans were not ignorant of the drift towards a federation of the South African colonies, and the implications thereof, is abundantly clear from this petition:

(e) The denial of the Franchise and Representation to the Natives under a Federal Union of the various States—which your Petitioners firmly believe is contemplated by the opponents of the Native franchise as aforesaid—would have an important bearing upon the relations of His Majesty's subjects, inasmuch as there is already a tendency to treat the Native Question as a 'domestic' one, and to eliminate the interference of the Imperial factor in the treatment of the Natives and the protection of their rights and liberties.

(f) While your Petitioners recognise and respect the absolute right of the several States to independent control of their domestic questions, your Petitioners respectfully submit, that having regard to the extreme racial antipathies at present existing in South Africa, and especially the strong prejudices manifested against the Natives, it would be unwise to treat such an important question as a domestic one. The proper arrangement of the relations of the various races is of supremest importance to the smooth and satisfactory working of the machinery of the future Federal Union. (79)

At its April 1906 conference the SANC also considered the possibility of sending a delegation to interview Lord Elgin to protest about any colour bar in the responsible government's constitutions. It felt that such a delegation should be as broadly-based as possible, and should include J. T. Jabavu. (80) Despite the proddings of the *Izwi Labantu* and enquiries about the SANC's plans from Dr Abdullah Abdurahman, who was busy preparing to lead a delegation of the African Political Organisation to Britain, the idea of a delegation fell through. (81) The SANC's actions were confined to the forwarding of resolutions to Lord Elgin. In asking for Imperial protection and extended political rights for Africans, these followed the same pattern as the various petitions. (82)

The recognition by the SANC of the desirability of forming an alliance which included leaders of all sections of the African community reflected the urgency with which Africans viewed the situation and the need they saw for unity. In this respect the willingness to co-operate with Jabavu is especially significant. Jabavu too, it seems, was appreciative of the need for unity at this time because the *Izwi* wrote that 'It is pleasant to record that the Editors of the Native Press are working in complete harmony on this great and paramount question which touches the interests of all the Natives.' (83)

*Natal*

The Africans in Natal were in general too preoccupied with their own precarious position in the rebellion-ravaged colony to give much attention to the constitutional plight of fellow Africans in the Transvaal and the Orange River Colony. However they were not unappreciative of the need for some form of African unity to meet the growing challenges facing them all. In September 1906 John L. Dube called for a conference of the Natal, Transvaal and 'Cape' (South African) Native Congresses in his newspaper, the *Ilanga lase Natal*. He noted that tribal antagonisms were dying down and declared that this was an indication of progress. (84) He said Africans should realise that 'Unity is Strength'. He gave the achievements of the *Het Volk* party in the Transvaal as an example: only a few years after the Anglo-Boer War, Louis Botha had become Prime Minister of the Transvaal. (85)

**The Imperial response to African opinion**

The pleas to Britain by African organisations for Imperial protection and for greater participation in the political systems of the ex-Republics were ignored. The new constitutions left the position of Africans practically unaltered, and such safeguards as there were in effect offered little protection for them. Under the new constitutions, the Governors were to exercise authority over all Africans in the two colonies according to the powers vested in them as Paramount Chiefs at the time of responsible government. The Governor-in-Council was empowered to summon African chiefs, and others with special knowledge and experience of the subject, to discuss the administration of native affairs and other matters of interest to Africans. He was to consider reports submitted to him by any such assembly and to take action which he considered proper. Land set aside for Africans was to be inalienable except in accordance with laws passed by the Legislatures. (86) Some Africans felt that these provisions provided them with a sufficient degree of Imperial protection, (87) but these hopes were groundless. Effective control of native affairs was in the hands of the Transvaal and Orange River Colony Ministers.

The constitutions were remarkable gestures of conciliation on the part of the British government towards the recently vanquished Afrikaners. They were intended to win the latter's loyalty to British paramountcy by persuasive means, rather than through the coercive policies adopted by Milner. To this end, Britain was prepared to give its approval to the political colour bar. In so doing the Liberal government sheltered behind the provisions of the Vereeniging Treaty. However, it need not have done so. Had Britain wanted to it could have exerted pressure for greater African political representation. (88) The fact of the matter was that such action would have defeated Britain's aim of winning the confidence of the Afrikaners. Britain sacrificed African interests in favour of placating the Afrikaners, thus hoping to pave the way for a strong, united and loyal white South Africa with its great military and economic potential for the British Empire. Nevertheless, the vague promises about protection for Africans in the constitutions that emerged from Whitehall, the continued confidence of many Africans in British paternalism, and the uncharacteristically sympathetic postures conveniently adopted by some statesmen in the ex-Republics towards native affairs at this time, although all in fact counting for little, kept alive amongst Africans hopes for the future.

Exemplifying the soft line taken by Afrikaner leaders, at a *Het Volk* gathering early in 1906 General Smuts said that if the mining magnates attempted to get African forced labour if the Chinese were repatriated, they would find the Afrikaners as strong in defence of African rights and liberties as they were of their own. Referring to statements in the same vein by General Botha, the *Izwi Labantu* welcomed in an editorial the 'modification of the hereditary anti-native attitude of the Boer leaders in the Transvaal' and said it raised the possibility of a united front of Bantu, Boer and Briton against the menace of unrestrained capitalism, which threatened the liberties of the whole people. However, 'Are they prepared to maintain the "Open Door" in the Transvaal and the Orange River Colony as in the Cape? That is the test of Dutch assurances. We have certainly not yet arrived as a people at a point where the Bantu can regard the Dutchman without suspicion.' (89) The South African Native Congress recorded its deep appreciation of the friendly attitude exhibited towards Africans by *Het Volk* leaders and said it trusted that this spirit of conciliation would continue to characterise the relations between the people of South Africa. At the same time, however, the Congress wished to impress upon the Afrikaner leaders the beneficence of the Cape system. The resolutions were forwarded to *Het Volk* and the Dutch press. (90) *Imvo* reported favourably that ex-President Steyn had said that he believed that the best class of Africans could not be justly deprived of the franchise and welcomed the new 'liberal and generous' approach of the Boer leaders. (91)

However, the reality of responsible government was that Africans were excluded from the political process for the foreseeable future. Britain had countenanced a constitutional system in two of its colonies which contradicted its own egalitarian democratic ideals. Humanitarian concern for blacks in South Africa was outweighed by matters of practical politics.

This was an important step in the evolution of a racially exclusive South African political system.

## Tentative moves towards African unity

By mid-1907, amidst a growing spirit of 'South Africanism' amongst whites, and in reaction both to this movement and to other stimuli, the idea of African political unity was taking shape. Throughout the various colonies groups had mobilised themselves into political organisations and around newspapers, and had begun to react in unison to events affecting them. Tentative moves towards realising some form of unity between these bodies had also begun. The programmes of some of the organisations embodied

aims for a broad African unity (92) and, as many examples in the
preceding pages have shown, resolutions were passed on matters
affecting Africans in areas outside the 'local' one.

Interchange between various organisations was taking place on a
small scale. The main bodies in the Transvaal joined forces to petition the Imperial government in 1905 and 1906 in connection
with responsible government. And it should be noted that the
Transvaal Native Congress was started as a branch association of
the Cape-based South African Native Congress, and although it
later functioned as an independent organisation, the two bodies
kept in contact. Saul Msane, a founder member of the Natal Native Congress, joined the Transvaal Native Congress while working on the Rand mines, but maintained his links with the NNC
at the same time. In 1907 the NNC entrusted him with promoting their *Isivivane* scheme for economic self-help in the Transvaal. (93) In that year, in order to protect 'members of our Congress in the Transvaal', the NNC also requested the Prime Minister
of Natal to appoint an official to give assistance to Natal Africans
working in the Transvaal. (94) H. R. Ngcayiya served on the executives of both the Orange River Colony and Transvaal Native Congresses in a short space of time. (95) Josiah Gumede of the NNC
acted on behalf of Basotho chiefs in the Orange River Colony in
their claims for land in that colony. (96) While in London in 1906,
Dr Rubusana of the South African Native Congress approached
the Colonial Office about land rights on behalf of Transvaal Africans. (97) We noted in the last chapter the founding of the short-
lived Native Press Association. Co-operation was further stimulated
by inter-colonial educational and religious activity, manifested
most obviously in the Inter-State Native College Scheme and the
workings of both the separatist and the established churches.

## Co-operation with the Ethiopian churches
The relationship between the so-called Ethiopian or separatist
church movement and the politically active groups at this time was
a highly significant factor in inter-African co-operation and in the
political activation of Africans at grassroots level. Hitherto, while
scholars have recognised the political implications of religious independency, they have had difficulty in establishing direct connections between the independent church movement and participation
in the emergent political organisations. (98) However, the link is
emphatic.

We must first ask to what extent was the Ethiopian movement

politically motivated. Dr James Stewart, one of the most prominent missionaries in South Africa at the time, assessed the movement as follows:

It began professedly as a religious movement, or more exactly, as an ecclesiastical one, seeking to create separate churches, i.e. corporate churches not congregations, wholly under native control. There was no real spiritual element
or spiritual life, and therefore it cannot be truly called a religious movement.
It was social, seeking for equality and freedom from white direction, and
though not intentionally or professedly political, sooner or later it must come
into collision with English or Imperial views or policy in this country. (99)

Fundamentally, this argument is sound. Differences with the white-
controlled mother churches arose over social rather than religious
matters, since the organisation and the biblical interpretation of the
secessionists were basically the same as the churches from which
they seceded. (100) And it is clear that their religious and social
programmes had political implications. 'Africa for the Africans'
and related catchphrases must have been like music to the ears of
the subordinate class, and a hugely convenient and effective means
of neutralising competitive white missionaries. They gave people
with little hope everything to hope for. None of the programmes
of the Ethiopian movement expressed explicit political aims, but
in practice African nationalist sentiments were frequently expressed
openly, albeit sometimes by individuals far removed from the
restraining influences of central organisations or leaders. There is
too much evidence from too many parts from people with first-
hand experience to conclude otherwise. Speaking from his own
experiences, Elijah Makiwane said, 'Those who refuse to join this
movement are now called white men or Britons. I have myself
been so called on several occasions and the meaning is that those
who have not joined have not been true to their nation, because the movement is regarded as the building up of the Africans
as a people. To be called *Mlungu* [white man] is therefore considered a great reproach.' (101) Another African minister, Elijah
Mdolomba, gave similar testimony: 'The old men [in Thembuland]
said that this thing [Ethiopianism] was separating them from their
children because it was being said by one to the other, "You are
on the white man's side, and you are no good now." '(102) James
Dwane testified that the official attitudes of the Ethiopians were
acceptable, 'but in the practical teaching and training the tendency
is to set the black race against the white race'. (103) *Imvo*'s policy
was that Ethiopianism was not compatible with loyalty and peace
because it preached that Africans should have nothing to do with

whites in Church, State and everything else. (104) On enquiry representatives of separatist churches regularly disclaimed any political intentions, (105) but they could hardly have been expected to be outspoken and candid in their testimony before an unsympathetic and powerful authority. That would only have served to incriminate themselves.

In fact, socio-religious and political issues were inextricably entwined. The constituency of the politican was the flock of the preacher. The disabilities the people suffered were the responsibilities of both. Therefore the religious movements should be seen as an extension of the political organisations—or perhaps it was the other way around, because the churches spread out more at grass-roots level than the political associations. As Christopher Saunders remarks, the pulpit could be an extremely effective means of politicisation in a largely non-literate society. (106) Ethiopian ideas were also imparted at schools started by the separatist churches. Thus the church got the masses involved, while the political associations drew their members from the educated. Politicians and churchmen complemented each other in stimulating the latent force of African political consciousness.

The most convincing support for these assertions is that many leading figures of the independent churches were also leading active politicians. Pambani Mzimba, of the Presbyterian Church of Africa, took part in electoral politics at the Cape, (107) and was nominated as a member of a proposed deputation to represent African grievances in Britain by the South African Native Congress in 1906. (108) James Dwane, (109) who forged the links between South African separatists and their American counterparts in the AME Church, and Jonas Goduka, (110) head of the African Native Mission Church, also took part in Congress activities. Edward Tsewu, Moderator of the Independent Presbyterian Church, was secretary of the *Iliso Lomzi* in the Transvaal and later a founder member of the African National Congress. (111) H. R. Ngcayiya, co-leader of the Ethiopian Church, served on the executive committees of the Transvaal and Orange River Colony Congresses. He too was a founder member of the African National Congress. The other co-leader of the Ethiopian Church, I. G. Sishuba, acted as an electoral agent for Cape politicians. (112) F. M. Gow of the AME Church was President of the African People's Organisation. (113) The Revds Kumalo and Mpela of the same church served on the executive of the Orange River Colony Native Vigilance Association. (114) Finally, the founder of the original Ethiopian Church, Man-

gena Mokone, was himself prominent for many years in African
politics in the Transvaal. He was connected with the Pretoria-based
African Political Society. (115) The examples do not end here.

Thus, an acute political awareness at the top levels of the Ethiopian movement was often expressed through the channels of political organisations, while a similar awareness at the lower levels
found expression in less sophisticated nationalist and sometimes
truly seditious utterances or actions. These were usually linked to
tribal politics.

In one particularly demonstrative instance, which caused a
flurry in Whitehall and Cape Town, two Ethiopian 'prophets'
excited a thousand-strong 'singing, shouting and haranguing'
crowd into a state of near revolt in Taungs. To continual cheers
the 'prophets' shouted exhortations such as 'The white man has
taken your country', 'The white man is oppressing you', 'You
must drive the white man off your land, his blood must flow',
'There must not be one white man alive when the sun sets.' (116)
Paul Kruger and Queen Victoria who had taxed them were said to
have died and been sent to hell for their sins. (117)

Outbursts such as these were not always completely in vain, as
they may have seemed. Although unsuccessful, they drew attention
to African grievances and aspirations. They also promoted the idea
of Africans as participants in a society and not merely passive on-
lookers which the ruling class could ignore with no second thought.

With many of the church separatists occupying leading roles in
African politics, it follows that they were accepted as community
leaders and that some, if not most, political organisations were
sympathetic to the broad aims of the Ethiopian movement.

The South African Native Congress declared that Ethiopianism
was a symptom of progress 'making itself felt in all departments
of the social, religious and economic structure', that the white
outcry against Ethiopianism was unjustified. According to the
SANC, no satisfactory evidence of disloyalty had been forthcoming.
(118) The Transvaal Native Congress also rejected the accusations
of disloyalty against the Ethiopians. It said the attitude taken by
the governments of Natal and the Orange River Colony bordered
on direct persecution. (119) Shula Marks has found that there was
also much to connect the influential John Dube of the *Ilanga lase
Natal* and the Natal Native Congress to the Ethiopian movement,
despite his disclaimers to the contrary. At one stage he was invited
to take over the leadership of the Zulu Congregational Church.
However, for strategic reasons Dube preferred to work for his ideal

of African unity within the system. (120)

This is not to say that there was no opposition to Ethiopianism in African politics. As the evidence of the Revds Makiwane and Mdolomba, and of the *Imvo Zabantsundu*, demonstrates, Ethiopianism gave rise to ideological and generational tensions in African communities. African ministers of the established churches and more conservative politicians were opposed to the radical doctrines espoused by the separatists. Ethiopianism was in conflict with their tone of cautious accommodation and striving for white support.

The participation of Ethiopians in political organisations seeking varying degrees of representation in white-dominated political structures brings to light an ambiguity in approach. This political approach was in contrast to the separatist nature of the church movements. Probably it was forced on them by political realities. It was possible to function independently of whites on a religious level (particularly in view of the AME Church connection) and to mobilise and influence religious, social and political attitudes, but to translate African political aspirations into political reality it was impossible to stand aloof from white politics. Only in the church was a total withdrawal from white rule possible. The abortive Bambatha Rebellion of 1906 showed that the black man could no longer provide an alternative power structure with which to assert his political and military independence. Therefore to help bring about change it was necessary to make demands and to seek involvement within the existing white political system.

It is clear that there was a definite link between Ethiopianism and the infant African political interest groups and that this broadened significantly the base of African political activity.

**International co-operation and influences**
The feelers of the organised African protest movement were not only extending throughout South Africa in the first years of the century, but were also coming into increasing contact with, and being influenced by, similar international streams of thought.

From the beginning, and through the whole period of its growth into a powerful international movement in the twentieth century, (121) Africans in South Africa were involved with the Pan-African movement. This was set in motion in September 1897 when an African Association, consisting of black expatriates from various countries, was formed in London. The main aim of the Association was to convene a conference of the 'African race from all parts of the world' so that British public opinion could be made aware of the adverse conditions under which blacks lived in places such as South Africa, West Africa, the West Indies and the United States. The chairman of the Association was H. Mason Joseph from Antigua in the West Indies. An African from South Africa, Mrs A. V. Kinloch, was elected to the executive in the capacity of Treasurer. (122)

The African Association sent circulars to people throughout the areas mentioned above and by June 1899 preparations had reached the stage where a preparatory session of the proposed conference was held in London. Several prominent Africans and Afro-Americans were present, including John Tengo Jabavu from South Africa. Mrs Kinloch was absent as she had returned to South Africa early in 1898. This preliminary meeting was followed by the conference proper in the next year. (123)

The first Pan-African conference, held in London from 23–25 July 1900, was attended by about thirty delegates from the United States, the West Indies, Africa, Britain and Canada. No people from the Cape, Natal, the Orange Free State or the South African Republic were present. (124) Jabavu and other leading Africans from South Africa, such as W. B. Rubusana and A. K. Soga, had been invited to attend but, while expressing the keenest interest, were unable to do so. Rubusana gave as his reasons to the organisers financial considerations and the prevailing war conditions in the country. (125)

Despite the absence of delegates from that part, the situation in South Africa featured prominently in the discussions at the conference. Several speakers criticised the racial inequalities that existed there and called on the British government to ensure a fairer dispensation for Africans at the end of the war. It was even suggested that the time had come for public protests about the state of affairs in South Africa. As a result, the conference sent a petition dealing specifically with this subject to Queen Victoria. The grievances listed included the 'compound' system on the mines, the system of indentured labour, the use of forced labour in public works, compulsory passes for blacks, segregation laws and the restriction of African land and voting rights. (126)

The conference received an assurance from the British government that it would not 'overlook the interests and welfare of the native races' but neither the petition nor the reply exerted any influence upon subsequent developments in South Africa. (127)

The convenor of the conference, and the 'father' of modern Pan-

Africanism, was a Trinidadian, Henry Sylvester Williams. While
practising at the Bar in London around the turn of the century, he
established close relationships with Africans by acting as legal adviser to several African Chiefs and other people who were in
England on political missions to the Colonial Office. (128) He
developed close connections with South Africa. Besides corresponding for several years with people like Jabavu (129) and Rubusana,
he actually stayed in South Africa for some time in the early
1900s. He was reported, incorrectly, to have been in the country
during the Anglo-Boer War, (130) but in 1903 he did settle temporarily in Cape Town. He was admitted as an Advocate of the Supreme Court in Cape Town on 29 October of that year, and had
his own office in the Metropolitan Chambers in Church Street.
(131)

Williams soon became involved in politics at the Cape. He contacted African and coloured political leaders, spoke at meetings,
helped organise delegations and sought audiences with Ministers.
(132) In March 1904, he presided at a mass meeting attended by
hundreds of people to protest against the treatment of coloured
people in the Transvaal, and was instrumental in having petitions in this regard forwarded to the Colonial and Imperial authorities. (133) He was also alleged to have travelled about South
Africa 'spreading the doctrine of the country for the black races
alone', (134) but the authorities in the Transvaal and Orange Free
State declared on enquiry that they knew nothing of him and
doubted that he had been in those colonies. (135)

He returned for a while to London and travelled in various British and French colonies in Africa, before finally going back to the
West Indies, (136) but continued to espouse the cause of Africans
in South Africa. In 1905 he helped bring the mass petition of
Transvaal Africans regarding responsible government to the
attention of the British government, and he and Rubusana petitioned the Colonial Office about the petitioners' land grievances;
(137) in the following year he acted on behalf of the Batlokwa
and Bakhulukwa tribes of the Orange River Colony in a similar
capacity; (138) and two years later he was reported, in Liberia, to
have made 'treasonable' remarks about the treatment by the
British Government of Africans in South Africa. (139)

Meanwhile, international contacts continued to increase. As we
have seen, the AME Church in the United States had a strong influence on the separatist church movements in the 1890s. This
influence persisted as the church established itself in South Africa

in the early years of the century. In 1901 it was recognised by the Cape government and subsequently a succession of bishops was sent out to South Africa to superintend the work of the church in the colonies. (140) It is of interest that leading personalities of the AME Church in the United States were involved with the first Pan-African Conference (141) and, of course, the designation 'Ethiopian' of the separatist church movement in South Africa, and its rallying cry of 'Africa for the Africans', were characteristically Pan-African as well.

Very importantly, the stream of Africans from South Africa to educational institutions abroad continued. In 1908 the Select Committee on Native Education in the Cape reported that upward of a hundred Africans from that colony alone had in recent years gone to colleges in the United States and elsewhere. (142) Some of these people distinguished themselves. In 1906, Pixley Ka Isaka Seme won a debating competition at Columbia University speaking on the topic of 'The Regeneration of Africa'. (143) Later he continued his studies at Jesus College, Oxford. (144) One of his contemporaries in England was Alfred Mangena who, in conjunction with another Pan-Africanist, Akilagpa Osabrampa Sawyer, (145) successfully took legal action against the Natal authorities in the English courts at the time of the Natal disturbances. He studied in London and after being called to the English Bar became the first African to practise as an attorney in South Africa. (146) Seme and Mangena are good examples of South African students going abroad and coming into contact with and being influenced by international ideas. Both were to achieve political prominence on their return to South Africa.

Another person to be lastingly influenced by overseas study was John L. Dube. While studying at Oberlin College in the United States in the late nineteenth century, he met Booker T. Washington (147) and was converted to Washington's philosophy of 'Negro' industrial self-help, as practised at his Tuskegee Institute. With the help of some patrons in the United States, and drawing on his experience there, he opened the Ohlange Institute for African industrial education in Natal. (148) After learning the trade of printing during his sojourns in the United States he established and edited the *Ilanga lase Natal* newspaper, as we have already noted. Dube rapidly became one of the most influential Africans in South Africa.

In general, the idea of international co-operation with blacks abroad was furthered by the African press. The *South African*

*Spectator* carried regular items on advancements being made by American blacks. The newspaper ran a series of articles documenting great achievements by black people, including figures such as Hannibal, 'one of the noblest men who ever lived'. All this was done with the aim of instilling race pride in blacks. (149) The *Izwi Labantu* followed a similar policy. Regular snippets of information and extracts from overseas appeared on Pan-African matters. (150) Through the newspapers local Africans could keep in touch and identify with the struggles for self-determination elsewhere. There was also a direct link between *Izwi* and Pan-African affairs. In an article on the 'distinguished South African', A. K. Soga, (editor of *Izwi*), the *Lagos Standard* reported in 1904 that he was engaged in arranging for a 'Conference of black men from the four quarters of the world, to be convened, probably in America, to discuss the black man's future'. The newspaper also reported that Soga was running a series of articles in the *Coloured American Magazine* and that he was preparing a book on 'The Problem of the Social and Political Regeneration of Africa'. (151) Other Pan-Africanists with whom Soga was in touch were Prince Bandele Amoniyas, the author of a book on the Ethiopian movement, who was a subscriber to *Izwi*, and the *Izwi*'s regular Edinburgh correspondent Moses da Rocha, who had been co-secretary with Henry Sylvester Williams of the Pan-African Association of London. (152) This latter body came into being after the first Pan-African conference in London in 1900, when the African Association, which had organised the conference, was transformed into a permanent organisation. The Pan-African Association elected Jabavu on to the executive committee and hoped to open branches in the four British colonies in South Africa, but this never materialised, and the Association soon ceased to exist. (153)

The success of so-called black nations in international conflicts against traditional world powers served as yet another source of identification and encouragement for black South Africans. The success of the Japanese against Russia in the war of 1902 (154) and the inability of German troops to crush local resistance in South West Africa were noted with great interest in South Africa and spawned the idea among Africans that they too could challenge with success the colonial power. (155) The Governor of Natal, Sir Henry McCallum, declared in 1906 that the disturbances in neighbouring South West Africa were 'giving rise to much unrest and adding to the confidence of the Natives throughout South Africa'. (156)

Clearly both the violent and non-violent struggles against injustice elsewhere were making an impact on black South Africans. Often sharing similar experiences of subordination, they were able to identify in varying degrees with the broader struggle. In some cases this identification was merely psychological, in others it was marked by active co-operation.

Thus, as this chapter shows, the stimuli which resulted in the increased politicisation of the African intelligentsia in the first few years of the twentieth century not only led to the formal mobilisation of interest groups in various parts of South Africa, but also generated domestic (and international) co-operation, thus providing a crude framework for political unity among the hitherto uncoordinated African groups. What was needed now was a trigger to precipitate formal African political unity. The political unification of South Africa, with its dire political, social and economic consequences for Africans and the emotions it engendered, was to provide this decisive impulse and set the latent force of African nationalism in motion.

# 5 Africans and the 'Closer Union' movement, 1907–08

The initiative in transforming the concept of federation from a vague aspiration into a concrete goal to unify the South African colonies was taken by members of the so-called Milner Kindergarten. This was a group of talented young men who had been brought out by Milner after the war to fill key posts in the four colonial administrations, and continued to serve under Lord Selborne after Milner's departure in 1905. One of this group, Richard Feetham, took the first step in this direction when he argued in a paper read in October 1906 that a definite start should be made towards the consummation of union. He gave several reasons for his thesis. They rested mainly on the contention that union was the best means of consolidating Imperial control in South Africa and ensuring economic stability. The other Kindergarten members agreed with Feetham's analysis and gave their full support to the closer union movement.

Lionel Curtis resigned from his post as Assistant Colonial Secretary of the Transvaal to devote himself fully to this ideal. After touring the various colonies he drew up a draft memorandum in conjunction with his colleagues arguing the case for union. The memorandum was then handed to the High Commissioner, Lord Selborne. He shared the Kindergarten's enthusiasm for union. They agreed that to have maximum effect the memorandum should be published under the authority of the High Commissioner, but to minimise the impression of Imperial interference the support of colonial politicians should be enlisted.

Curtis therefore approached Dr Jameson, the Prime Minister of the Cape. Jameson became a willing collaborator. (1) Accordingly, on 28 November 1906 the Cape government brought to the attention of the Governor the multiplicity of problems caused by the continued division of the various colonies in South Africa and recommended that he should ask Lord Selborne in his capacity as High Commissioner to review the general situation in South Africa with a view to creating public awareness about the desirability of a central South African government and an interest in the best means of achieving this. (2) When approached, the governments of the other colonies concurred with the recommendations of the Cape ministers. (3)

On 7 January 1907 Curtis's memorandum, modified slightly by Lord Selborne, was sent to the various governments. (4) At the next session of the Cape parliament in Cape Town in July, the Selborne Memorandum was tabled by Jameson. This was followed by a successful motion by F. S. Malan that the Cape government should approach its counterparts in the other colonies during the recess to consider the advisability of taking preliminary steps towards union. (5) Malan was a prominent member of the Afrikaner Bond, who himself had come out as a strong advocate of federation in a series of six articles in *Ons Land*, (6) the newspaper of which he was editor. The Selborne Memorandum was published and widely distributed. (7) Federation, the term loosely used at this stage to describe any scheme for closer union, became a public issue.

The Selborne Memorandum played carefully on the sentiments of the South African colonists. It was directed to the white people of the various colonies and emphasised that no enduring federation could be formed unless it emanated from them. Unless they united they would not realise their full potential or enjoy the full freedom of self-government. Unity would bring political, economic and industrial stability. It would solve the vexing railways and customs questions and maximise the benefits to be gained from uniform legal, defence, agricultural and mining systems. It would also help defuse the potentially dangerous Asiatic, coloured and Native questions. 'All South Africans are agreed', declared Selborne, 'that the native question is at once the most important and the most profoundly difficult question which confronts themselves and their children; but by the perpetuation of five or six totally different native administrations and policies, they are doing all that is in their power to make the question more grave and the problem more difficult.' (8) He did not elaborate on what form a united policy should take.

Africans were not unaware of the importance of the Selborne Memorandum. The vernacular newspapers discussed the issues involved and a conference was held to ventilate the attitudes of Africans to federation.

### African newspaper responses to the Selborne memorandum

In mid-1907, when the Selborne memorandum was made public, the *Ilanga lase Natal* published several editorials on federation. The newspaper urged the Imperial government on behalf of the bulk of the people of South Africa not to hand over the Africans to a not 'very scrupulous white autocracy'. The newspaper said that while it appreciated Lord Selborne's sincerity, federation involved far greater principles than merely settling railway disabilities. Federation, it warned, would increase beyond contemplation the trouble and expense already incurred by Britain in her South African colonies. A powerful Afrikaner caucus, which could not be relied on to 'hold the scales of justice', would rule the Federal Parliament. Britain would gradually become a merely tolerated colonial power which would eventually lose its hold on South African markets. (9)

At the same time the *Ilanga* posed the question whether Cape Africans, the only Africans who had a right to vote, were aware of the implications of federation:

... we may ask do they know how important the matter is? Do they know what it means to them and their fellow countrymen? We should like to see evidence in the *Izwi Labantu* and *Imvo* as to the extent of their knowledge. For we fear they are somewhere in the clouds concerning it; and who shall say what their courage is when they do know? (10)

The *Ilanga*'s fears were not unfounded as far as the *Imvo* was concerned. The newspaper's response to the Selborne memorandum and the concomitant question of federation was at first strangely non-committal. Except for a few passing references, it hardly mentioned the issue until mid-October as the Cape elections approached. Responding to reported hostile utterances against the Cape franchise by politicians in the Orange River Colony, *Imvo* declared, 'With Federation looming large gentlemen are required [in the election] who are convinced supporters of the moderate and just Native policy of the Cape, otherwise we are undone.' (11)

Shortly afterwards *Imvo* published correspondence between F. S. Malan, one of the prime movers of federation, and John Alfred Sishuba, an influential African electoral agent for the South African Party, to counter Progressive Party election propaganda in the Transkei. Sishuba wrote to Malan that rumours were being circulated by the Progressives that the Afrikaner Bond would remove liberal allies of the Bond in the South African Party such as J. X. Merriman and J. W. Sauer from positions of power as soon as the SAP assumed office, and that they would install a Prime Minster who would support moves to disenfranchise Africans at the proposed inter-colonial conference on federation. Malan's own attitude to the federation and his position on the franchise for Africans were also being questioned by many people, he said. (12)

In reply Malan said that he had always been in favour of the traditional Cape native policy. When the question of Closer Union was discussed he would do his best to defend the Cape franchise. In presenting these views, Malan said he was confident that he was voicing the opinion of the great majority of Bond and SAP supporters. (13) Jabavu enthusiastically supported Malan's statements.

Jabavu explained his virtual silence on the question of federation in January 1908 when he said that the great issue of federation seemed to him to be a question of high politics, far above the level of Africans who, whether they liked it or not, could no more affect the issues than 'the proverbial fly on the wheel, trying to stop the wagon from going forward'. (14) This was a rather uncharacteristic utterance on the part of Jabavu, but it was not far out in its description of the ineffectiveness of Africans to influence the federation process.

In contrast to the *Imvo*, the *Izwi Labantu*, the vociferous mouthpiece of the South African Native Congress, expressed itself strongly on federation, probably more so than any of the African newspapers. In keeping with his socialist interpretation of events, the editor A. K. Soga described the federation movement as part of a grand design for a capitalist-dominated South Africa, controlled by Rand magnates. He expanded on this theme in an editorial subheaded 'people vs capitalists':

We hear a good deal about federation and Lord Selborne is being applauded to the skies for his interesting historical contribution to the scheme, but when we remember that those people who are shouting so loudly for federation are the same gentry (the capitalists) who attempted to steal a march on the Cape Constitution to further their own ends; who set up spurious Labour Commissions; who shouted the glories of the Chinese from the housetops; and who showed us how a country could be redeemed by a Native Affairs Commission which strove to upset the orderly legislation of half a century and to throw the native franchise to the dogs, and which is driving honest white workers out to Australia and elsewhere. We feel . . . sure that if federation was to come in on their pretentions—woe betide the people. . . . These land and other sharks hold all the public resources and utilise them as the trump card in this great game of gamble, scramble and beggar-my-neighbour which is dignified with the name of government. Unless some miracle happens to fend off federation under their auspices, . . . this will be a glorious country for corporation pythons and political puff-adders, forced labour and commercial despotism, but no fit place for freemen to live in. (15)

And it is clear from extant copies, reports and extracts that the *Koranta ea Becoana*, the *Naledi ea Lesotho* and the *South African Spectator* shared in the general apprehension of federation.

Around the time the Selborne memorandum was released, the *Naledi* printed an article by Dr Emile Vollet in which he stated that federation raised a cloud on the horizon and that all Africans should be accommodated in Imperial protectorates, for the good of Africans and of Great Britain itself. (16) Later articles reveal the newspaper's strong antagonism to federation. (17) This reflected the wide concern which prevailed in Basutoland at the time about the probable incorporation of that territory in a union with its white-dominated neighbours. (18)

In July/August 1907 the newly resuscitated *Koranta ea Becoana* declared that it was important that Africans should ask themselves how the question of federation would affect them as a people. They should then make known their views on the matter before any action was taken by the various governments. The *Koranta* criticised Lord Selborne for drawing distinctions between Africans and coloured people and added, 'The moment racial prejudice gets into the minds of governments, federation is bound to prove a difficult task.' (19)

No files of the *South African Spectator* of this period remain, but the views on federation of its editor, F. Z. S. Peregrino, are well known from letters and reports in contemporary newspapers. Peregrino said the outlook for blacks with federation was one either of Afrikaner domination and political slavery in a common area or of territorial segregation. Therefore, in the face of the threat from the North, it was the responsibility of blacks in the Cape to demand from their representatives in parliament that no concessions or compromises would be made with regard to the Cape franchise. (20)

We have no knowledge of early African opinions on federation in the Orange River Colony and the Transvaal. No African newspaper existed in the former region, no files of the *Leihlo la Babatsho* newspaper in the Transvaal have been preserved, and the African political organisations in the two territories made representations to the authorities on federation only late in 1908. Nevertheless it is clear that Africans in these colonies were dissatisfied with their condition and that they desired an expanded political role in any new dispensation.

**The Queenstown conference**

At the annual conference of the South African Native Congress in August 1907 the question of federation was raised, but owing to 'pressure of time' it was not discussed and left to the executive to handle. (21) This SANC leaders like Soga and Rubusana did by publishing a 'Call to Conference' under the auspices of the *Izwi Labantu* newspaper. In a prominent notice, the *Izwi* called on sixty-two African and, significantly, coloured leaders, representing various interest groups in the Cape, to meet at a conference in Queenstown to decide on a united plan of action in view of the fact that serious attempts would be made to undermine the interests of blacks in the projected federation of the different states of South Africa. Unity was essential to counter the forthcoming attack on the constitutional rights of blacks in the Cape, the attempts to keep Africans in the other colonies excluded from political representation, and the unconstitutional devices used in these colonies to keep blacks in lasting servitude under oppressive class legislation. The *Izwi* therefore suggested that a conference be held to frame a manifesto to which parliamentary candidates in African and coloured constituencies would be expected to adhere in the forthcoming elections, and which they would pledge themselves to apply if elected to Parliament. The manifesto would embody the matter of federation, the franchise, education, land, liquor and labour. The chosen delegates were asked each to nominate two other representatives to accompany them. (22)

The Queenstown conference was held on 27 and 28 November 1907. It was attended by over 80 delegates from 29 centres thoughout the Cape Colony. (23)

The conference was a landmark in African politics. It was an important event in two respects. First, it was an attempt to end the factional nature of African politics in the Cape Colony by forming a broad alliance, including all politically conscious Africans, to face the challenges of union. Secondly, formal co-operation with coloured politicians took place for the first time. The African Political Organisation (APO)–the first coloured political organisation of importance to emerge in South Africa–was prominently represented, having decided at its annual conference in Port Elizabeth to accept the invitation to attend. (24)

Like many of the African organisations, the APO had been formed in September 1902 in the mood of post-war disillusion. For several years its activities revolved around the failure of the Imperial government to free coloured people from their legal disabilities in the Transvaal and the Orange River Colony after the demise of the Boer republics. It made concerted efforts to persuade Great Britain to extend the Cape system to the northern colonies. (25) These activities reached a climax when an APO delegation went to London in 1906 to protest against the 'Europeans only' clauses in the responsible government constitutions about to be conferred on the two ex-republics. (26)

The history of the organisation is inextricably linked with the name of Dr Abdullah Abdurahman, who was its president for 35 years. Dr Abdurahman was a man of exceptional ability. Not only was he one of the most outstanding leaders the coloured people have produced, he was also one of the greatest figures in the history of Cape Town's civic affairs and the Cape Provincial Council. He was the first black medical doctor in South Africa, the first black Cape Town City Councillor and the second (after Dr Rubusana) black member of the Cape Provincial Council. His tenure of office in these two bodies spanned thirty-four and twenty-six years respectively, and was severed only by his death in 1940. (27) Dr Abdurahman assumed the presidency, and virtual sole control, of the APO in 1905 after being asked to take over the leadership of an organisation which was then on the verge of floundering. Within five years the organisation had asserted itself as a representative mass movement with 111 branches throughout South Africa. (28)

Given the antipathy which generally had hitherto existed between African and coloured politicians, the joint conference of 1907 was an important landmark in the evolution of a united black front against white domination. Previously the APO had made clear distinctions between coloured people and Africans. Dr Abdurahman himself had on occasion referred to Africans as 'barbarous natives'. In its vigorous lobbying for an extension of the franchise to coloured people in the ex-republics under responsible government, the APO was content to leave Africans disenfranchised. (30) For their part African leaders had also had reservations about forming alliances with coloured people. African leaders of the time deprecated inter-racial sexual contact just as vigorously as whites did. John L. Dube with his strong Zulu heritage was a ready example of this. He wrote, 'I am as jealous of the purity of the black race as the Anglo-Saxon is of his.' (31) Regional separation also militated against co-operation. However, common disabilities gradually drew the leaders of the two groups together. After the turn of the century a number of calls for greater

co-operation were made. It took the shock of Vereeniging, responsible government and the threat of union to bring them together.

John Tengo Jabavu, who favoured co-operation between African
and coloured people, (32) and who had corresponded with coloured
leaders with this aim in mind, (33) did not, however, attend the
Queenstown conference. Once again he shunned the opportunity
of joining in a broad alliance with other sections of the African
political élite. His refusal to co-operate brought him criticism from
several quarters and bitter condemnation from the *Izwi*. The
newspaper accused him of selfish personal interests and emphasised
that the aim of the conference was to sink differences in the
interests of the common safety of Africans in a time of crisis, not
to promote sectarian party political ideals. (34) It must be said,
however, that it would have required a magnanimous gesture
on Jabavu's part for him to participate in a project sponsored by
inveterate rivals to his newspaper (*Imvo*), his party political (South
African Party) and his educational (Inter-State Native College
Scheme) activities. The *Izwi*/South African Native Congress group
was constantly trying to undermine his personal appeal, and he
their growing stature. And indeed his failure to discern evolving
trends in African politics and his stubbornness in not co-operating
with other African politicians would eventually lead to his political
demise.

Besides Dr Abdurahman and a number of APO delegates from
as far afield as Cape Town, Kimberley and Port Elizabeth, the list
of delegates included a large group of South African Native Congress members. Among those present were Congress stalwarts like
Dr Rubusana, Mesach Pelem, Jonathan Tunyiswa, Thomas Mqanda
and, of course, A. K. Soga. Silas Molema travelled from Bechuanaland as the personal representative of Chief Badirile Montsioa, Paramount Chief of the Baralongs. Other notable figures included Jonas
Goduka, head of the African Native Mission Church, and Samuel
Mqhayi, the Xhosa writer and part time editor of the *Imvo Zabantsundu*. Apologies were received from F. Z. S. Peregrino, editor of
the *South African Spectator,* and Enoch Mamba, who had their
papers read by proxy, as well as P. J. Mzimba, moderator of the
Presbyterian Church of Africa. (35) Two delegates from the Transvaal, the Transvaal Native Congress Vice-president J. G. Kaiyana
and J. Molofe, also signalled their intention to attend and requested
the convenor to forward rail tickets, but did not make it to Queenstown, probably because of problems with the travel arrangements.
(36)

A host of prominent Jabavu and South African Party supporters followed Jabavu's lead in rejecting the 'Call to Conference'. They included John Alfred Sishuba, Simon P. Sihlali, Isaac Wauchope and Elijah Makiwane. So too did John Tobin, Dr Abdurahman's main rival in coloured politics and also a staunch supporter of the South African Party.

Thus unavoidably the conference took on a party flavour. A large majority of the delegates were Progressive Party supporters, but a small contingent of South African Party supporters was also in attendance. It was composed of men such as Chief Mhlambiso, Headman Sol Kalipa, R. B. Mlilwane and Titus Mahe. (37)

When the conference proceedings opened Daniel Dwanya, a law agent and experienced politician, was appointed chairman. The question of federation was discussed at once. After the chairman had briefly alluded to the issue, lengthy speeches were made by A. K. Soga, Dr Abdurahman, Dr Rubusana and H. McCorn, an APO delegate from Port Elizabeth. (38)

Soga retraced in detail the constitutional history of the Cape and said its non-racial provisions should be made mandatory in the federal parliament. If Downing Street failed to fulfil its heavy responsibilities towards blacks in this matter, they could still resort to the highest courts in England in order to obtain justice. (39) Dr Abdurahman dwelt on the desirability of a federal rather than a unitary system for South Africa. Under the latter the sound policy of the Cape would be submerged to the detriment of blacks. (40) Dr Rubusana said blacks were speaking about the colour line, but there had long been a colour line between Africans and coloured people themselves. He hoped this was the beginning of unity. Broader aspirations were reflected in his claim that the meeting represented not only the Cape Colony and Transkeian Territories, but also the Transvaal and the Orange River Colony. (41) After a full day's discussion, the following resolutions were unanimously adopted and forwarded to the Cape and Imperial governments and to the heads of churches in the Cape:

That this Conference of the coloured people and natives of the Cape Colony assembled at Queenstown is of the opinion that in the event of the adoption of any form of closer union of the South African colonies:

(a) Federation is preferable to unification.

(b) That form of federation should be adopted in which the Federal Parliament exercises such powers only as are specifically given to it in the federal constitution.

(c) The Cape Franchise should be the basis of federal franchise.

(d) The basis of representation of the Federal Parliament should be the voters' list.

(e) The present so-called native territories (Swaziland, Basutoland and British Bechuanaland) should be regarded as outside Federal territory and under the protection of the Imperial Government represented by the High Commissioner for such native territories, unless or until provision shall be made for the representatation of such territories in the Federal Parliament by members elected on the same basis as in Colonies forming the federation. (42)

On the following day the conference turned to a discussion of the question of the prohibition of liquor, another topic of the day of particular interest to blacks. After a long discussion the Conference resolved that the free and unrestricted sale of liquor was detrimental to the welfare of blacks. Five more resolutions along these lines were passed: the conference denounced recent attempts in Parliament to extend outlet facilities for the brandy farmers; it called for more uniform and strict liquor restrictions; and asked churches, temperance societies and other associations to advocate the boycott of European liquor. Then the conference took on a party political flavour.

With time pressing and the questions of education, land and labour still to be discussed, a proposal was carried to set these aside and to discuss the forthcoming elections. The conference decided that, as many black voters needed guidance, it should lay down guidelines for black voters by pledging its support to the party which had the best interests of blacks at heart. The result was a foregone conclusion. The delegates voted overwhelmingly to support the Unionist candidates against the South African Party. (43) The Unionists were an alliance of the Progressive Party and a group of independents. Attempts by the small group of South African Party supporters to prevent the decision to discuss party politics were unsuccessful. The fact that this issue was raised can be seen as a consequence of the imbalance caused by the failure of more South African Party sympathisers to avail themselves of the invitation to attend the conference. The APO delegates did not take part in this discussion as they were prohibited from pledging themselves to either party before the APO annual conference at Indwe the following month decided on the matter. On that occasion the APO also came out in support of the Unionists. (44)

### Responses to the Queenstown conference
The reaction of Jabavu's *Imvo Zabantsundu* was that the Queenstown Conference was a 'pantomime' with 'crusted old Progressives'

as the players, (45) but the African newspapers in Natal and
Basutoland hailed the conference as an historic occasion and an
augury for future black unity. Both the *Ilanga lase Natal* and the
*Naledi ea Lesotho* criticised Jabavu's attitude to the conference
and said it was harmful to the African cause. (46) The editor of
the *Naledi*, S. M. Phamotse, described his uncooperativeness as
'very disgusting'. (47) Starr Jameson, the Cape Prime Minister and
leader of the Unionists, also reacted positively to the conference.
He expressed his appreciation of the support promised by the
conference to his party and reiterated his determination to stand
by Rhodes's dictum of equal rights for every civilised man. (48)

In response to the Queenstown Conference, Jabavu summoned
a Native Electoral Convention at Debe Nek on 17 and 18 January
1908. He encouraged local committees of registered voters to hold
meetings to elect area delegates to the Convention, and to give
them a mandate so that, unlike the Queenstown Conference, which
was attended by 'individuals representing nobody but themselves',
the Debe Convention could be truly representative of African
opinion. (49)

Fifty delegates and three hundred observers attended the meeting, which in fact was nothing more than a convention of South
African Party supporters, something which the chairman, Isaac
Wauchope, readily confirmed. The delegate for Peddie, Ben Tele,
one of the few South African Native Congress/Unionist Party
sympathisers present, accused the chairman of having misled Africans when he invited the 'whole nation' to participate. (50) He
had been instructed by the Peddie voters to adhere to the resolutions of the Queenstown Conference. The question of federation
was raised at the meeting, but it did not form a major part of the
discussions. After a number of resolutions on African education,
land tenure, the question of liquor prohibition and Africans in
towns, the government was simply asked 'to see that the rights of
natives were as far as possible secured' under federation. (51)

In his address on the subject, Jabavu took an unusual line. Far
from fearing that federation might lead to the downfall of the
Cape system as many others thought, he foresaw the opposite.
To his mind only by bringing the other colonies into a union or
federation with the Cape would the enlightened native policy of
the Cape be extended to the other colonies. Jabavu compared the
effect this would have with 'the light which has ever chased away
darkness'. Only through educative contact with the Cape system
would Natal, for example, be persuaded to depart from its degra-

ding policies. (52) (This was the attitude that the Cape delegates would take when compromising on the Cape franchise during the National Convention.)

The most important decision taken by the Debe Convention was to endorse its support for the South African Party in the elections. Jabavu said that in his opinion the best thing Africans could do was to return to parliament for their own protection the likes of Merriman and Sauer, the natural successors of the great old liberals like Sir George Grey and Sir John Molteno who had secured them the vote. (53) The convention advised all its 'constituents and friends' to cast their vote for South African Party candidates. (54)

As expected, the South African Party won the election handsomely. John X. Merriman, one of Jabavu's political champions, succeeded Jameson as Prime Minister. Jabavu revelled in the election results. (55) Through the demise of Jameson, he declared, Africans stood to lose nothing and win a great deal. Jameson stood for only one of the three groups in the country, but the SAP, with the old stalwarts Merriman and Sauer at the helm, represented all sections of the population. (56)

The Queenstown conference, despite the recalcitrant attitude of Jabavu towards it, had a rejuvenating and unifying effect on African politics. Besides bringing together a host of delegates from all over the Cape, the conference also aroused a greater sense of unity between African newspapers such as the *Ilanga lase Natal*, *Naledi ea Lesotho*, *Izwi Labantu* and *South African Spectator*. These newspapers wished to see a greater degree of political cohesion amongst blacks and were therefore unanimous in their criticism of Jabavu for his refusal to co-operate in the interests of the 'nation'. Besides his individualism, the main reason why Jabavu stood alone was his support of the Afrikaner-dominated South African Party. The other newspapers (and political organisations) were distinguished by their uncompromising enmity to any form of Afrikaner control. (57)

After the Queenstown conference a close exchange of thoughts began to take place and new, more uniform, strategies emerged. Thus when the *Naledi ea Lesotho* re-opened the idea of a Native Press Association and called for a pan-African conference organised by a united black press to find ways of freeing the Zulus from the repressive control of the Natal government in March 1908, the other three newspapers reacted readily to the proposal.

The *Naledi* declared:

Speaking of ties of blood, where are the *Imvo*, the *Izwi*, the *Koranta*, the *S.A. Spectator*, the *Ilanga lase Natal* and the *Naledi*? Why have they not sounded the bugle-horn and called their countrymen together to meet at some convenient place to deliberate on the advisability of petitioning the Imperial Parliament to constitute Zululand into a Native reserve like Basutoland in order to free it from the ravages of war that will always follow year after year? Are we not all Bantu and therefore of the same blood? Our cousins the Zulus cannot under the circumstances help themselves and it behoves those of us favourably placed to take up the cudgels in their behalf. There is not the time to cavil or recall the tribal feuds of days gone by. These have long gone into blessed oblivion and there remains the grim fact that the white man intends turning this into a white man's country. ... Yet, we sincerely believe that if we can unite and petition the Home Government we might yet be allowed to live in this country as worthy citizens of the mighty British Empire. (58)

The *Izwi Labantu* welcomed the idea of a meeting of the editors of the African press and said it would be glad to help any practicable scheme to ameliorate the sad condition of the Zulus. However, in view of past failures to co-operate, the newspaper asked whether the *Naledi* could guarantee the support of the other African newspapers for the proposal. (59) F. Z. S. Peregrino pledged the co-operation of the *Spectator* in any tangible arrangements made by the *Naledi* in this direction. Peregrino said the inability of the African newspapers to sink their petty differences made them the laughing stock of all intelligent people. He deeply regretted that Jabavu was resolutely unwilling to co-operate 'in spite of all advances made to him towards the amalgamation of the press with a view to presenting an intelligent organisation to combat the forces of prejudice which confront us'. (60)

*Izwi* said that too much reliance had been placed on *Imvo* in the past. The other newspapers should agree on some way of presenting a united front on vital issues affecting Africans. They should also enlist the help of the British and foreign press. (61) The *Izwi* suggested an annual conference of editors. In the meantime an exchange of correspondence and special articles should take place. It blamed the *Imvo*'s reluctance to co-operate for the difficulties the *Koranta ea Becoana* and other papers had already suffered.

The *Ilanga* published the *Izwi*'s views and adopted a similar standpoint: 'Wise people have long since learned that Unity is strength. If the *Imvo* is playing the fool with so serious a question as that of uplifting the Bantu people, let us ignore it and unite our efforts in the great cause. . . .' (62) Later Dube begged Jabavu not to lose sight of his sacred duty to his people, meaning 'the whole of the Bantu tribes of South Africa', and to reconsider his position. (63)

Despite the clear desire for co-operation between the newspapers, no formal press association was formed. The matter of African press unity continued to be raised, but without any success. The need for such an organisation subsequently also became less necessary because within a year the *Koranta ea Becoana*, the *South African Spectator* (with the different titles it came to acquire) and the *Izwi Labantu* were crippled by financial problems and forced out of circulation.

The *Naledi ea Lesotho*'s idea of holding a conference representing the various tribes of South Africa also died with the failure to establish press unity.

## Organisational activity 1907–08

The conference held at Queenstown in December 1907 was the only direct action taken by Africans on the question of unification in the period from the release of the Selborne memorandum until well into the second half of 1908. During this time African political organisations in the three northern colonies were too involved with survival politics, concentrating on issues immediately affecting them (economic and social conditions and local politics), to focus their energies on the still hazy issue of federation. Because of the strict limitations imposed on them in the respective societies their role was reactive rather than innovative and forward-looking. They reacted specifically to the issue of unification only when the four South African governments took concrete steps to bring this about by convening a National Convention to draw up a blueprint for a united South Africa.

In Natal the attention of Africans in 1907 and 1908 was focused mainly on continuing disturbances in the aftermath of the 1906 rebellion, the arrest of Dinizulu in connection with the troubles, the activities of the Natal Native Affairs Commission of 1907, which had been appointed to pinpoint the causes of the unrest, and three contentious bills dealing with native affairs introduced by the government early in 1908 in response to the findings of the Commission.

The Bambatha rebellion in Natal was followed in late 1907 by a recrudescence of the earlier unrest. Martial law was once again proclaimed and a strong militia force was sent to the area. Dinizulu and certain chiefs were arrested on charges of rebellion. (64) When Dinizulu, who denied the charges against him, was arrested in

December 1907, African dissatisfaction heightened considerably. As Paramount Chief of the strongest tribe, Dinizulu was regarded as the symbolic head of the African tribes in South Africa. The treatment he received was regarded as an 'unparalleled insult' to Africans. *Izwi Labantu* stated, 'We pray to God to defend our Dinizulu.' A correspondent wrote, 'We are all Zulus, Mr Editor, every black man under the sun is a Zulu practically. . . . Is this not worse than slavery? Brethren, is this not bondage?' (65)

The Natal Native Affairs Commission which investigated these troubles criticised the management of native affairs in the colony in its report and found that there was widespread African distrust and dissatisfaction in Natal. (66) The Commission was in a good position to make such a judgement as at least 5 500 Africans of all classes testified before it. (67) These numbers indicate that there was considerable political activity amongst Africans at the time.

When the government responded to the report with three unpopular bills, the political interest which Africans had shown in testifying before the Commission was maintained. The bills made provision for four new nominated members representing Africans in the Legislative Council; the appointment of Native Commissioners, a Native Council of government officials, a permanent secretary for Native Affairs and an annual meeting of chiefs and indunas in each division; and systems of land tenure and local government similar to those applying under the Glen Grey Act in the Cape Colony, (68) but without direct representation for Africans. The Glen Grey and Transkeian models, which politically-conscious Africans in Natal wished to see implemented in that colony too, (69) were followed to a large extent, but with the important exception that Africans themselves would not be directly represented. White and African government nominees were to fulfil all representative functions. (70) African dissatisfaction revolved around this issue and the land settlement provisions, which they wanted scrapped in favour of existing freehold title deeds, with minor modifications in certain cases.

There was widespread reaction to the bills. From April through to the end of the year Africans held numerous meetings, sent petitions to the Legislative Assembly, Governor and Secretary of State, and held interviews with the Prime Minister and Minister of Native Affairs, and other officials of the Native Affairs department. (71) At one of these meetings more than 150 African representatives from 35 centres were present. (72) The opposition to the bills was led by the *Ilanga lase Natal*, the Natal Native Congress, which appointed a special committee of fifteen people to watch the progress of the bills, and the *Iliso Lesizwe Esimnyama* (Eye of the Black Tribe), a new organisation which had emerged.

The *Iliso Lesizwi Esimnyama* (originally the *Iliso lo Muzi*) (73) was formed in 1907. It was formally constituted after a meeting held at Blaau Bosch in the Newcastle Division in March resolved to draw up a constitution for the body. The meeting was attended by three hundred 'chiefs and ordinary people'. (74) The main aims of the *Iliso*, as set out in the constitution, were the avoidance of causes of distrust and division, and the union of the people of Natal-Zululand into a contented, prosperous and united people; to bring about harmony and mutual cooperation between the people of Natal-Zululand; and to advance the general prosperity and progress of the country and people who found themselves in a 'deplorable condition'.

The *Iliso* was directed primarily towards organising tribal Africans. In fact the conditions of membership as laid down in the constitution applied solely to tribal Africans. All Africans in Natal and Zululand, under tribal chiefs, and over the age of eighteen years, were eligible for membership. An executive was to guide the *Iliso*'s activities, but at grassroots level it was to be represented by 'Tribal Committees' affiliated to the mother body and subject to its regulations. (75)

It appears that the *Iliso Lesizwe Esimnyama* emerged as a result of attempts by *Kolwas* to broaden African political activity to include tribal Africans. *Kolwas* controlled the proceedings at meetings and served in the executive. An observer at an *Iliso* meeting remarked, 'The desire of the *Kolwas* (who were in charge of the meeting) was clearly to be at one with the rest of the Natives.' (76) The Natal Native Congress may have had a hand in the formation of the organisation. Prominent Congress members such as Martin Lutuli, Mark Radebe, H. C. C. Matiwane, Abner Mtimkulu, Cleophas Kunene and J. T. Gumede were involved with its activities. Kunene and Gumede were at various stages respectively Secretary and Acting Secretary of the *Iliso*. (77)

Meetings of the organisation were well attended. They often exceeded a hundred people in number, and sometimes turned into marathon sessions, one such assembly lasting from the afternoon of one day through until daylight the following morning. (78)

In an effort to publicise its activities the *Iliso Lesizwe Esimnyama* also discussed the formation of a newspaper which would

serve as a mouthpiece for the organistion. Abner Mtimukulu was
given the task of investigating the feasibility of setting up a syndi-
cate to finance such a venture. The scheme he proposed was accepted, and a committee was appointed to collect funds. All chiefs
belonging to the organisation were to contribute a certain sum.
However, despite the good intentions, the newspaper did not mat-
erialisc. (79) The value of a vernacular newspaper in influencing
African public opinion was realised by the Natal government as
well. In 1908 the Cabinet considered the publication of a newspaper for Africans, (80) but for some reason this project too got
nowhere and the *Ilanga lase Natal* continued to monopolise the
field.

\* \* \*

In the Orange River Colony the attention of African interest
groups after responsible government in July 1907 was concentrated primarily on two measures which most Africans opposed.
These were the 'Rights of Coloured Persons in Respect of Fixed
Property Act, 1908', which aimed at weakening the position of
African squatter-peasants on farms, (81) and the decision to abolish the Native Affairs department.

The department was abolished after the government decided
that it did not justify the expenditure incurred. (82) Africans,
already without representation, felt that this move would mean
that they would be even more indirectly represented than before.
They not only desired the continuation of the department, but
wished to see it brought under the direct control of the Governor
in his position as the Paramount Chief of Africans in the colony
under the terms of the 1907 Letters Patent. (83)

In the agitation against these measures the Orange River Colony
Native Congress was once again prominent. (84) So too were the
African Political Organisation, which was directly affected because
of the fact that no distinctions were made between coloured
people and Africans in the Orange River Colony, (85) and another
political organisation, the Becoana Mutual Improvement Association, which came to the attention of the authorities for the first
time. (86)

This Association represented the Baralongs in the Thaba Nchu
district. This district was formerly the independent Baralong enclave of Moroka, which lay within the borders of the Orange Free
State Republic. The 850 square mile territory was annexed by the
Free State government in 1884 after trouble arose as a result of

a leadership struggle in which Chief Moroka's designated successor Tshipinare was killed by his rival Samuel. The government then safeguarded the land grants made by Tshipinare and appropriated the rest of the territory for itself. Under the new arrangements, ninety-five farms were granted to the traditional Baralong ruling class; fifteen or twenty were granted to whites, including three to the Methodist and Anglican churches; two areas, the Seliba and Thaba Nchu reserves, covering an area of 49 000 acres, were set aside for Baralongs not otherwise accommodated; and twenty-nine farms were reserved by the Free State government (and later sold to British soldiers after the war). By 1900 the number of Baralong farms had decreased to fifty-four. They were 185 000 acres in extent. Thus the area occupied by Africans in their former territory now amounted to 234 000 acres while European and government farms (124) covered an area of 395 000 acres. A large proportion of the African population in the district were resident on these farms. (87)

The land-owning class that emerged in Thaba Nchu provided the local political leaders. The Chairman of the Becoana Mutual Improvement Association, Joel Goronyane, for example, owned three farms. (88) Although 'mortgaged up to the eyebrows', according to Murray, these people were relatively wealthy and influential, and the men at the helm of the Becoana Mutual Improvement Association were recognised as the leaders (89) of the predominantly Baralong population of over 20 000 people in the district. (90) Chiefs no longer had any authority over tribesmen, although to some extent their status was nominally recognised. (91)

Joel Goronyane (who was also a minister of the Wesleyan Church) had long been the leading spokesman of the Baralong tribe in the colony. Over a period of at least ten years his name featured prominently in letters and petitions to the authorities, and as the Baralong representative before government commissions. He claimed to speak for 'all the natives in the land'. (92) Other prominent members of the Becoana Mutual Improvement Association were Moses Masisi, Jeremiah Makgothi and John Mokitlane Nyokong. The latter was the paternal grandfather of Dr James Moroka, who later became the President-General of the African National Congress. Dr Moroka's maternal grandmother was one of Tshipinare's wives.

The agitation of the various organisations in the Orange River Colony against the two measures—again following the familiar pattern of letters, petitions and interviews with the authorities—was partly successful. On the advice of the Colonial Office, (93) the government shelved the implementation of the Fixed Property Act pending the decision of the four colonies concerning union. (94)

\* \* \*

African grievances in the Transvaal during 1907 and 1908 were mainly of a general nature, encompassing economic and social matters and municipal issues. (95) Two Acts affecting Africans were passed during 1908. The one was the so-called Gold Law which prohibited blacks from hiring or owning property in municipal areas and proclaimed residential segregation. (96) The other was the Native Tax Act which differentiated between squatter-peasants and labour tenants on farms. The squatter-peasants were more heavily taxed. This was an attempt to restrict the economic freedom of this group and to force them into the labour market. (97)

The frustration and powerlessness felt by Africans in some quarters could not have been more aptly illustrated than by the call by the New Kleinfontein and Boksburg Native Vigilance Associations for a day of humiliation and prayer on 24 May 1908, Empire Day. At meetings of the Associations it was decided that, as the use of constitutional avenues for a redress of black grievances was futile, the only remaining resort was to appeal directly to God to help them. All 'the sons and daughters of the South African Races (Coloured and Native)' were entreated to get together on 24 May

... to ask Almighty God to help us and deliver us out of all our difficulties, oppressions and disabilities, of which there is abundant proof if we take into consideration the numerous deputations and petitions which have since the cessation of the war been brought before [the Imperial government] ... setting forth the grievances and disabilities of the different sections of the coloured and native races of South Africa. These deputations and petitions have failed to ameliorate the positions of the petitioners, for they have in every case been referred to their own administrators for redress. ... It was felt and therefore resolved that we follow the only course still open for us; that is, to petition God. (98)

Unmistakable overtones of Ethiopianism and Pan-Africanism were evident in the religious and universal ideas expressed in the appeal:

We feel that our sympathies should be broad enough to include the whole of the African races when we approach our Maker. For instance, the atrocities which our brethren are suffering under the administrators of the Congo Free State should appeal to us with a loud voice for our sympathy and prayers.

Undoubtedly the time has come for the sons of Africa to stretch forth their hands unto God unitedly, as was prophesised of us in Psalm 68 verse 31.

Let us, who are enlightened and led by the Spirit of God, lead our brethren to make a covenant with God, the Ruler of the Universe, in all sincerity and truth, with the assurance that if God is approached by us in the right attitude and spirit, He *will* bless us and send us a wave of His Spirit, which will pass through the whole of Africa from the Cape to Egypt, the effects of which will be felt even by our brethren in America, who come from the same original stock as ourselves. God grant this to His people. Amen. (99)

The appeal went on to lay down the order of service that should be followed in the prayer meetings.

The *Izwi Labantu* commented sympathetically upon the appeal and solemnly approved of the 'race' coming to

. . . Fall with all their load of cares
Upon the world's great altar stairs
That slope through darkness unto God

but warned that the black man should not forget that God helps those who help themselves. No amount of prayers could remove their disabilities and grievances if ignorance and apathy prevailed. (100)

The political associations in Natal, the Orange River Colony and the Transvaal, while active and responsive to local stimuli, did not initially concern themselves with the debate about federation which had been set in motion by the release of the Selborne memorandum. They were only to do so when positive steps were taken to translate the idea of union into reality in mid-1908. However, newspaper reports show that Africans followed the whole unification issue with interest from the time Lord Selborne published his views right through 1908.

### African responses as the impetus to union increases

The impetus to union gathered strength when the South African Party, dominated by the Afrikaner Bond, was elected to power in the Cape elections of early 1908. The change in government marked the success of a remarkable anti-imperial reaction in which the Afrikaners had regained the reins of power in the space of a few years in three of the four South African colonies. The stage was now set for the unification of South Africa on their terms.

It was decided to make the inter-colonial conference on customs and railway questions of May 1908 'the starting point of a united South Africa'. The Kindergarten, acting mainly as propagandists and organisers, assumed a subordinate role to South African politicians. White public opinion had by now been thoroughly aroused by intensive press coverage of the issue and the formation of Closer Union Societies. (101)

The inter-colonial conference met in Pretoria on 4 May 1908. To avoid differences which might arise from other matters, it was decided to place the question of 'Closer Union' before the conference first. By the following day resolutions on 'Closer Union' had been finalised. The conference resolved that 'the best interests and permanent prosperity of South Africa' could be secured only by an early union. It was decided that the legislatures of the various colonies should be asked to appoint delegates to a National South African Convention whose object would be to consider and report on the most desirable form of union and to prepare a draft constitution for a united South Africa. (102) The conference then considered the customs and railway matters for which it had been called, but no agreement could be reached. It was reconvened in Cape Town on 26 May, but complete deadlock resulted, and it was decided to leave these questions pending until after political union, which was now perceived as a probability. (103)

Africans were fully aware of the importance of these developments. Jabavu's *Imvo Zabantsundu* described the conference as an event of momentous importance where the foundation of the long-awaited, much-discussed union would be laid. (104) 'Great things are expected of the conference. May its decision be a blessing to South Africa as a whole,' declared the *Imvo*. (105) It expressed the hope that union would be in 'the broadest and most liberal spirit as possible' and said that the Cape could not be more strongly represented than by J. X. Merriman, J. W. Sauer and F. S. Malan. (106) The *Izwi Labantu*, in contrast, expressed doubts about the make-up of the conference and said, '. . . it will be harder for the more liberal ideas of the Cape Colony to penetrate than it would be for the camel to pass through the eye of a needle.' The newspaper warned Africans, 'Put not your trust in Princes,' and urged them to protect their own interests by shaking off their apathy and organising and standing up for their sacred rights. (107)

The tone of the two newspapers remained the same after the conference. After the adjournment of the Pretoria session, the *Imvo* noted optimistically, 'It does not appear that the bug-bear of the so-called Native Question frightened any members of the conference. This is as it ought to be.' If Africans were treated justly, there would be no native problem. 'There is only a Native Question when Governments endeavour to pursue towards the governed devious methods of treatment.' (108) But the *Izwi* placed without comment an unfounded report from the *South African Review* which stated that it had been heard on good authority that the conference had taken an unbending stand on native affairs and that the Cape had been threatened with exclusion from union unless the African vote was abolished. (109)

Another question which was broached at the inter-colonial conference was the Inter-State Native College scheme. Africans looked with particular interest to see what the result of these discussions would be. With a convention scheduled for Lovedale in July, interest in the subject was high. The scheme was at a well-advanced stage and it was hoped that the various governments would agree to give the go-ahead for a start to be made with the Inter-State College. To minimise expenses, closer union was necessary in this as in other matters, the *Imvo* said. (110) However, no firm decision was taken. Merriman raised the subject, but he found that feelings were so strong that it would have done more harm than good to force a formal discussion. Prime Ministers Fischer of the Orange River Colony and Moor of Natal were strongly opposed to the scheme, while Botha of the Transvaal, though not enthusiastic, was 'still fairly favourable'. Although the Cape government was entirely sympathetic to the scheme, its financial position prevented it from providing monetary support. The idea in fact only materialised after union. (111)

By June, as the *Imvo* correctly noted, the question of closer union was paramount, all other matters being of subsidiary importance. (112) Many Africans in the Cape were full of optimism for the new era that was dawning. Not only did they believe that their rights would remain untampered with, but they foresaw the extension of privileges similar to theirs to the northern colonies. The *Imvo* observed that

... there does not appear any disposition amongst those working for the Closer Union of the South African Colonies to be either unfair or unjust to the Natives in their treatment in the Union arrangements; that the existing rights and privileges of the Natives in the Cape Colony will be safeguarded we have no doubt. We are equally persuaded that something, even though not on a par with what our Cape people possess, will be done for our Native friends in the other Colonies in the direction of securing them some form of representation in the Union. (113)

Jabavu's views were coloured by his loyalty to Merriman and the South African Party, but, although the *Izwi* was more sceptical, Cape Africans generally evinced a measure of complacency about their political future. They felt that their rights were secure, as leaders of both major Cape political parties had declared themselves opposed to any tampering with the constitutional rights enjoyed by Africans in the Cape in any scheme for union. (114) This feeling of complacency amongst Cape Africans was to last until the release of the draft South Africa Act in February 1909, when they were dealt a rude shock and galvanised into resorting to extraordinary actions to safeguard their interests.

Counterposed to the confidence of Africans in the Cape was the open alarm shown by the *Ilanga lase Natal* and the *Naledi ea Lesotho* at the prospects of union. These newspapers had little faith that colonial statesmen would voluntarily extend the political rights of Africans. Indeed they feared the opposite.

To justify its opposition to union, the *Ilanga* quoted an article in the *Natal Advertiser* which recalled that Louis Botha had stated before the Transvaal Labour Commission that if he had his way he would break up the native reserves and force the Africans on to the labour market. According to the *Ilanga* this was the type of prospect union held for Africans. (115) It would accentuate rather than lessen the difficulties Africans lived under. (116) Dube's strong fear of and opposition to an Afrikaner-dominated union was derived largely from the deep suspicion of union that prevailed generally in the predominantly English colony of Natal.

The *Naledi ea Lesotho*, which wrote several editorials on the question at this time, (117) was equally suspicious. It viewed the situation in the Cape in a favourable light, (118) but it was generally hostile to the idea of Africans being governed under union according to the prevailing colonial systems. It said that if the South African colonists had their way there would be no African franchise and no Protectorates. (119) It was especially critical of the Natal administration and declared that, if the Natal system held sway at union, what had taken place there recently would be repeated in a united South Africa. (120) It asserted that as union would directly affect Africans throughout South Africa, they should not wait to see what happened in the forthcoming months, but should band together in unity and approach the Imperial government for protection. It would be to the Imperial government that Africans would have to look when the question of union was finalised. (121)

The position of Africans under South African union was also discussed in Britain at this time and Africans eagerly followed what was said. During May the matter was raised in the House of

Commons and Lord Milner spoke on the subject before the Imperial South Africa Association in London. Africans were particularly interested in these views because they looked to Britain for protection, and British ideals formed the essence of their political aspirations. They believed that as a union could not be obtained without the consent of Britain, their rights would be protected under union. (122)

All the speakers in the debate in the Commons spoke in favour of political representation based on the Cape franchise system for Africans. The Under-Secretary for the Colonies, Colonel Seely, said the franchise was the key to the situation. There were many things pressing for solution—African land, African education, African rights of every kind. Given the franchise these things would solve themselves. The feeling in the Commons was that the self-governing colonies would give Africans some form of representation. This would go a long way in reciprocating the magnanimous gesture of the Imperial government in granting the ex-republics self-government with a racially exclusive constitution. (123)

Milner concurred with the feeling that a more liberal attitude towards Africans on the part of leading men in South Africa was evident. He said African interests should be protected under union. The colour-bar was incompatible with African progress. Although the question of union was a matter for the people of South Africa to decide, it was the duty of friends in Britain to express well-instructed opinions. (124)

The optimism that existed in Britain that Africans would be given political representation under union was illusory. Lord Selborne informed the Secretary of State about this. Commenting on the debates in the House of Commons, he said the views expresssed by Sir Charles Dilke, Colonel Seely and others were 'founded on a complete misapprehension'. Selborne said he regarded it as his duty to say so. To a man the ministers in the Transvaal and the Orange River Colony were opposed to African representation. In holding these views, he regretted to say, they faithfully reflected the views of their constituents. (125)

### African strategies regarding the impending National Convention

As the National Convention—which was scheduled to meet in Durban on 12 October 1908—drew closer, politically conscious Africans in the various colonies began to respond more keenly to the developments. In August African political associations joined the newspapers in the debate about union and well-meaning white sympathisers also entered the fray on behalf of Africans.

There were two lines of thought with regard to the Convention. Cape Africans generally were disposed to put their faith in the Cape delegates and not to interfere. The feeling in the other colonies inclined towards direct action.

The Becoana Mutual Improvement Association in the Orange River Colony requested an interview early in August with the Governor, Sir Hamilton Goold-Adams, and cited as its first reason 'the position of Natives under the proposed Federation or Unification of S. A. States'. (126) The Governor granted the request soon afterwards. A delegation from the Orange River Colony Native Congress was also in attendance at the interview, but they were concerned mainly with other matters. (127) The Association deputation consisted of the Chairman Joel Goronyane, John Mokitlane Nyokong, Timothy Seiphimo and Jeremiah Makgothi, (128) while the Congress was represented by the Chairman Jacob Lavers, J. B. Twayi, Jan Mocher, Peter Phatlane, H. C. Msikinya and T. Mtobi Mapikela. (129)

At the meeting, and in a subsequent petition, the Africans informed the Governor that they wished to be allowed to express their opinion on Closer Union before the question was discussed at the forthcoming Convention. They asked that Goold-Adams, in his capacity as Paramount Chief of the Africans and in terms of Clause 2 of Article 52 of the Letters Patent, should call together the leading Africans in the colony, 'with such other persons having special knowledge and experience and who are interested in native affairs', to hear their views. (130)

However, the Governor informed the delegates that their interpretation of the Letters Patent was wrong and that the control of Africans was in the hands of his ministers. As no special provision existed in the pre-responsible government laws or under the constitution granted in 1901 for the Governor to exercise any special powers as Paramount Chief, no such powers were subsequently taken over by him when the existing constituion was granted in 1907. Article 52 stated that the Governor was empowered only to exercise such powers and authority as were vested in him at the time of the granting of responsible government. (131) Goold-Adams notified Prime Minister Fischer about the various points raised by the two organisations and the latter consented to meet the two deputations. (132) The meeting apparently took place on 6 October, (133) a few days before the Convention met. It is likely, therefore, that Fischer proceeded to

Durban knowing at immediate first hand the feelings of politically conscious Africans in the Orange River Colony on the subject of unification.

The Congress also made attempts to bring the question of future African representation to the attention of the Imperial authorities. In view of Goold-Adams's impending departure for a visit to Britain, the executive committee again communicated with him in September 1908. It asked him to convey its loyalty to the Imperial government and expressed the hope that 'the question of vouchsafing the Natives in the new Colonies a militant voice in connection with matters affecting them is at present receiving the favourable consideration of His Majesty's Government'. (134)

In neighbouring Basutoland, the Basutoland Progressive Association, an organisation which had been formed in December 1907 along the lines of the political groups in the various colonies, (135) discussed the Closer Union question for two days at a meeting in Maseru in August. The Association decided that it could not support either federation or unification until the ruling classes made up their minds to open the door of equal rights to all subjects of the Empire, irrespective of colour or means. It expressed the hope that Basutoland and other native territories would remain outside any scheme of Closer Union, under the protection of the Imperial government. (136) Similarly, the *Naledi ea Lesotho* newspaper, referring to union, declared, 'No self-respecting Native would accept any form of representation short of direct representation in the legislatures of the country.' (137)

Africans in the Transvaal also now began to respond to the developments concerning union. In August 1908 Sefako Mapogo Makgatho's African National Political Union forwarded a lengthy petition to Prime Minister Botha, listing grievances and reforms it wanted implemented, 'especially at this moment when the question of the Unification or the Federation of the South African colonies is on the eve of consideration, and as our interests and our future prospects will therein be involved'. (138)

The petition was on behalf of the Africans of the Pretoria district and Chiefs Sekhukhuni, Makapan, Matlala, Kehane, Mphahlele and Ramambe representing their respective areas. It asked for equal rights, protection, privileges, liberty and freedom for all British subjects. In addition attention was drawn to general pass regulations, the harshness of the hut and dog taxes, the viciousness of Zulus enlisted as policemen in the Transvaal, the execution and shooting of Africans, church and education matters, trading rights, the sale of liquor, and the wish for a government-appointed committee to look after African orphans, and for African post offices.

Late in September 1908 the Secretary of the main Natal organisation, the Natal Native Congress, H. C. C. Matiwane, issued a notice calling a meeting of the Congress for 15 October to discuss the Convention. The whole black race was invited to come in great numbers to record its final word. It was reported that from what Africans were saying it would appear as if the meeting would be a large one. (139) It was eventually held on 23 October during the sitting of the National Convention and the Congress duly requested the Secretary for Native Affairs to put its views before the Convention. (140)

With less than a month remaining before the Convention was due to meet, two almost simultaneous calls were made for active steps to be taken to co-ordinate African opinion and to make a united appeal for representation to the Convention. On 18 September the *Ilanga lase Natal* appealed for a 'Committee of Vigilance' to be formed during the conference and a few days later Theophilus L. Schreiner, a former member of the Cape Legislative Assembly and a long-standing champion of African rights, called on Africans to combine to secure their rights.

The *Ilanga* called on the *Imvo Zabantsundu*, the *Izwi Labantu*, the *Naledi ea Lesotho*, the *Koranta ea Becoana* and the *South African Spectator* by name to rally all blacks and to realise the need for closer union amongst themselves. It asked them to urge Africans and coloured people through their various political organisations to send delegates to Durban for the duration of the session of the Convention. These delegates should form a Committee of Vigilance and request that their views be heard by the Convention. It was also desirable that whites like James Henderson, Theophilus Schreiner, Joseph Orpen and Marshall Campbell should be present to assist the delegates in formulating and pressing their claims. If it was too late for some to send delegates, they should petition the Convention. The *Ilanga* remarked that a British naval squadron would be in Durban for the opening of the Convention, 'and there will be a great firing of cannons and other demonstrations of this meeting as a great and grand historical event', but it should be remembered that the majority of people in South Africa would not be represented. Therefore, it was the duty of African leaders to make representations to the Convention. (141) It was clear that the *Ilanga*'s editor, John L. Dube, contemplated the forthcoming union with apprehension. He had been warned by the Natal government early in September to curtail his political activities and moderate his newspaper's views as he was 'playing with fire', (142) but after the *Ilanga* had published its appeal he continued to draw the attention of his African readers to the dangers of union in a series of long editorials in Zulu and English. (143)

In the editorials Dube stated that while the time was not ripe for union as African interests had not yet received proper consideration, union was inevitable and Africans should take cognisance of the matter. It seemed they would be excluded from the union. It would be a union of the white people only. He said this was not a good thing. No people in the world were fit to govern another class without any representation whatsoever. They could never adequately understand or care about the wholly unrepresented group, or act impartially towards them. (144) People in the self-governing colonies were calling for union to be decided on in South Africa without British interference, but it was inconsistent to contemplate a union which did not do justice to all the people and expect non-interference from the Imperial government. To ensure the well-being of the country, the *Ilanga* felt, Britain should interfere in South African affairs. (145) The fact that the British government had to approve any scheme devised by colonial statesmen for union gave the *Ilanga* hope for the future.

The *Ilanga*'s appeal on 18 September for a 'Committee of Vigilance' during the National Convention was followed a few days later by an appeal, circularised in the form of a letter to the African press, from Theophilus Schreiner for Africans to combine and to petition the Convention, the Imperial government and the House of Commons asking for their rights to be safeguarded:

I send this letter to the Native Press in South African under a deep sense of duty and responsibility, in the hope that the leading men amongst the Natives, sinking all petty jealousies and ignoring all dividing lines in view of the importance of the crisis, may combine in united action so as to produce a unanimous expression of opinion such as will carry weight both with the Convention, and the Imperial Government and Parliament, and will strengthen the hands of those who are fighting the battle of justice and fair play irrespective of colour. (146)

As the issue also affected the coloured people, Schreiner felt that they should unite with the Africans. Time was at a premium, so he suggested that all Africans and coloured organisations and committees should at once ask and empower Joseph Orpen in Durban to do whatever was possible to safeguard their interests before the

Convention, and to forward all resolutions and petitions to him.

Schreiner regarded the following as the most important points to be included in the petitions to the Convention:

That the Imperial Government should continue its rule and administration over the Native Reserves which are under its control, and not hand them over to any Colony or proposed Federation or Unification of Colonies, until and unless irrevocable guarantees are given beforehand by the Governments of the various Colonies that such Colony or Federation or Unification of Colonies will recognise:

1 The inalienable right of the Natives in those Reserves as a whole to the land in such Reserves unoccupied by Europeans;

2 Their right eventually to receive individual tenure and title for the same;

3 Their right to the establishment of some system of local self-government;

4 The right of the civilised Native, whether in the Reserves or elsewhere, to genuine and adequate parliamentary representation based upon a civilisation franchise.

It is the duty of the Imperial Government either to continue its control over these Reserves or to obtain these guarantees; but to hand these Natives over to a federated and unified European South Africa without doing so will be a base betrayal of the King's loyal Native Subjects that will prove evil for them, evil for South Africa as a whole, and evil for the Empire. (147)

Theophilus Schreiner was one of four members of a family who were to distinguish themselves in their outspoken defence of the rights of Africans under union in the ensuing months. Ever since the Anglo-Boer War, he had been one of a small group of whites, including Joseph Orpen, J. S. Moffat, Edouard Jacottet, F. B. Bridgman, Harriette Colenso and Dewdney Drew, who had helped articulate as yet imperfectly formed African opinions. (148) Schreiner was recognised as one of the most tireless of these spokesmen. (149) He was the first member of Parliament to emphasise the need to protect Africans in any scheme for union, (150) and shortly before the National Convention he published a pamphlet attacking the much-favoured idea of separate representation of Africans as propounded by the South African Native Commission. (151)

The appeals by the *Ilanga* and Schreiner met with a disappointing response. The only significant support came from Pambani J. Mzimba, the influential head of the separatist Presbyterian Church of Africa. (152) Both the *Imvo Zabantsundu* and the *Izwi Labantu* poured cold water on the idea. That the African response to these calls was negligible can be seen from the list of representations made to the Convention. The suggested committee did not materialise and only one or two individuals addressed themselves to the Convention.

The reaction of the *Imvo* and the *Izwi* and that of Cape Africans in general was that it was the responsibility of the Cape and British governments to safeguard and represent African interests. If Africans appealed above the heads of their representatives to the Convention they would be displaying a lack of faith in them. These newspapers, in fact, were pointedly hostile to the idea of any African agitation during the Convention.

The *Imvo*'s attitude was that

A meeting of African people in connection with union at this stage seems unnecessary. At this stage the Africans have nothing good or bad before them on which to base their discussions at such a meeting. Union is still going to be discussed by the National Convention which meets in Durban and the results of which are as yet unknown. If the African nation should meet, what direction will its discussions take since there is as yet nothing before the nation? It is reasonable for the Africans of the Northern colonies to be restless; they have always been excluded from the enjoyment of civil rights because of the antagonism of the Europeans in those colonies, there being also no doubt that the delegates of those colonies will enter the convention still imbued with their old and bad spirit of antipathy towards Africans. There would be nothing wrong in the holding of meetings by the Africans of the Northern colonies. The Cape Africans are in a different position altogether. Their civil rights are not doubted by anyone. There is no fear that the Cape delegates will speak for anything other than the retention of civil rights by the Cape African, of whom they have wide experience. Any agitation by Cape Africans at this stage would have the effect of discouraging our delegates and also make them appear as though they are ignorant of obligation. (153)

Agitation on the part of Africans would also

. . . give some force to the contention of certain individuals who would treat Natives as an evil, and refuse point blank to regard them, as they should be considered, as identical with the body politic save for the disadvantage of lack of education in civilised modes of life. It would, moreover, be an assumption that the delegates to the Convention are prejudiced persons who are incapable of seeing right and justice done to all sections of the community. Certainly nobody has a right to make such an assumption in respect of the delegates from the Cape, no matter to which political party they may belong. In our opinion a propaganda of this sort, at this stage, would be prejudicial to the best interests of the Natives. It would very greatly hamper the Cape delegates in the fight for the rights of all that they may encounter from those coming from Colonies with systems in which the repromoniation [*sic*] of the people is incomplete through prejudice, born of ignorance. . . . Altogether, an agitation by Natives is much to be deplored. There would be reason for it when the proposals of the Convention are found seriously and unjustly to threaten the rights of any section of the people, but we fail to see any ground for Natives crying before they are hurt. (154)

The *Izwi* fundamentally agreed with the *Imvo*'s conclusion. In its opinion, Africans should wait and see what stand the Cape delegates, who all belonged to parties which had frequently claimed to support the African franchise, would put up. However, any modifications to or the abolition of the much-valued Cape franchise by the Convention could be taken as a sign of hostility and would justify united action by Africans and their friends. (155) It was also not necessary to petition the Convention because the British Government would not let the Africans down. The discussions at the Queenstown Conference of November 1907 had made the Imperial authorities aware of the fears and grievances of Africans. (156)

The *Izwi* played down the support of 'the Reverend from Alice' (Mzimba) for 'unrepresentative committees' which slept on their laurels all year round and then emerged in a time of crisis to represent the nation. (157) A correspondent, in turn, expressed his disappointment at the *Izwi*'s attitude towards Mzimba and appealed to Dr Rubusana and A. K. Soga, who were the leaders of the people, to call a conference and not let the nation down at this crucial time. If these gentlemen responded, the people in the correspondent's district would also call a conference to gauge African opinion on the subject. It was not too late yet. (158)

But Africans in the Cape were also mollified by the choice of delegates appointed by the Cape parliament to represent the colony at the Convention. They were Sir Henry de Villiers, Chief Justice and Chairman of the Legislative Council, who was an Independent, John X. Merriman and J. W. Sauer, Jabavu's political champions, F. S. Malan, J. H. M. Beck, H. C. van Heerden and G. H. Maasdorp (all South African Party), Starr Jameson, Thomas Smartt, E. H. Walton, and J. W. Jagger (Unionist) and W. P. Schreiner (Independent). (159) An erstwhile Prime Minister, a brilliant constitutional lawyer and an ardent spokesman for Africans, W. P. Schreiner was seen as the man to look after African interests at the convention. In his Queenstown election manifesto of 1907 he had come out firmly against a political colour bar in the coming federation/unification of the South African colonies. (160)

Speeches in the Cape parliament and by the delegates seemed

to confirm that Africans had nothing to fear under union. During
the last session of the Cape parliament members on both sides had
made it clear that the Cape franchise should be respected. (161) In
moving the adoption of the inter-colonial conference resolutions
in the Legislative Assembly, Merriman had declared that both sides
of the House were pledged to maintain up to the hilt the rights of
Africans with regard to the franchise. (162) Jabavu believed that
one of the most important features of the parliamentary session
had been 'the jealous defence by the government of Native interests'.
He said the performance of the government had shown how
unnecessary the bitter jeers and jibes were that had been hurled at
South African Party supporters during the election. (163) Speeches
in support of the Cape franchise by Sir Henry de Villiers and J. H.
Hofmeyr at a farewell party for the Convention delegates in Cape
Town reinforced the belief that African interests would be protected. (164)

African hopes received a setback when Schreiner withdrew as a
delegate to the Convention. He had gladly accepted nomination as
a Cape delegate when Merriman asked him to do so in June 1908.
(165) Earlier, however, realising the political and social implications
involved in the trial of Dinizulu in Natal, Schreiner had agreed to
defend the Zulu chief despite pressing parliamentary and other
commitments. He had anticipated that the trial would be over by
October/November. (166) When he saw that the two events would
coincide, he asked the Natal Prime Minsiter to postpone the trial
until later, (167) but Moor refused. (168) Schreiner was left with
a difficult decision. He chose what appeared to be the less attractive and more idealistic alternative when he announced his resig-
nation from the Convention to a surprised Legislative Assembly on
4 September. He declared that his first duty was with the person
whose defence he had undertaken, and he could not set that aside,
even for the high duty of attending the Convention. It was one of
the disappointments of his life, he added. (169)

Thus the one person who would most probably have fought
hardest for a multi-racial policy in a federal system against the
idea of a white unitary state was excluded from the deliberations
on a common future for South Africa. Although Merriman voiced
his indignation at Schreiner's withdrawal, (170) he was secretly
pleased about it. Indicating signs of compromise which would
come later, Merriman wrote to Louis Botha, 'It's a very good job
that Schreiner retired and it will shorten our proceedings material-
ly. Stanford [Schreiner's replacement] is a good fellow and has

seen and knows too much about natives to be an ultra-negrophile. Whatever he agrees to will be accepted by the other side. . . .' (171) Merriman had earlier expressed his wariness of Schreiner in a letter to ex-President Steyn. (172)

Colonel Stanford had vast experience in African affairs and was widely, (173) but not unanimously, (174) regarded as a good replacement for Schreiner by Africans and sympathetic newspapers, but he was first and foremost a civil servant, not a politician. Although he was to put up a fight for the Cape franchise at the Convention, he was not equal to the overwhelming odds he faced in opposing the viewpoints of the other colonies. However, it is doubtful whether even the presence of someone with the statesman-like qualities of Schreiner would have significantly affected the final decisions reached by the Convention.

# 6 The National Convention

Only nine years to the day after the outbreak of the Anglo-Boer War in 1899 the National Convention assembled in Durban on 12 October 1908, thus bringing to a culmination a remarkable process of reconciliation between Boer and Briton in South Africa.

When the proceedings got under way, Sir Henry de Villiers was unanimously elected President. He made a short speech in which he called on the delegates to display mutual faith, co-operation and perseverance in bringing about a strong and united South Africa. Ex-President Steyn of the Orange River Colony was chosen as Vice-president. (1)

Thirty-three delegates representing the four colonies and Rhodesia attended.* They included the four colonial Prime Ministers, as well as leading government and opposition members from each colony. The three Rhodesian delegates were given the right to speak, but not to vote. (2) Except for the opening address by the Governor of Natal, Sir Mathew Nathan, the Imperial factor was excluded. The proceedings were entirely in the hands of colonial statesmen. However, Sir Henry de Villiers kept in regular contact with the British High Commissioner, Lord Selborne, to gauge the views of the Imperial government, especially on the vital questions of the franchise and the Protectorates, and the Imperial connection was emphasised by the presence of a British naval squadron in

* The delegates were: *Cape Colony* J. H. de Villiers (Chief Justice and President of the National Convention), J. X. Merriman (Prime Minister), J. W. Sauer, F. S. Malan, L. S. Jameson, T. W. Smartt, E. H. Walton, W. E. M. Stanford, J. W. Jagger, H. C. van Heerden, G. H. Maasdorp, J. H. M. Beck; *Natal* F. R. Moor (Prime Minister), E. M. Greene, T. Hyslop, C. J. Smythe, W. B. Morcom, T. Watt; *Transvaal* L. Botha (Prime Minister), J. C. Smuts, H. C. Hull, G. Farrar, P. Fitzpatrick, H. L. Lindsay, S. W. Burger, J. H. de la Rey; *Orange River Colony* A. Fischer (Prime Minister), M. T. Steyn, J. B. M. Hertzog, C. R. de Wet, A. Browne; *Rhodesia* W. Milton, C. P. J. Coghlan, L. Michell.

Durban for the occasion. The Governors of the different colonies also were supplied with the minutes of the proceedings. (3)

The first point to be discussed was the form union should take. (4) The protagonists of a unitary system were not hard put to carry their views against those who preferred federation. The Convention then went on to the language question. Here the equality of the Dutch and English languages was recognised. These discussions took up the first week of the session. (5)

### The franchise

During this first week, the vital question of the franchise for blacks, a delicate matter which underlay all South African politics and could make or break union, was raised briefly. On 19 October, Merriman moved that the existing colonial franchise laws should remain as they were, being alterable only under special conditions for changing the Union constitution. (6) Later he said that these conditions should be a majority of not less than three-quarters of the members of both Houses sitting and voting together. (7) Stanford moved instead that 'All subjects of His Majesty resident in South Africa shall be entitled to franchise rights irrespective of race or colour upon such qualifications as may be determined by this Convention.' (8) Stanford, therefore, proposed that the electoral colour bar should be abolished in all the colonies, while Merriman saw the retention of the status quo in each territory as the only means of reaching an agreement satisfactory to all.

From 20 to 22 October there was an intensive debate on the subject. Several franchise proposals were forthcoming, but no unanimity could be reached. Opinions accorded with the traditional conceptions prevailing in the respective colonies. Broadly speaking, the Cape delegates wished to extend, or at least preserve, the nonracial franchise of the Cape, while the opposite applied to the representatives of all three northern colonies. They were unanimous in their hostility to African participation in the political system.

In starting the discussions both Merriman and Stanford reiterated their earlier proposals. Merriman said that there were those who wished to get rid of every black man in South Africa, but they had to face realities and the fact that the Cape delegates had special responsibilities towards blacks. They were trustees for these people and had to guard the rights which had been granted to them and never abused. The whole matter of political rights for blacks should be left as it stood until after union. Stanford said the franchise was the crux of the whole native question in South

Africa. Africans should be granted not only freedom, but citizenship. In his opinion the extraordinary advances shown by Africans in the Cape Colony during the past century were due to a great extent to their having the franchise. Africans appreciated this privilege. The franchise was a safety valve which provided an outlet for their grievances. Grievances were not left to simmer until they led to disorder and rebellion. (10)

Sir Percy Fitzpatrick, who represented the opposition Progressive Party in the Transvaal, spoke next. He advocated a high franchise qualification based on a 'civilisation test' carried out by a permanent tribunal. According to him the success of the Cape in dealing with the native problem was due to the excellence of its administration rather than to the franchise or any other law. (11)

Prime Minister Moor of Natal then spoke. He called for a total colour bar. He felt that the white and black races in South Africa could never be amalgamated: the history of the world showed that the black man was incapable of civilisation. (12)

Thus the first four speakers had all advocated widely differing policies towards Africans. Merriman's proposal received the most support from the speakers who followed before the proceedings of 20 October were terminated. While J. W. Sauer supported Stanford's motion, Abraham Fischer, J. W. Jagger and J. C. Smuts spoke in favour of a retention of the status quo in the various colonies. (13) Fischer declared that only a Union Parliament could work out the uniform native policy which everyone desired. (14) Smuts said Stanford's proposals were unacceptable to the northern colonies, while Moor's ideas would be rejected by the Imperial government; Fitzpatrick's suggestion would meet with opposition in all four colonies as it would be regarded as too severe in the Cape and too generous in the other colonies. Therefore, the franchise should be left as it stood in the various colonies until after Union when it could be amended by a simple majority in the Union Parliament. (15)

The compromise strategy of making the solution to the so-called native problem secondary to the more pressing need for union, decided on by Smuts and Merriman before the Convention, was beginning to assert itself. It is certain that they would have sounded out other delegates on the matter before raising it; and as they were the two dominant personalities of the Convention, the odds were that their approach would be accepted in the end.

Meanwhile, the adroit Sir Henry de Villiers had realised that the approval of the Imperial government was imperative for union to succeed, and for some months he had kept in touch with Imperial officials on the franchise question. As the debate entered its second day on 21 October, De Villiers informed the Convention of the conclusions he had drawn from his observations, and read a letter he had elicited from Lord Selborne on the subject.

He said that during a visit to England in June he had met the Colonial Secretary, Lord Crewe, and other British ministers to ascertain their views. He said they were willing to give a free hand to South Africa on the question of union, except on two points: the African franchise and the protectorates. In respect of the first matter, the Imperial government wished to see a franchise qualification which would leave the door open for Africans to qualify for full rights of citizenship in the future. Secondly, it felt it would be best for all the Native territories to be incorporated into South Africa from the start, but if the franchise question was not dealt with satisfactorily the protectorates would not be handed over. De Villiers had also asked the High Commissioner, Lord Selborne, to make certain observations about the franchise, especially with a view to elucidating the position of the Imperial government on the matter. (16) Lord Selborne had hastened to comply.

The High Commissioner had proposed a franchise for blacks based on a laborious 'civilisation test'. The idea was similar to that suggested by Fitzpatrick. Lord Selborne had reservations about Merriman's motion that the status quo should be retained in every colony: 'If it succeeds in making the franchise secure to the Cape natives, it will also make it practically impossible at any time to extend the franchise to any of the natives of the Transvaal, Natal or the Orange River Colony.' He said the Imperial government was greatly concerned about the franchise question. It would be placed in an invidious position 'if a Constitution is established for South Africa which leaves no open door whatever to the franchise for the native, however civilised, or for the coloured man, however civilised. . . .' (17) Such a constitution would lead to strong protests to the Imperial government and would raise the undesirable possibility of Imperial interference.

According to Lord Selborne, the Imperial government interpreted clause eight of the Vereeniging peace terms to mean that the question of the African franchise would be dealt with shortly after responsible government had come into existence. No more appropriate moment for dealing with this question could occur than during the National Convention.

Furthermore, as the Imperial government had already informed

De Villiers, the question of the franchise was closely bound to the conditions of the expected transfer of the protectorates to the union. If the Cape franchise was left untampered with and 'a permanent adequate door to the franchise was opened to the natives' in the other colonies, the prospects for a transfer would be favourable. A closed door policy would have the opposite effect. (18)

With De Villiers's entry into the debate, the delegates now knew more or less what was the attitude of the Imperial government, which had the final say in the matter, but succeeding speakers almost without exception stuck doggedly to the broad principles of 'native policy' in their various colonies. While Cape representatives like Malan, Smartt, Jagger and Walton forcefully defended a non-racial franchise, the delegates from the north, with Louis Botha at the helm, were equally forceful in their support of a colour-bar. (19)

C. R. de Wet touched on the fundamental attitude of the north when he said, 'Providence has drawn the line between black and white and we must make that clear to the natives, not instil into their minds false ideas of equality.' (20) Morcom, Hyslop and Greene of Natal supported an absolute colour bar for South Africa. The latter moved an amendment to exclude blacks from membership of both Houses of Parliament. (21)

Although the depth of commitment to the respective policies varied, the only real dissenting forces in the various colonial delegations were those of Fitzpatrick, who continued to defend his original proposal, (22) and G. H. Maasdorp of the Cape, who, speaking as a representative of the Cape farmers, said they feared the African franchise and wished to see it restricted. He would be happy with some form of separate representation based on the recommendations of the South African Native Affairs Commision. (23)

With the Cape and the northern colonies insistent in their support of the prevailing policies in the respective colonies, the big question was whether the Convention should formulate a uniform franchise system for South Africa or whether it should leave the franchise as it was in each colony until after union. It was clear that unless the latter avenue was followed deadlock would be reached. Louis Botha put it bluntly when he said that if the view of F. S. Malan that there should be no union before a settlement was reached was accepted, then the question of union was finished. He saw in Malan's approach a desire to force the rest of South Africa to accept the principle of Cape franchise. If this was done he might just as well go home. (24)

In order to reach some sort of agreement, Botha proposed that the task of framing resolutions in regard to the future 'native policy' be entrusted to a committee nominated by the various Prime Ministers. The proposal was adopted.

The franchise committee was composed of J. W. Sauer and E. H. Walton (Cape Colony), C. J. Smythe and E. M. Greene (Natal), Percy Fitzpatrick and J. C. Smuts (Transvaal), J. B. M. Hertzog and Abraham Fischer (Orange River Colony), and C. P. J. Coghlan, who was nominated by the Administrator of Rhodesia, Sir William Milton. (25) Abraham Fischer acted as chairman of the committee. As the Convention proceedings could not be held up while the delegates waited for the franchise committee to complete its deliberations, the committee met during spare hours in the evenings and the Convention turned meanwhile to discussions of other matters.

Sir Henry de Villiers, who had continued his consultation with Lord Selborne on the franchise issue, was able to provide the committee with important advice on this matter. (26) On 21 October he had written to Lord Selborne responding to the latter's suggestion of a 'civilisation test' and informing him of the general feeling of the Convention on the franchise for Africans. De Villiers said it would be extremely difficult to devise a scheme for applying the test which Selborne suggested. He asked whether the High Commissioner intended this scheme for the Cape as well. If this was the case it would place a restriction on the Cape vote.

In addition, De Villiers posed three more questions on which he desired clarification:

1 It seems to me extremely desirable that before any resolution is arrived at I should know whether, in your opinion, the Home Government would agree to the application of the test of civilisation to coloured persons and not to Europeans.

2 I should like also to know whether, in case no satisfactory test of that kind can be agreed upon, the Home Government would agree to allow the present franchise to remain in the different Provinces until altered by the Union Parliament either with or without the proviso that such alteration shall not be allowed in regard to the qualification of coloured persons in the Cape Colony unless carried by a majority of not less than three-fourths of the members of both Houses, sitting together.

3 It is very important that I should know whether the Home Government would agree to a provision that only persons of European descent shall be eligible as Members of either House of the Union Parliament. The Cape delegates

seem to be prepared to accept such a provision seeing that without it an agreement on the matter of franchise would be almost hopeless. (27)

The last point of De Villiers's letter was of cardinal importance. It indicated that the Cape had bowed to the demands of the other colonies on the matter, and indeed Merriman had already agreed to support the Greene motion to bar blacks from the Union Parliament. Assurances from the Imperial government, the final arbiter in the matter, were now being sought.

Lord Selborne's response on 22 October to the four questions posed by De Villiers cleared the way for a settlement based on colonial principles:

1 ... My private opinon, for what it is worth, is that such a scheme [the 'civilisation test'], if evolved, should eventually be applied to the whole of South Africa. In no case do I think it would be reasonable to remove from the voters' list the names of any voters already on them, whether white or black. As regards the prospective expectation of men not yet voters, of course a disappointment of such an expectation must always be involved in any raising of the franchise. This would apply in the case of whites as well as in the case of natives.

2 ... I believe they would, as part of a general settlement of the franchise question in South Africa which gave an adequate permanent access to the franchise to the coloured people and natives in all the British South African Colonies.

3 ... I think His Majesty's Government would feel that they would not satisfactorily answer the question until they were aware of all the main details of the general scheme of closer union, and how each part reflected upon another, and also until they knew how far the general scheme agreed upon represented the unanimous or practically unanimous opinion of the members of the National Convention, or whether the opinion of the delegates was divided in nearly equal proportions on any of the more important parts of the scheme. I am confident, however, that in default of a general settlement of the native franchise question they would warmly sympathise with any provision securing to the Cape Coloured persons and natives that access to the franchise which they at present enjoy.

4 ... I do not think that His Majesty's Government would object to such a provision as part of an otherwise satisfactory settlement of the native franchise question. (28)

As a result of this letter, De Villiers was able to inform the franchise committee that Britain would probably agree to the continuance of the discriminatory Transvaal, Orange River Colony and Natal franchise systems, and even to the exclusion of blacks in the Cape from the right to sit in Parliament, a right which they had always enjoyed but had not yet exercised. With Britain's willingness to co-operate virtually confirmed, the constraints against drawing up a colour bar constitution were weakened and the fears of a Royal Veto of a constituion embodying differential principles diminished. Instead of actively supporting the non-racial Cape franchise system, Selborne weakened the chances of its being adopted elsewhere in South Africa. The Colonial Secretary, Lord Crewe, with whom he was in constant communication during the Convention, also was not insistent on the matter. Crewe's response to Selborne's answers was that they were not at variance with the general policy of the British government, although it was perhaps inclined more in the direction of the Cape system than Lord Selborne had made out. The main aim was union. While Crewe favoured the non-racial franchise, he said he was sensible of the difficulties of its being applied in the northern colonies. (29)

After considering the various resolutions and amendments of the Convention, and the suggestions for a qualified franchise from Lord Selborne, the franchise committee presented its report to the Convention on 2 November. It was discussed the following day.

The last two parts of the four-part report, dealing with non-controversial formalities, were quickly passed, but the first two parts, concerning safeguards for existing black franchise rights and a 'European descent' provision for parliamentary eligibility, were vaguely worded and gave rise to contention. (30) It soon became clear that a long debate would ensue. The Convention, therefore, decided that the amendments and the disputed sections of the report be referred back to the franchise committee with instructions that it present a report the following day. (31)

The final report received the approval of the Convention. Part I of the report recommended that no law should disqualify any persons in the Cape from the vote by reason of their race or colour only, unless it was passed by a majority of two-thirds of the members of each House of Parliament. Until such a law was passed, the existing franchise qualifications in the various colonies would prevail in elections of members of the central Parliament. Moreover, no registered voters in any province should be removed from the register by reason only of any disqualification based on race or colour. (32)

Part II was submitted in the same form as it had appeared in the original report of the previous day: 'Only persons of European descent shall be eligible as members of either House of Parliament.' (33) Supporters and opponents of political rights for blacks now made a final attempt to influence the constitution towards their way of thinking. Stanford gave notice of a motion opposing the exclusion of blacks from Parliament, but he withdrew the notice and it was not even discussed. (34) Similarly, Malan moved that the 'two-thirds' safeguard for black voters in the Cape apply to Natal as well, but he too withdrew the amendment. (35)

The hardliners on the colour question were more resilient, and gained a final concession before the resolutions of the franchise committee were adopted by the Convention. Louis Botha moved that instead of the approval of two-thirds of the members of each House being required to disqualify Cape blacks from the franchise, the clause in question should provide for two-thirds of the total number of members of both Houses of Parliament, sitting together, to pass the disqualification. The amendment was agreed to. (36) Prior to this Smythe of Natal had moved that the proposed safeguards for black franchise rights in the constitution should be removed. However, Smythe had been supported only by his Natal co-delegates and J. D. de la Rey of the Transvaal. (37)

With the acceptance of the franchise committee's recommendations, the Convention virtually concluded its deliberations on the question of the franchise for blacks. The matter was raised only briefly again during subsequent discussions. This happened, for example, during the Convention's deliberations on female suffrage, (38) and on the Provincial Councils; in the latter regard it was decided that, in the Cape, all voters regardless of colour could become members. (39)

In the draft South Africa Act, which embodied the final decisions of the delegates before the proposed constitution was put to the country at large, the colour bar clauses decided on by the Convention were contained in sections 25, 33 and 44. Sections 25 and 44 dealt with the qualifications for members of the Senate and the House of Assembly respectively. Only British subjects 'of European descent' were eligible for these positions. Section 33 and its seven subsections provided for increases in the size of the House of Assembly in proportion to the numbers of European male adults, rather than the number of registered voters or adult males of all colours, in each province. Other provisions of the draft Act which concern us here were Sections 35 and 153, dealing with amendments to the constitution. The latter stipulated that the entrenched clauses of the constitution could only be altered by a majority of two-thirds of the total number of members of both Houses of Parliament sitting together, while the former specified that one of the entrenched clauses was that no person in the Cape could be disqualified as a voter except under the above conditions. Altogether there were 153 sections and a Schedule which dealt with the protectorates. (40)

In the final analysis the Convention's recommendations on the franchise question were a compromise between the Cape and the northern colonies. The latter agreed to the continuation of franchise rights for blacks in the Cape, while that colony countenanced the continuation of the colour bar in the north and the principle that blacks should be excluded from sitting in parliament.

## The protectorates
The future position of the British protectorates or High Commission Territories in South Africa, a question narrowly related to the discussion on what role Africans should be allocated in the new political system, was also discussed by the Convention.

It was generally expected by colonial whites that the protectorates—Basutoland (Lesotho), Bechuanaland (Botswana) and Swaziland—would in due course be incorporated into a white South African government. The consummation of closer union was seen as an ideal opportunity to realise this expectation. (41)

However, this was not to be. While the British government generally accepted that it had effectively relinquished control of native affairs in the self-governing colonies, it was determined to exert itself fully in the protectorates. These areas were still directly under Imperial control. They had come under British rule under special circumstances and the Imperial government, therefore, had special responsibilities towards these people. (42) As a specially obligated trustee, Britain decided that it would not transfer the protectorates to a united South African government unless firm and liberal assurances had been given. Local pressure helped in making this resolve concrete. (43)

The traditional leaders in the protectorates had expressed their apprehension at reports about union as early as May 1908. On 12 May Paramount Chief Letsie Moshweshwe of the Basothos asked the Imperial authorities for clarification: what were the reasons for those who planned union, how was it to be effected and was Basutoland also considered in this scheme? (44) Similar enquiries were made by Sebele Sechele, Paramount chief of the Bakwena in Bechuanaland on 23 May, (45) and by the Queen Regent of Swaziland, Labotsibeni, in July. (46) The Basothos felt so strongly on the subject that Letsie asked for authority in

September for a Basotho delegation to be allowed to convey in person the loyalty of the Basotho nation, and their fears of union, to King Edward VII. (47) The chiefs were assured that their fears were groundless and that their interests would be safeguarded by the British government. (48)

Meanwhile the High Commissioner, Lord Selborne, had been actively involved in working out a scheme for the protectorates once South Africa became a union. In contrast to his half-hearted defence of African political rights in the South African colonies, he exerted strong pressures on the colonial and British governments in his efforts to protect the interests of the indigenous peoples in the protectorates. (49) His standpoint was that it was in the interests of both the South African and Imperial governments that the protectorates should fall within the union, but that as Britain had special obligations towards these territories this transfer should not take place until a future date, when definite safeguards for Africans in the protectorates, embodied in the union constitution, had been met. Selborne argued that these safeguards should include respect for the inalienability of African land, the prohibition of liquor sales, a fair distribution of union custom duties and a degree of political autonomy. In respect of the last matter, Selborne wanted the Basutoland National Council to be preserved and a special Commission with wide-ranging powers to be appointed in place of the High Commissioner to administer in detail the government of the protectorates. In this way, the protectorates would not be directly administered by the union government. (50)

Lord Selborne's scheme was put to the four prime ministers and J. C. Smuts at the end of October. The respondents were unhappy about the proposals. With the exception of Moor, who thought the time was inopportune even to discuss the matter of the transfer of the protectorates, they wished to include the protectorates in the union at once and were strongly opposed to any interference which would affect the sovereignty of the South African government over the territories. Hence their opposition to the proposed Commission, with powers independent of the union government. (51)

Further negotiations ensued. On 29 November Botha, Fischer and Merriman agreed to accept all the proposals except for the one regarding the composition and powers of the Commission, which they wanted to see merely as an advisory body. They agreed to delay the transfer of the protectorates. Moor stuck to his previous standpoint, but said he would support his fellow prime ministers if the issue was handled then instead of in the future. (52) In an attempt to reach a compromise, Selborne too was prepared to make minor alterations to his plans for the Commission. (53)

On the morning of 10 December, at a meeting between Selborne, De Villiers and the four prime ministers, the matter of the protectorates was taken further. (54) That afternoon it was discussed by the Convention. The question was referred to a committee consisting of De Villiers, the prime ministers, Sir Lewis Michell and Colonel Stanford. (55) After keeping in close touch with Lord Selborne during its deliberations, (56) the committee submitted its report on 17 December. It was received with mixed feelings by the Convention. However, with leading delegates like De Villiers, Merriman, Fischer, Botha, Smuts, Steyn, Stanford, Malan, Farrar, Jameson and Beck providing support, the report was carried with only a few minor modifications. (57)

The Convention's resolutions regarding the protectorates were embodied in a special 25-point schedule to the draft constitution. After the transfer of a protectorate to the union, the Governor-General-in-Council would be the legislative authority and could by proclamation make laws provided that these were first laid before both Houses of Parliament. The Prime Minister, advised by a Commission of not less than three members and a secretary, would be charged with the administration of the territory. The members of the Commission would be appointed for ten years, but this could be extended. They would not be permitted to be members of either House of Parliament. It would be the duty of the members of the Commission to advise the Prime Minister on all administrative and legislative matters. If the Prime Minister refused to accept a recommendation of the Commission or proposed to take some action contrary to their advice, the matter would be laid before the Governor-General-in-Council, whose decision would be final. A Resident Commissioner would be appointed in the territory. Amongst other things, he was to prepare the annual estimates for revenue and expenditure and act in accordance with such estimates.

Several other provisions were set out in the schedule. The union treasury would pay each territory its proportion of the total custom revenues towards the cost of administration. In the case of shortfalls between revenue and expenditure, the union government would make good the deficiency. Land belonging to Africans could not be alienated. The sale of liquor would be pro-

hibited. The custom of holding a *pitso* or any other recognised
form of native assembly would be maintained. No differential
customs laws would apply to the territory. Subject to the laws
of the union, including the pass laws, there would be free intercourse between the whites and blacks of these territories and the
rest of South Africa. The rights of civil servants would be protected. Annual reports would be presented before the union
parliament. In addition, the King could disallow any law made by
the Governor-General-in-Council, and all bills to amend or alter
the provisions of the schedule would be reserved for the King's
pleasure. (58)

This schedule was a compromise. Its effects cut both ways.
While the South African statesmen had surrendered their desire
immediately to incorporate the protectorates under union, their
appeasing approach went a long way towards minimising the risk
that Britain would veto the political colour bar in the new constitution. Furthermore, the terms which Selborne had persuaded the
Convention to accept in regard to the protectorates provided an
important sop to the consciences of the Home rulers. Although
the Africans in the colonies had been left without Imperial protection, the interests of those in the protectorates had been safeguarded.

### Representations on behalf of Africans

While the discussions were taking place at the National Convention, the African people, whose destinies were being determined,
were unrepresented. However, nothing prevented Africans and
their sympathisers from addressing themselves to the Convention.
Some took the opportunity to do so. A number of petitions emanating from or on behalf of Africans were laid before the Convention.

On the day the Convention assembled in Durban, it had before
it a telegram from W. P. Schreiner. (59) He expressed the wish that
the labours of the Convention would advance the true welfare and
union of all South Africa and its people. (60) The following day a
detailed, more urgent address from Joseph Millard Orpen, an octogenarian champion of African interests, was submitted. (61) As
was the case when the issue of responsible government for the
Transvaal and the Orange River Colony was current, Orpen took it
upon himself to speak out on behalf of the Africans who were
without effective spokesmen. (62)

With more than half a century of practical involvement in parliamentary politics and African affairs in several territories in South Africa, Orpen was well qualified to speak on the so-called 'native problem'. He was, at one time or another, a member of the first Volksraad in the Orange Free State, a member of the Cape Parliament, a government representative among African tribes in the Transkei, East Griqualand, Bechuanaland and Basutoland, and Surveyor-General for Rhodesia, an executive post. Orpen was also a prolific writer. (63) In recent years he had endeared himself to many blacks for his outspoken defence of African rights. (64) He had been appreciative of Theophilus Schreiner's call for blacks to appoint him to represent their interests at the Convention, and had supported the *Ilanga lase Natal*'s appeal for African and coloured organisations to send delegates to Durban to work in conjunction with white sympathisers in defending the interests of blacks. With this aim in mind he had written to W. P. Schreiner at the end of September, saying, 'We want you and if you cannot be here in person I hope you will kindly give your advice as to what representations should be made and what should be asked for and how to ask it.' And further, 'Perhaps you would publish your views.' (65)

As we have seen, owing to lack of time, initiative and co-ordination, nothing came of the *Ilanga*'s proposal. Orpen, therefore, approached the Convention in a private capacity and without any mandate from others. He asked the Convention, in the interests of both black and white in South Africa, to include in its decisions some liberal scheme for the granting of a fair measure of representation to blacks throughout South Africa, with due regard to the safe-guarding of white supremacy. (Even the most ardent advocates of African rights at that time regarded white supremacy as essential.) However, as the example of the Cape and the Transkeian Territories had demonstrated, the only way to uplift the Africans and keep them content was to give them representation. 'Representation is the sovereign cure for every ill,' said Orpen quoting Charles James Fox. Without representation there could be no lasting solution to the most fundamental question in South African politics:

There never has been, there is not and cannot be any section of the community which, if alone represented in the Government of any country, would not, consciously or unconsciously, prefer its own interest to those of the unrepresented section and do it injustice. . . . The more humble and weak any section of the community may be, the more widely separated from the rest by race-feeling, language and customs, the more urgent is the necessity for its representation, the more eloquent its appeal to the higher race on the grounds of common humanity, common interests and common dangers. Representation is no discovery of. an advanced civilisation. It has always existed even in the most rudimentary forms of government. It is a fundamental necessity in any good government, the very root and existence for such a government. (66)

To emphasise his point Orpen quoted at length from W. P. Schreiner's speech at the farewell function for the Cape delegates to the Convention as well as from utterances by Lord Selborne and the late Harry Escombe. He had not suggested a scheme for representation in his letter, Orpen concluded, but he would be happy to place at the disposal of the Convention copies of what he had written on the subject. (67)

Orpen and the Schreiner brothers were not the only white sympathisers to act with concern for the position of Africans when the Convention sat. The Revd J. S. Moffat wrote to the High Commissioner, Lord Selborne, expressing his interest in and anxiety at the approach of union, (68) and a similar letter was directed to Sir Henry de Villiers by Sir James Rose Innes, Judge President of the Transvaal. (69) In addition, the Bishop of Pretoria forwarded to the Convention two letters with resolutions from the Diocesan and Episcopal synods of the Church of the Province of South Africa. The resolutions expressed the hope that union would be established on the foundations of co-operation, trust and justice towards all sections of the population. (70) Later this concern was to spread to other church bodies as well.

## Representations by Africans

The first representation to the Convention from the African population group was a letter from Charles Daniel of Imbizana, Natal. It was presented by Mr Moor on 3 November, (71) the day the franchise committee reported for the first time and a day before the whole franchise question was resolved.

Charles Daniel was a member of the Natal Native Congress. He represented the Lower Umzimkulu Division on that body. His letter, dated 15 October, and directed to the Natal Secretary for Native Affairs, was written in Zulu. A translated copy was presented to the Convention. 'On behalf of all the people of Lower Umzimkulu and the Division of Ixopo and Harding', Daniel hoped that while the Convention discussed the new constitution it would resolve on a scheme by which Africans would be 'drawn into proper enlightenment' and given the exemption and franchise rights theoretically granted to civilised Africans in Natal in 1865. Despite having rejected traditionalism and remained loyal and law-abiding, 'We have not been given these rights although we were promised them.' They hoped their rights would not be ignored under the new union.

In an argument clearly reflecting the influences of modernisation and acculturation, Daniel said further that not only should 'civilised' Africans be granted just rights, but that heathenism and traditional customs should be actively combated through agricultural improvement, advanced education, Christianity and the prohibition of customs such as polygamy. The 'Governor of South Africa' should 'strive to diminish heathenism'. It was the heathenism under which most Africans still lived, and the attitudes of some whites who saw Africans as nothing more than labour units, which caused rights to be withheld from Africans. If possible, the petitioner said he would like to be given the opportunity of appearing personally before the Convention so that he could give his views on these matters. (72)

The most substantial direct approaches by Africans to the Convention were two petitions presented by the Transvaal National Natives Union (TNNU) in November and December 1908. Designated the successor of the Transvaal Basotho Committee, the TNNU developed from the perceived need for greater unity amongst various African groups in the Transvaal at this critical period. It was only formally constituted as an organisation at a meeting on 1 January 1909. (73) Whether earlier the TNNU was simply a designation conveniently used by the Basotho Committee, whether the petition emanated from an *ad hoc* committee of several groups, or whether unity only developed from the actual circulation of the petitions is not certain.

On 22 October the organisers circulated numerous copies of the petition, handsomely printed on quality paper, throughout the Transvaal. However, owing to the urgency caused by the uncertainty as to when the Convention would complete its deliberations and rise, the petitions were not circulated as extensively as desired. Nevertheless within a month, W. P. Letseleba, the TNNU Chairman, and Z. More, its Secretary, were able to forward eighteen copies of the petition to the National Convention. These contained the signatures of 1994 Africans from Johannesburg, Pietersburg, Barberton, Germiston, Standerton, Boksburg and Potchefstroom. (74) The petition was laid before the Convention on 23 November. (75) A further sixteen copies of the petition were forwarded to

the Convention on 17 December (76) through David Pollock, secretary of the Transvaal Native Affairs Society. (77) (This organisation had been founded in January 1908 'to promote the study and
discussion of the South African question, with a view to enuncia-
ting and advocating a liberal, consistent and practical Native policy
throughout South Africa'.) (78) This channel was used to communicate with the Convention on the second occasion because the
petitioners had received no acknowledgement after forwarding the
first batch of petition lists. (79) The supplementary petitions were
signed by 1770 people, bringing the total number of petitioners to
3764. In addition to some of the districts already mentioned, the
following centres were represented: Vereeniging, Pretoria, Kilnerton, Marabastad, Mphahlele's Location, Saulspoort, Klerksdorp
and Rustenburg. As the Convention had already adjourned for the
Christmas recess, these petitions were submitted to the Convention
only on 11 January 1909. (80)

The petition of the TNNU was a clear indication of the anxiety
of Africans, particularly those outside the Cape, at the coming
union. The petition requested representation for Africans in the
parliament of a united South Africa:

We desire to remind the Convention that the natives in this Colony have
hitherto been totally unrepresented in the local Parliament, notwithstanding
the fact that they contribute largely in direct taxation to the Treasury, in
addition to bearing a full share of the indirect taxation through Pass-Fees, the
Railways and the Customs Tariff.

We attribute the advancement in prosperity, contentment and loyalty,
which is such a marked characteristic of the natives of Cape Colony, to the
generous policy which has permitted them to qualify themselves as citizens
and to enjoy the privileges of citizenship. And we submit that the same happy
result may be expected to follow the extension of the Cape Franchise to our
people throughout South Africa.

We therefore submit to the favourable consideration of your Honourable
Convention our claim to be permitted to qualify for the full political privileges, such as may be granted to the European population in the Constitution
you are preparing for submission to His Majesty the King, while praying that
the interests of those of our people who may be unable to qualify for this
Franchise may be protected by a measure of separate representation following
in part the method suggested in the Report of the South African Native
Affairs Commission. (81)

Among the prominent Africans who signed the petition and
canvassed signatures were S. M. Makgatho and Phillip Maeta, Chairman and Secretary respectively of the African National Political

Union, Chief Mphahlele, who had close ties with this body, Mangena M. Mokone of the African Methodist Episcopal Church, Samuel James Brander of the Ethiopian Catholic Church in Zion and H. R. Ngcayiya of the Ethiopian Church. Mangena and Brander were connected with the Pretoria-based African Political Society and Ngcayiya was a member of the executive of the Transvaal Native Congress.

This petition of the Transvaal Africans did not go unnoticed. It was, for instance, reported in colonial newspapers such as the East London *Daily Dispatch* (82) and the *Natal Mercury* (83) and, of course, in the vernacular *Izwi Labantu* (84) and *Ilanga lase Natal*. (85) The *Natal Mercury* said no thoughtful South African could view with unconcern the spectacle which the petition conjured up. It brought the Convention face to face with the African view of an important question which would have to be settled on an intelligent basis at the outset by a union government. The newspaper said it was difficult to see how Mr Merriman and his fellow Cape delegates could logically withhold their sympathy from the petitioners. (86)

On 23 October, the Natal Native Congress convened a special meeting in Pietermaritzburg to discuss the franchise question, with a view to submitting its decisions to the Convention. (87) The question of representation was paramount in the minds of the delegates. In an address intended for the National Convention, the Natal Native Congress declared:

We Natives of Natal, though loyal subjects of the Crown and sharing the burden of taxation, are labouring under serious disabilities by being excluded from free access to the Franchise, and having no efficient means of making our wants known to Parliament and no say in matters regarding our most vital interests such as taxation and other things. We humbly beg, with regard to our future government, for some degree of representation in the Legislature. This would go far to remove all causes of complaint and make the Natives a more contented and devoted people under His Majesty's gracious rule. ... Any scheme for the Closer Union of the Colonies under the British Crown should include a provision that representation should be accorded fairly to all sections of the community, without distinction of colour, and that in Natal, as a precedent to any union with the other Colonies of South Africa, the Native population should first be placed in the fair position Natives hold in the Cape Colony. . . . (88)

The petitioners stated that this position was believed to have been guaranteed to Africans in Natal by the British government when it annexed Natal, but that it had not been borne out in practice.

For some reason or another this address of the Natal Native Congress was never submitted to the National Convention. It was delivered to the Natal Native Affairs Department at 4.20 p.m. on the afternoon of 5 November (89) (shortly after the Durban session had ended) for submission to the Convention, but it was never tabled. It could have been that in view of the adjournment of almost three weeks and the fact that a basic agreement on the African franchise had already been reached, Moor considered it unnecessary to lay the address before the Convention.

The only other approach from Africans to the Convention during its first and second sessions was a letter in January 1909 from the white Chairman and Secretary of the 'Native Section' of the Kimberley and Bloemfontein synod of the Wesleyan Methodist Church of South Africa. This body claimed to represent 40 000 members and adherents in the above area and roughly 200 000 people throughout South Africa It expressed the sincere hope that the Convention would 'fully safeguard the interests of the Native Races in this sub-continent'. (90)

It is clear that the direct representations made by Africans to the National Convention had no effect whatsoever on the deliberations of the delegates, who, gathered in secret discourse, and unknown to the country at large, had already reached finality on the matter of the franchise for Africans.

## Coloured representations on behalf of all black people

When the coloured African Political Organisation petitioned the Convention for a redress of grievances, it appealed on behalf of all blacks. As the Queenstown conference of November 1907 had demonstrated, there was now a greater sense of solidarity amongst blacks than in earlier years. Because its organisation extended across colonial boundaries, Dr Abdurahman's APO was able to co-ordinate coloured opinion in the various colonies more effectively than the Africans had been able to do. The Cape, the Orange River Colony and the Transvaal affiliates of the APO all sent petitions to the Convention. (91) The wording of these petitions differed only slightly.

The petitions urged that the principle of 'equal rights for all civilised persons in South Africa' should be respected and that no colour line should be drawn in the new constitution. They pointed out that the 23 000 African and coloured electors in the Cape had never abused the privilege of the franchise or used it to the detriment of Europeans. It had been an agent of rapid and peaceful progress. The extension of this successful system to the other colonies would be an act of wisdom which would be in the interests of whites and blacks alike. If this was not done hardship and dissatisfaction would result. And if the status quo was maintained in the various colonies an intolerable and unworkable situation would arise when people enjoying certain privileges in one colony proceeded to another colony where other conditions existed.

Petitions were also received from a meeting of 'the Cape Coloured People of Johannesburg (Witwatersrand)' and the Wynberg Coloured Men's Political Organisation. Africans were not specifically referred to, but the political colour bar was deprecated. (92)

## Other African attitudes and activities

What were the attitudes and activities of Africans apart from the representations to the Convention at this time?

In the Cape, Africans maintained their passive wait-and-see attitude. (93) Once the Convention had settled down to its discussions, the *Imvo Zabantsundu* and the *Izwi Labantu* newspapers focused their attention on other matters. Nothing was heard from the South African Native Congress. Except for odd rumours about the Convention's proceedings, (94) which gave rise to speculative reports from time to time, no definite news penetrated the tight veil of secrecy surrounding the Convention to give any cause for alarm. On the other hand, John Dube, close to where the constitutional discussions on South Africa's future were taking place, kept the spotlight on the Convention and the closer union issue in the columns of the *Ilanga lase Natal*. The thread of the *Ilanga*'s arguments remained the same as in the past: the need for representation; fear of Afrikaner domination and racial differentiation; and heavy reliance on Imperial protection. (95)

In the Transvaal, the intense political activity that took place from October to December 1908, when almost 4 000 signatures were collected for submission to the Convention, led to greater co-operation among Africans in the colony. On 1 January 1909, a number of political organisations, including the Transvaal Basotho Committee, the Transvaal Native Congress and the *Iliso Lomzi*, formed a united body, the Transvaal Native Union (TNU), to defend their common rights. (96) This was an attempt to consolidate the co-operation of the previous few months.

The formation of the Transvaal Native Union was an important event in an area with probably the greatest population diversity of all the colonies. The spread of 'universal' ideas among Transvaal

Africans was reflected in the proviso that coloured people could become members and that the organisation would act on their behalf. Current political developments clearly were bringing home the need for increased organisation and united action amongst blacks. Moreover, to co-operate with members of the white ruling class was also thought desirable. One of the objects embodied in the constitution of the TNU was 'co-operation with all friends of law, order, liberty and justice . . . without distinction of race'. (97)

At the well-attended inaugural meeting of the TNU in the Nancefield location, attended by delegates from fourteen centres, a central executive was elected to control the activities of the organisation. The committee consisted of a cross-section of members of the various affiliated bodies. (98) They were Edward Tsewu, Jesse Makhothe, M. R. Ruoele, J. K. Moikangoa, Z. More, E. Moeletsi, the Revd Mvuyane and Messrs Gunza and Monakali. The South African Native Congress stalwart and editor of the *Izwi Labantu*, A. K. Soga, who was in the Transvaal at this time, possibly to seek financial relief for his hard-pressed newspaper, also attended the TNU inaugural meeting. After being given a special welcome, Soga impressed on the delegates the need for unity. (99)

Understandably, Africans looked for reassurances from the Imperial authorities at this crossroads in South African politics. Without a voice in the discussions on a new constitutional model for their country, they were anxious to receive some kind of guarantee from Britain, as the ultimate authority, that their interests would not be ignored. Statements by high-ranking people in Britain raised hope in this respect. When the Colonial Secretary, Lord Crewe, declared in November 1908 that, while the British government had left colonial statesmen to decide on the machinery for union, it had a real and distinct obligation towards the Africans, *Ilanga* commented that never in the history of the land was such an assurance more valuable, and that it was bound to have an influence on current politics. (100)

In December, the *Izwi Labantu* noted a similar speech by the Under-Secretary of State for the Colonies, Colonel Seely, who stated that Britain's obligations to the Africans who were looking to the Imperial government and the King for protection would never be lost sight of in any settlement arrived at. (101) And the King's speech in January to 'the Princes and Peoples of India', in which he said that steps were being continually taken to obliterate distinctions of race, was seen as a hopeful sign. The *Imvo Zabantsundu* said it revealed 'the heart of a great King towards the Coloured subjects of his Empire'. (102)

## Responses in the protectorates

If the Africans in the South African colonies hoped for British intervention on their behalf, those in the protectorates expected it. Since the protectorates were directly controlled by the Imperial government, which in the very nature of the political arrangement had special obligations towards the African inhabitants, they had every right to insist strongly that their interests be safeguarded.

The nature of African political leadership in the protectorates was another factor that distinguished them from the colonies. While the westernised, educated élite were usually in the vanguard in expressing African attitudes towards union and other matters in the colonies, the traditional leaders fulfilled this function in the protectorates. The reason was simple: with the partial exception of Basutoland, the people in these territories were hardly affected by modernising influences. Educational opportunities were minimal and the people were governed through traditional leaders.

Early in January, soon after the National Convention had passed its basic resolutions on the future of the protectorates, Lord Selborne informed the principal chiefs in these territories through the local Commissioners that at first they would remain outside union, but it was likely that they would be incorporated at an early date. The chiefs all reacted adversely to this news. The Acting Resident Commissioner of Bechuanaland, Barry May, travelled from Mafeking to Serowe and Gaberones to convey Selborne's message to the Tswana chiefs and their followers. At meetings with him, Chiefs Khama, Sebele, Bathoen, Linchiwe and Baitlotle Ikanenge –Paramount Chiefs of the Bamangwato, Bakwena, Bangwaketse, Bakhatla and Bamalete respectively–all expressed strong opposition to being incorporated in the union. (103) With the exception of Khama, they also subsequently put their views in writing to the Imperial authorities. (104)

The Tswana chiefs declared that they did not wish to live under the laws of the South African government. They regarded these as being restrictive. Even in the Cape Colony there were oppressive laws, said chief Sebele Sechele. The chiefs implored Britain to honour the pledge it had given to protect them and to allow them to govern themselves along traditional lines.

The Swazis shared similar feelings. The Acting Resident Commissioner of Swaziland informed Lord Selborne that the news that Swaziland probably would be incorporated in the union at some future date was 'repugnant' to the Swazis. He had conveyed the proposals to the Chief Regent, the Chief Mother and the Swazi Council on 12 January. In attendance were 71 leading chiefs and 28 representatives of absent chiefs. He said it was clear that the Swazis looked upon the inclusion of their territory in any form of closer union as a prelude to the annexation of Swaziland to South Africa. (105)

The Basotho refused to let the subject of union rest merely with assurances from Lord Selborne. (106) Even the willingness of the High Commissioner to pay a personal visit to explain the matter was not enough to satisfy them. They wished to present their views directly to the King. In the face of this insistence, Selborne had little option but to allow a Basotho deputation to travel to Britain in January 1909 for this purpose. (107)

The deputation was composed of chiefs Seeiso, Mojela Letsie, Masupha Lepogo, Masupha and Leshoboro Majara, as well as two African interpreters, a secretary and an attendant. Paramount Chief Letsie was unable to travel on account of ill-health. The deputation met the Colonial Secretary, Lord Crewe, on 15 February, (108) and three days later it presented the Basotho petition to the King. (109) In the petition the Basotho chiefs and people asked the King not to include Basutoland in any union. They were satisfied with their form of government and desired no change:

Thus we do humbly beseech thee O King! to make us easy in our minds by telling us we need have no fear, in the event of South African unification or federation, that our nation will be absorbed in any of Your Majesty's Colonies, and thereby lose our national existence and our old native laws and customs, which are so well administered by Your Majesty's representatives in Basutoland. . . . (110)

If it was inevitable that the Basotho would be included in union, they wished to maintain their present form of government, customs and native laws. Furthermore, land should be inalienable and the Basotho National Council should be preserved.

The reply of the Imperial government to the petition was given to the deputation by Lord Crewe at a final interview on 25 February. The reply embodied the principles agreed to by the National Convention. (111) The Basotho were unable to extract the assurance that Basutoland would continue as a separate entity, but to a large extent their demands in the event of incorporation were met.

The constitutional attempts by the Basotho to safeguard their autonomy were accompanied by rumours of tribal discontent. It was reported that the Basotho would rather fight than be incorporated in a union. Despite vigorous denials from the Basutoland authorities, these rumours continued through the period leading up to unification. (112) They also had an effect on developments in the Cape Colony. Traditionalist unrest in the East Griqualand region, which bordered on Basutoland, in the early part of 1909 was ascribed in part by colonial intelligence sources to the Basotho unrest about union.

In a communication to the military authorities in Pietermaritzburg, the Officer Commanding Natal Guides, Polela, reported that unrest was brewing in East Griqualand (113) where Pata, the chief of the twelve-thousand-strong Hlangwini tribe located in the districts of Umzimkulu, Matatiele and Mount Currie, (114) was often in communication with the disaffected Basotho Chief Griffith. The report alleged that Griffith, a brother of the Paramount Chief Letsie and high on the succession list, told his people that if the Basotho deputation to England 'failed to obtain satisfaction, it would be a good chance to start a row'. To back up his intention, the report said, Griffith in late January had the riding horses of his tribe brought down from the mountains and sent messages to members of his tribe away working to return to their homes. At the same time, it was reported, members of the Hlangwini tribe working in Durban had been notified to return to their kraals. Pata had allegedly held two big meetings of his tribes in December where their grievances were discussed and money was subscribed, ostensibly to purchase land, but secretly to obtain arms and ammunition. Pata had also been in contact with other chiefs and headmen to sound out their views on the native situation. (115)

Unrest was prevalent in the districts in question, but it is unlikely that it was specifically related to the question of union, although this issue might have contributed to the dissatisfaction. The Secretary of Native Affairs in the Cape said the chief cause of unrest was the extension of the unpopular Proclamation 79 of 1906 (which promulgated regulations for the control of African townships on private property and the prevention of squatting) to the Umzimkulu district. (116) The magistrates in the various districts cited food shortages, the financial impoverishment of many of the people, the circulation of wild rumours about Dinizulu and talk of the banished Griqua leader Le Fleur being about to return to take over the country as additional causes. They made no mention of dissatisfaction about the impending union and described the Natal report as on the whole much exaggerated, (117) a view shared by the Basutoland authorities. (118)

As the reports from the *Naledi ea Lesotho* during 1908 and the resolutions of the Basutoland Progressive Association (detailed in the previous chapter) show, the small westernised section of the African population in Basutoland approved of the actions of the traditional leaders with regard to union. In fact, it seems they could have been responsible for these actions. S. M. Phamotse, editor of the *Naledi ea Lesotho*, informed W. P. Schreiner in July 1909 that 'Since the very first sitting of the National Convention I have been in communication with the Paramount Chief Letsie and have had interviews with him urging him to secure the services of a legal adviser, as I was sure Basutoland would be affected by Union.' (119) Phamotse, incidentally, had close ties with African politicians in the Transvaal. Up until 1908, when he returned to his native Basutoland to become the official secretary to Chief Jonathan and editor of the *Naledi ea Lesotho*, he had been one of the guiding forces behind the *Leihlo la Babathso* newspaper in the Transvaal. (120)

The small Basutoland educated class was becoming increasingly critical of the authorities at this time, much to the disquiet of the latter. In his report for 1908, the Resident Commissioner, H. C. Sloley, said that it was discouraging to note that old scholars of government-aided schools were showing impatience with the authorities and writing critically about them in the vernacular press. By 'misapplying the benefits of their school training' they would spread disaffection amongst the rest of the population. If the educated class exceeded the 'limits of tolerance', its actions should be checked. (121) And indeed, Phamotse was deported from Basutoland soon after union.

Africans in the South African colonies inclined to sympathise with the actions of the Africans in the protectorates. They identified with protectorate Africans in the same way that the Cape Afrikaners sympathised with Afrikaners in the ex-republics. This can be seen from the resolutions of the Queenstown conference and in contemporary newspaper comments. The *Ilanga lase Natal* said the eyes of hundreds of thousands of Africans were focused on the Basotho deputation to England to see what would be the attitude towards the rightful plea for the protection of African interests. (122) The *Imvo Zabantsundu* declared that it would be a pity if the promising system of native administration that was developing in Basutoland was interrupted by union. (123)

Thus in contrast to the ideas held by the great majority of delegates to the National Convention, the desire of Africans in South Africa was to gain political participation for the educated group, and at the same time to ensure autonomy for traditional communities.

# 7 African responses to the draft South Africa Act

The full report of the National Convention, the draft South Africa Act, was released to the press on 9 February 1909. (1) Although many of the details were criticised, the whites of the Transvaal and the Orange River Colony generally gave the draft a favourable reception. However, it was widely opposed in Natal. That colony feared being 'submerged' by its neighbours. But in respect of the provisions pertaining to Africans under union, the draft succeeded to a large degree in placating white public opinion in the three northern colonies. Most whites were opposed to the principle of Africans having the franchise, but they accepted the compromise with the Cape as being necessary to achieve the greater goal of union. (2) A vocal minority, however, did not. Botha informed Merriman that there were some people who were quite prepared to wreck union on this question. (3)

In the Cape, with its relatively non-racial traditions, it was the proposed colour bar which caused considerable dissatisfaction. A powerful lobby developed, led by W. P. Schreiner, demanding amendments to the colour bar provisions in the draft when it came before the Cape parliament. (4) When the report was released Schreiner was in Greytown where he was still involved in Dinizulu's trial. His immediate reaction was that the draft was 'narrow, illiberal and shortsighted in conception'. It was unjust to the black majority and did not safeguard adequately their rights. (5) He later repeated this theme in well-publicised speeches in Queenstown (6) and Cape Town. (7)

Other critics of the draft were J. G. van der Horst, editor of the *Cape Times*, the influential veteran Afrikaner Bond leader, J. H. Hofmeyr, and a number of ecclesiastical and liberal personalities, mainly in Cape Town. (8) Under Hofmeyr's influence, the Cape Town branch of the Afrikaner Bond strongly denounced the draft and called for a referendum in the Cape before it was passed. Its main criticism was levelled at the under-representation of the Cape in the union parliament, the strong centralisation of powers in the union government and the colour restrictions and the inadequate protection given to black voters by the two-thirds majority clause. (9) Hofmeyr's opposition seriously embarrassed Prime Minister Merriman. He feared that the 'hornet's nest' which it had stirred up in Cape Town could jeopardise the passage of the draft. (10) When the annual conference of the Bond repeated, but more cautiously, most of the objections of the Cape Town branch, including the question of protecting black franchise rights, (11) Merriman's concern deepened. (12)

Thus while whites in the northern colonies, with a few 'negrophile' exceptions, either accepted the franchise provisions regarding Africans, or considered them too generous, a vocal minority in the Cape demanded the repeal of the colour bar sections. This group found ready allies in the majority black population, which mobilised on an unprecedented scale to demonstrate its opposition to the proposed constitution. Throughout South Africa, African newspapers, political groups and spokesmen were virtually unanimous in their condemnation of its provisions.

### Newspaper responses

The response of the African press to the draft was one of undisguised hostility. All four newspapers—the *Imvo Zabantsundu, Izwi Labantu, Ilanga lase Natal* and *Naledi ea Lesotho* (13)—were outspoken in their criticism of the colour bar.

Jabavu's *Imvo* was first to comment. It described the report as illiberal and said it 'stereotyped vicious, flagitious and immoral colour distinctions among the King's subjects'. No opening was provided for the reasonable aspirations of the black man. The 'unreasoning and unreasonable prejudices' against Africans of the delegates from the Transvaal, the Orange River Colony, Natal and perhaps Rhodesia, had overwhelmed the Cape. While Africans were grateful to the Cape delegates for preserving their voting rights, the colour bar in parliament took away the prized guarantee of political freedom and political contentment and made the African franchise 'illusory'. (14) The franchise 'has been given with one hand and taken away with the other', *Imvo* added. (15) To alienate Africans at the very outset of union was 'very, very bad policy indeed. May our beloved country be spared from it.' (16)

As usual, A. K. Soga did not mince his words in the *Izwi Labantu*. 'This is treachery! It is worse. It is successful betrayal, for the

Act has virtually disenfranchised the black man already even before the meeting of the Union Parliament, which will complete the
crime by solemn vote of the two Assemblies. . . . This is a replica
of the treaty of Vereeniging.' (17) 'At one stroke they sweep away
the work of half a century and the dearest possessions of 20 000
voters who represent the more errant millions.' (18)

*Izwi* saw the report as part of 'a calculating and deliberate compact' to get rid of the African vote. (19) It had been engineered in
the Transvaal by the 'plutocrats', who ruled the world and were
perverting British principles, with their Afrikaner collaborators.
The plot had unfolded with the treaty of Vereeniging, the attempts
to suspend the Cape Constitution and the Randlords 'getting a
little of their own back' out of Bambatha and reasserting their
power after Africans had defeated them in their attempts to corner
the African labour market after the war. The *Izwi* said it had seen
this whole plot developing a long time ago. That is why it had
called the 1907 Queenstown conference to discuss the question of
union. (20) The Cape delegates, particularly the Progressive leaders,
had finally shown their true colours by shamelessly co-operating in
this compact. Their smirky assurances could not stand up to their
dishonesty which could be read in the draft report. They could
never again be trusted. With such a 'pack of hucksterers and hug-
germuggers' as the Cape Progressive leaders had proved themselves
to be, could there be any doubt of the result when an 'ignorant
Boer member' stood up in parliament one day to propose the abolition of the African franchise? (21)

When the *Daily Dispatch* accused the *Izwi* of adopting 'an in-
flammatory tone and language calculated to appeal to the worst
passions of its readers', the *Izwi* replied that the *Dispatch* need not
be afraid of its dividing blacks against whites. This could not be
more surely done than by the passing of the 'South African Conspiracy Act' in its existing form. (22) The *Izwi* warned that blacks
would never be satisfied with an inferior status:

'Equal rights for all South of the Zambesi' is the motto that will yet float at
the masthead of this new ship of state which has been launched under the
Union, and no other will be permanently substituted while there is one black
or coloured man of any consequence or self-respect in the country, or any
white man who respects the traditions of free Government—so help us God.
(23)

The *Ilange lase Natal* was even more explicit. It warned of the
threat of future violence if the constitution was implemented. The
*Ilanga* said Africans believed in union, but only in a just 'Manly

Christian Union'. They could not accept the 'spurious' plans devised by the National Convention. These ignored the interests of
all except Cape Africans and would leave a residue of doubt and
suspicion among blacks. 'It was naive to believe that millions of
people would willingly be made into mere political chattels to suit
the whims and avarice of a privileged few.' Africans hoped there
would be amendments. (24) The only solution was to follow
Rhodes' dictum that all civilised men should have equal rights. The
term civilised should be properly defined and then evolution should
be left to take its course. (25) If racial prejudice persisted and
Africans continued to be regarded only as exploitable labour units,
the prospect for a future filled with 'bitter hatred', (26) and even
violence, loomed ahead. There was 'a great body of natives who
never will be ready to submit themselves to the tyranny of the minority. . . . They think themselves entitled to boss the show.' (27)

The *Ilanga lase Natal* also offered some practical suggestions on
amendments which would make union more acceptable. It suggested that there should be a 'strong' Senate. The Upper Chamber
should not be an ineffectual rubber stamp. Very importantly, the
native senators should be elected directly by the Africans themselves. Each senator should represent one of the four main regions
of the union. (28) Also, the Governor-General should have personal
powers in making appointments. The decision should not be left
to his council. Finally, the Administrators of the provinces should
be nominated by the Imperial government, whose steadying influence it was important to maintain. (29)

### A national convention for Africans proposed
The Orange River Colony Native Congress meanwhile had anticipated the decisions of the National Convention and had decided to
act. Even before the release of the draft Act, the Congress had
made preparatory plans to arrange a joint convention of Africans
from throughout South Africa. The aim of this convention would
be to formulate and publicise the views on union of the unrepresented out-group. Immediately the draft was released, the ORCNC's
plan was set in motion and promoted through private correspondence between political leaders and newspaper editors in the
various colonies, and through the columns of an affronted African
press. A committee of the ORCNC under its Secretary, Thomas
Mtobi Mapikela, set about organising the convention. It was to be
held in Bloemfontein, the most central venue for an inter-colonial
meeting.

The decision to organise a convention for Africans was first released in the *Imvo Zabantsundu* on 9 February, the same day that the draft was made public. Jabavu gave the plan his full support. He said it was necessary that the 'black house' should hold council and voice its opinion before the constitution was enacted, and, if necessary, also take its grievances to Britain. He expressed his willingness to publish the names of the delegates in the *Imvo* and to make any other preparations which would make the meeting a success. He urged all African organisations in the four colonies to meet as soon as possible to prepare for the convention, which was scheduled to take place before the various colonial parliaments were to meet to decide on whether or not any amendment should be made to the decisions of the National Convention. (30)

In the following two issues of his newspaper, he placed a special advertisement publicising the proposed convention. The secretaries of the local associations in the various districts were encouraged to organise meetings to discuss the issue and elect delegates to represent them. Their names were to be forwarded to the *Imvo* and 'other' offices before the end of February. (31)

Within days of the release of the draft constitution, the ORCNC organising committee circularised letters to the various regions informing interested groups of the proposed convention. (32) In view of the threat to African interests, they appealed to all associations 'guarding the rights of the people' to prepare for a *Pitso* or *Ngqu* at which South African native opinion would be expressed. This applied as much to the enfranchised Africans in the Cape as to those in the Transvaal and the Orange River Colony, who were without any franchise rights whatsoever. Although Cape Africans retained the franchise under the new constitution, the ORCNC predicted that the 'voteless masses of Natives in other Colonies will be utilised as an instrument by the anti-native franchise majority to disenfranchise the Cape Natives.' Only the speedy extension of the vote to the northern colonies would permanently secure the African franchise in the Cape. Therefore it was important that the Africans joined forces as soon as possible to pursue this goal.

The ORCNC proposed in addition that, prior to the national convention for Africans in Bloemfontein, a joint conference restricted to Africans from the Orange River Colony and the Transvaal should be held. The aim of this conference would be to protest against the failure of the governments of the two colonies to extend franchise rights to Africans after the grant of responsible government, as Africans contended the governments were obligated to do under the treaty of Vereeniging, and to request the Imperial government to reserve the draft South Africa Act until this was done. The ORCNC believed that the eagerness of the ex-republics to enter a union was an attempt to evade the responsibility of giving Africans some form of representation. (34) However, this proposal was not acted upon and the conference never materialised.

But the appeal for an African national convention in Bloemfontein found a ready response. Such was the hostility to the draft constitution that the convention took place scarcely six weeks after its release. In that time Africans mobilised to an extent not hitherto achieved. Both the *Izwi Labantu* (35) and the *Ilanga lase Natal* (36) added their support to that already given by the *Imvo*. Urged on by the African press and political leaders, local committees from far and wide organised meetings to express African opposition to the draft and to elect delegates to the regional meetings that were being organised in the various colonies. At these meetings preparations were made for representation at the central convention.

The *Imvo Zabantsundu*, celebrating its twenty-fifth year of existence, commented, 'Conferences are the order of the day among the natives of South Africa on the ugly colour line that is being imposed on them in the draft constitution. We have never known our people so united and determined to contest, constitutionally, of course, a political issue.' (37) In one issue the *Imvo* reported on no less than sixteen protest meetings in its vernacular columns. These ranged from Vredefort in the Orange River Colony to Kimberley in the northern Cape, Cape Town in the south and Tsomo in the Transkeian Territories. (38) Even African women joined in the fray. In Somerset East the local ladies organised interdenominational prayer groups to pray for the success of those who were opposing the draft constitution. (39)

## Protest activities

### The Orange River Colony

The first colony-wide organisation to meet after the release of the draft Act was the Orange River Colony Native Congress. It held its annual Congress at Winburg on 17 and 18 February 1909, (40) little more than a week after the National Convention had made its draft public. There are conflicting reports about the meeting, but representatives from at least eleven centres (41) in the Orange River Colony attended. According to a report by Dr Rubusana, the meeting was attended by forty-eight delegates from fifteen centres. The *Friend* newspaper reported the number of delegates as twenty-one and the towns represented as eleven. The proceedings were started by an address by Thomas Mtobi Mapikela in which he 'surveyed the important events and radical changes affecting natives'. During the discussions that ensued, the initiative of the central committee in arranging a convention for Africans was put to the delegates. The idea was unanimously accepted. (42)

In the customary placatory message of loyalty, (43) and in a subsequent petition to the Prime Minister, (44) the ORCNC made no mention of the question of union. However, for some reason the Chairman and Secretary of the local branch in Bloemfontein were summoned to the Governor's office on the day after the Winburg congress ended. (45) Whether this was in connection with the convention arrangements or the ORCNC's allegations about the maltreatment of Africans that became the topic for local newspaper comment is a matter for conjecture. The *Friend* took the ORCNC to task for giving vent to its feelings about the 'barbarities' and suffering experienced by Africans at the hands of farm owners and the police under the Masters and Servants Act. It had been said that this act, originally intended to secure Africans against arbitrary treatment, was now wielded as a 'weapon of oppression' against them. The newspaper declared that the African leaders should for their own good withdraw the 'absurd allegation' made at Winburg. (46) Instead Mapikela took issue with the editor on the matter. (47)

After the meeting Mapikela, helped by other members of the ORCNC committee, like Elijah Tshongwana and J. S. Mocher, continued with arrangements for the convention. It is clear from reports in the vernacular newspapers that they were corresponding with various leaders. For example, in a letter to Jabavu on 23 February, Mocher referred to his communication with Soga and asked Jabavu to contact the people in the Transvaal because they had not replied to a letter from the ORCNC. (48) On 5 March, Mapikela circularised a second notice through the African press. This was aimed at involving traditional leaders in the convention as well. It was directed to the *Zinkosi na Mapakati, na Manene* (Chiefs, Councillors and Headmen):

Let us meet together before it is too late. Remember what happened at Vereeniging and what was done to the black man. Let not union be brought through you Chiefs Letsie, Jonathan, Ntsane, Dalindyebo, Sandile, Gwenbinkumbi, Nqwiliso, Ngangelizwe, Njokwini, Mhlabiso, Mabandla, Bakleni, Ndhlangazi, Makawula, U'Mhalla, Siwane, Molema, Falo. You also our Chiefs from Natal, Transvaal, Swaziland, Zambesi and M'Zilikazi [Matabeleland]. (49)

Shortly afterwards the dates for the convention were fixed for 24–26 March. Mapikela also posted advertisements informing delegates that special accommodation would be provided (50) and received permission from the government to hold the meeting. Prime Minister Fischer explained to Prime Minister Moor that the government had decided not to interfere, as it considered it inadvisable 'to manufacture cheap martyrs' and better to learn publicly what would be said. (51)

The Becoana Mutual Improvement Association held a meeting at Thaba Nchu on 20 March, at which the provisions of the draft Act were strongly deprecated. They deplored the colour bar in the constitution, saying that this 'repugnant' principle was contrary to accepted British constitutional and egalitarian traditions. The constitution was 'illiberal and unjust' and did not sufficiently safeguard the rights of Africans as British subjects. Unless altered, it would be permanently detrimental to the peace, progress and prosperity of South Africa, as there would be 'constant unrest and agitation' on the part of Africans. They asked for the draft to be 'considerably amended', asserting that the history of the Cape franchise system had shown that Africans appreciated and respected the privilege and could be trusted with the vote.

Local matters also were raised. They wished to include the Thaba Nchu and Witsieshoek native reserves under the protective terms of Section 14 of the Schedule to the constitution. The reserve at Witsieshoek had been set aside for Chief Paulus Mopeli and his tribe at the outset of republican government in the Orange Free State, and Thaba Nchu (or the ward of Moroka) had been an independent Baralong enclave until it was taken over by the Orange Free State in 1884. Africans in these areas therefore had been accustomed to land possession and self-government. Against this background the Association wished to ensure that their land would remain inalienable and that they would not be subjected to still more stringent white control. (52)

It is probable that arrangements for participation at the convention at Bloemfontein a few days later were also discussed.

## The Cape Colony
While the initiative for inter-colonial African co-operation came

from the Orange River Colony, the release of the draft Act triggered the most extensive response among the Africans of the Cape. The protests were led by the *Izwi Labantu* and *Imvo Zabantsundu* newspapers. They maintained a constant clamour against the proposed colour bar, encouraging local groups to do likewise and to elect delegates to represent them at proposed regional conferences. (53) Numerous meetings were held in urban and rural areas throughout the colony, particularly in the eastern Cape. They ranged from well-reported gatherings at places like Ndabeni in Cape Town to briefly detailed meetings in areas such as Engqushwa (Peddie) and Qoboqobo (Keiskamma Hoek). (54) Some were attended by hundreds of people, others were small. From everywhere the message was the same. The 'nation' was against the 'blot' on the constitution. The correspondence columns of the newspapers emphasised the point. In areas such as the Karoo where Africans were thinly spread, and in places where organisation was lacking, Africans took part in protest gatherings organised by the African Political Organisation. Their role was not merely passive. At meetings in Graaff-Reinet and Kimberley, for example, local Africans played a major part in the proceedings. (55) The APO was at the helm of the concerted agitation of the coloured people against the draft constitution.

Delegates to the National Convention such as Stanford, (56) Smartt, (57) Jameson (58) and Walton (59) also held special meetings for Africans in the Eastern Cape constituencies. This was part of the general campaign by Convention delegates to market the draft Act to the country. In the case of Stanford, to give an example, his itinerary was Butterworth (3 March), followed by Idutywa, Umtata, Engcobo and Elliott on the 4th, 6th, 9th and 11th respectively. In each town he held meetings with the whites in the mornings and Africans in the afternoons. (60) In his diary Stanford alludes to the concern among Africans about union. The Thembu paramount Chief, Dalindyebo, was one of those present at the well-attended meeting in Umtata. (61)

The attitude usually adopted by the Convention delegates at the meetings was that far from endangering the Cape African franchise, the draft constitution with its two-thirds majority requirement protected African interests. They said they felt that in due course the liberal ideas of the Cape would influence the other colonies, leading to a better dispensation for all Africans. (62) Most Africans who attended these meetings accepted the assurances given to them. After they had expressed concern about the

'Europeans only' clauses, and asked the delegates to do their best to have them removed, the meetings usually ended with votes of confidence being passed in the draft. However, the *Imvo* and the *Izwi* responded differently. Commenting on the speeches of delegates along these lines, the *Imvo* warned that the European-descent clause would make it impossible for liberal views to prevail. (63)

What did give hope to the *Imvo* and the *Izwi* were the dissenting voices of white political and church leaders in the passionate debate which was taking place in colonial circles over the merits of the two-thirds safeguard and the 'Europeans only' limitation. The two newspapers provided extensive coverage of the various views. Responding to W. P. Schreiner's powerful denunciation of the colour line in his Queenstown speech, the *Imvo* praised this 'vigorous and eloquent effort', (64) and the *Izwi* expressed the indebtedness of the Africans to Schreiner for his bold stand. (65) As at the start of the National Convention, the *Izwi* set aside space for the views of W. P. Schreiner's brother, Theophilus. (66) The reservations about the draft constitution aired by J. H. Hofmeyr and other Afrikaner Bond members such as J. G. van der Horst, J. A. C. Graaff and J. J. Michau also were welcomed. (67) Similarly, when Lord Selborne spoke in favour of a more liberal solution to South Africa's race relations question at the degree day of the University in Cape Town in March, (68) the *Imvo* said his speech gave 'intense satisfaction to Natives and friends of justice'. (67) Africans hoped that these utterances would evoke a more critical analysis of the Convention's decisions and influence the colonial parliaments in the direction of 'eliminating the deplorable and unstatesmanlike colour bar which at present disfigures the new South African Draft Act'. (70) And not only did Africans appreciate the opposition that white liberals were expressing, but they also wished to see white sympathisers participating in the meetings Africans were holding to discuss union. The *Izwi* said they should not wait for invitations, but should consider themselves welcome at these meetings. Their advice was never more needed than in this time of crisis. (71) Africans in other colonies similarly invited sympathetic whites to join with them in protests against the draft Act. (72)

Against this background of African solidarity, and in the light of the fact that both the *Izwi* and the *Imvo* had initially welcomed the call by the Orange River Colony Native Congress for a united African convention, it seemed that there was a chance that the traditional Xhosa-Thembu/*Izwi Labantu*/South African Native Congress/Progressive Party versus Mfengu/*Imvo Zabantsundu*/Jabavu/South African Party differences in Cape African politics would be resolved. This optimism soon proved groundless. Despite the common disillusionment over the draft Act and the logic in favour of united protest action, the rift in Cape African politics remained as deep as ever.

The feeling of the organisers of the Bloemfontein convention, (73) of political leaders in the Transvaal and Natal, and of the South African Native Congress in the Cape, was that the various delegations should be representative of the respective colonies, not of local organisations. (74) However Jabavu, who did not have a broad organisation as a power base, did not share this attitude. His influence had been built up around his own person, not within an organisation. Nominally delegated by his local King William's Town Native Association, he intended going to Bloemfontein on behalf of himself and his large informal following. The South African Native Congress claimed that Jabavu's King William's Town Native Association should, like other associations, first attend the regional conference it had called for in Emgwali near Stutterheim on 17 March. The people would then elect delegates to represent the Cape at the national convention. Only through this procedure could a properly representative delegation be sent to Bloemfontein. (75)

As matters turned out, Jabavu attended neither this meeting nor the one at Bloemfontein. In March he withdrew his active support for the Bloemfontein convention, and then proceeded to organise his own conference. The decision to do so was taken at a meeting in King William's Town on 5 March. The *Imvo* reported that it had been decided that King William's Town would be a better venue than Bloemfontein, and that the conference should be moved there. A committee was appointed to arrange this. It consisted of Jabavu and five other people, Messrs Mtyaku, Mtoba, Nobako, Haye and Solilo. (76) The well-known N. C. Umhalla, who had fallen out with the SANC, was also involved in the meeting. Notices in the *Imvo* advertising the Bloemfontein convention and signed by Jabavu (77) were now dropped and replaced by similar ones summoning Africans to King William's Town. (78) The date was set for 7 April.

The spurious argument used by the *Imvo* to explain this turnabout was that the Bloemfontein venue had been decided on before the publication of the draft Act, and before it became known to what extent the rights of Africans in the Cape had been affected, and in view of the subsequent developments a different approach was now called for. The Cape Africans would have gone to Bloemfontein for a demonstration against the continued inferior status of Africans in the other colonies, but now unexpectedly the political future of Cape Africans was being threatened and they should therefore organise more strenuously amongst themselves. This does not explain why the *Imvo* continued to support the idea of a conference in Bloemfontein for a few weeks after the release of the draft. (79)

Meanwhile the SANC regional conference was being planned. The notice convening this meeting captured the urgent and anxious mood of the times:

. . . We are rushing to meet so as to have the people's word before the Parliament assembles. The branches must send delegates and give their views. The places which have no branches must also send people. The people as a whole must be present so as to give advice. The house [i.e. the black people] is in danger because of the decisions of the Convention of the colonies.

The call ended with the popular expression *'Zemk' Inkomo Magwalandini!'* ('There go your cattle [i.e. rights] you cowards!'). (80)

The Emgwali conference lasted three days, from 17–19 March. (81) It was attended by eighty delegates. (82) Among them were several chiefs who had responded to a call by the *Izwi* for chiefs to attend. (83) They included Chief Gamma Sandile, Chief Sigonyela Mapassa and Chief Mbingwe. SANC stalwarts such as the President, Thomas Mqanda, the Secretary, Jonathan Tunyiswa, W. B. Rubusana, A. K. Soga, Eben Koti and William Siyo were also present. (84) Groups from Beaufort West, Cape Town, Colesberg, East London, Emgwali, Fort Beaufort, Glen Grey, King William's Town, Kimberley, Komgha, Peddie, Port Elizabeth, Queenstown, Stutterheim, Umtata and Wodehouse sent delegates or messages of support. (85)

The conference was opened by G. S. Stewart with a religious service. Before the discussions got under way, Walter Rubusana explained the aim of the meeting to the chiefs and councillors, saying, 'The nation must be proud of itself and stand up for its rights.' Congress wanted to be the mouthpiece of the whole nation. It wished to create the unity among Africans that the famous Ntsikana had foretold. A. K. Soga also developed this theme. He thanked the chiefs for attending as they were the natural leaders. He stressed that petty differences and jealousies should be set aside in view of the great dangers facing Africans. (86) The conference accepted the decision of the SANC leaders to send delegates to the Bloemfontein convention rather than to the conference being organised by Jabavu. After a lively discussion on the draft Act, Walter Rubusana, A. K. Soga and Thomas Mqanda were delegated to attend the convention in Bloemfontein a week later. (87) Jabavu's name was also put forward for selection, but the nomination was outvoted. (88) Those in attendance at the meeting contributed generously to a collection to help cover the delegates' travelling costs. (89)

### British Bechuanaland

The Baralong in British Bechuanaland—isolated from African political activity in the eastern Cape by their geographical situation in the north-western Cape, and in closer touch with their ethnic counterparts in the Orange River Colony, particularly at Thaba Nchu, than with the Xhosa-speaking groups to the east—saw the proposed constitution as another in a series of threats from the authorities to the autonomy the tribe had been promised when the area was made part of the Cape Colony in 1895. They mobilised promptly to meet the challenge.

On 27 February the chiefs and headmen convened a meeting in Mafeking to consider the draft Act. The Acting Paramount Chief, Lekoko Montsioa, presided. J. Gerrans, who was soon to come into the limelight for his activities on behalf of the Bechuana chiefs, addressed the meeting and explained the draft. (90) The meeting resolved that 'The Baralong nation cannot regard the native clauses in the Draft Constitution as giving sufficient protection to the Cape coloured franchise.' It pledged itself to oppose the recommendations of the National Convention in their existing form. The Baralong wanted steps to be taken 'to induce the Cape Legislature to get more adequate protection for them in the Constitution'. (91)

Shortly afterwards the matter was taken further. On 8 March Paramount Chief Badirile Montsioa wrote to the Governor and Prime Minister asking for clarification. Would the chiefs still be allowed to govern their people as before and decide cases of purely native character under the constitution? Was it correct that if less than one-third of the members of parliament were not sympathetic to Africans, their vote would be taken away from them? (92)

To the first question, the government replied that people in Bechuanaland would be put in the same position under union as they were at the present time under the Annexation Act. Clause 149 of the draft Act stipulated that 'All rights and obligations under any conventions or agreements which are binding of any of the Colonies shall devolve upon the Union at its establishment.'

To the second question, the reply was that the Prime Minister was of the opinion that the African franchise was sufficiently safe-guarded by the draft constitution, and further that Mr Merriman felt that it would be the height of imprudence for the Africans to 'raise an agitation' in this respect. Instead of advancing their cause, this would increase the prejudice that all their well-wishers were anxious to remove. (93)

When the draft was released, the Baralong took the precaution of approaching the heads of the Wesleyan Missions who were the custodians of certain documents relating to guarantees given to the Baralong chiefs at the time of their annexation to the Cape. The Acting General Superintendent of the Missions, F. J. Briscoe, sought an interview with the High Commissioner, Lord Selborne, to discuss the matter, but he was informed that it concerned the Cape government, and that therefore the proper person to approach would be the Cape Governor. Lord Selborne said, however, that it appeared clear to him that according to the draft Act the union government would inherit the responsibility of the Cape govern-ment for the reserve. (94) This answer accorded with the terms of the communication directed to Chief Badirile Montsioa by the Secretary for Native Affairs.

Further proof of the concern felt by the Baralong about the im-pending union was the appointment of a high-ranking delegation to attend the Bloemfontein convention. It consisted of Chief Le-koko Montsioa (the second most senior chief), Chief Silas Molema (the confidant and assistant to the Paramount) and T. Lefenya. (95) The absence of Sol Plaatje, who would normally have been a natural choice for the delegation, raises an interesting question. It has been suggested that Plaatje, who was susceptible to illness, could have been indisposed or, more probably, engaged in recruit-ing labour for the mines. (96) Paramount Chief Badirile Montsioa was at this stage an alcoholic, and not active in tribal affairs, hence Lekoko's lead at the meetings in Mafeking and Bloemfontein. (97) Drink was to result in Badirile's death in the space of two years. (98)

## The Transvaal

Although the organisers of the Bloemfontein convention initial-ly received no reply from the Transvaal to their suggestions, (99) and although the proposed joint preliminary meeting of Africans in the two ex-republics never materialised, Africans in the Transvaal were also responding to developments at this time.

Following a meeting a few days earlier, (100) J. G. Kaiyana, the Vice-president of the Transvaal Native Congress, wrote to Jabavu on 22 February informing him that he and the General Secretary, Jesse Makhothe, would be representing their organisation at Bloemfontein. (101) For some reason, however, they were not in fact there. It could have been that the Congress was represented instead by the two delegates of the Transvaal Native Union, of which the Congress was an associate member, or by one or more of the three other Transvaal delegates, A. Mpinda, S. Ndima and J. Ndaba, whose political affiliations are unknown. The first possibility seems the most likely. Newspaper reports suggest that the three above-mentioned men represented local associations, not regional bodies. (102) No mention is made of the Transvaal Native Congress in the newspaper reports of the convention.

The Transvaal Native Union responded to the appeal by the Orange River Colony Native Congress by summoning a meeting on 8 March. The aim was to inform Africans of what was happening and to discuss the draft constitution. The meeting was held in the Nancefield location in Johannesburg. It was attended by 365 people. These included delegates from the Krugersdorp, Roodepoort, Boksburg, Roodekop, Evaton, Johannesburg and New Primrose branches of the Transvaal Native Union. The proceedings were controlled by William Letseleba, who was in the chair, and the secretary, Z. More. Edward Tsewu was also prominent.

The meeting strongly condemned the draft Act, and sent a report containing its main criticisms to the government. (103) It stated that not only were Africans not consulted in the drawing up of the constitution, but their interests were also neglected. Instead of extending the privileges of Africans in the north, the Convention had sought ways of doing away with their vote in the Cape. The members of the South African Parliament would represent the wishes of the white people, and legislation too would reflect these wishes. The legislation would be passed no matter how detrimental it was to the interests of Africans. To make matters worse, Africans were to be wrenched from the protection of the Imperial government which would have no powers of veto. Africans were now in 'the most dangerous position in which a nation can possibly be'.

Repeating verbatim parts of the circular sent out by the ORCNC when it launched its initiative for a convention of Africans, (104) the TNU declared further that the ex-republics were using union to escape the responsibility of granting Africans the franchise, as in the opinion of the meeting they were bound to do according to the treaty of Vereeniging. Unless Africans in the rest of South Africa were also given the vote, Cape Africans would soon be deprived of their franchise rights in the face of encroaching northern illiberalism. It denounced the delegates of the National Convention in the 'strongest terms' for shamefully neglecting the interests of Africans, who formed the majority of the population, whose loyalty to the Empire was unimpeachable and who shouldered the greatest share of taxation in the Transvaal. The High Commissioner was to be asked to convey to the King the meeting's request that unification should not be allowed until the interests of the 'defenceless' Africans had been properly and adequately safeguarded. (105)

The TNU also delegated Z. More and E. T. Moeletsi to represent it at the forthcoming convention in Bloemfontein. (106)

*Natal*

Natal was the only colony where no regional meeting was held before the convention in Bloemfontein at the end of March. According to Rubusana, the Natal Native Congress met on 13 and 14 March, (107) but this is incorrect. The Congress did not convene a meeting to discuss the effects of union till April. (108) And the *Iliso Lesizwe Esimnyama* did not discuss the subject until the beginning of June. (109)

In the absence of organisational activity, individuals took the lead in responding to the draft Constitution. Early in March a prominent member of the Congress, Abner Mtimkulu, made an attempt to get the government to convene a meeting for Africans on the question of union. Writing from Dundee to the Under-Secretary for Native Affairs, Mtimkulu said, 'The men here in the north wish to have the matter of union explained to them. The government should gather together the "black race" for this purpose.' (110) Mtimkulu probably had in mind a meeting similar to the large gatherings that were held the previous year for the government to explain the three native administration bills it introduced after the report of the Natal Native Affairs Commission, and to hear African grievances against these measures. (111) He added, 'We think that this would help with regard to the prevailing opinion that the black race is being sold by the British to the Dutch.' (112) Like the predominantly British white population, from whom they had partly inherited this attitude, Africans in Natal feared Afrikaner domination. (113)

In reply to Mtimkulu's letter, the Prime Minister and Minister of Native Affairs, Frederick Moor, informed him that as the draft Act was still under consideration, he had nothing to communicate to the Africans. (114)

In a similar individual initiative an unnamed minister of religion from Natal communicated with Jabavu in the Cape on the matter of African protests against union. The correspondent stated that Africans in Natal wished to co-operate with other blacks to oppose the colour bar. He asked for details about the arrangements for a joint meeting of Africans in South Africa. Jabavu advised that Natal should hold its own meeting and elect five delegates to meet representatives from other colonies at some still unspecified date in the future. (115) A. K. Soga, editor of the *Izwi Labantu*, was also in touch with Africans in Natal at this time, (116) and there were letters in the *Ilanga lase Natal* voicing opposition to the draft constitution. (117)

But it was John Dube's *Ilanga* that took the lead in opposing the draft Act in Natal. He saw the newspaper as the mouthpiece of the 'voteless but not voiceless' outsiders. (118) A constant stream of comment poured from the presses at Ohlange. The 'nation' was exhorted to shake off its lethargy and to unite to show its opposition to the terms of union; the '*Vukani Bantu!*' call was made. (119) Up to the end of April, when Dube declared that the time had now come for the *Ilanga* to close the chapter of its 'fearless and dutiful' comment on unification, only one editorial in the newspaper's English columns—on Roman Catholic deviousness in an alleged case of exorcism of evil spirits (121)—deviated from the subjects of union and political representation for Africans.

Dube saw the necessity of convening a meeting similar to those that were being held in the other colonies, and continually urged the Natal Native Congress to organise one. He warned, '*Madoda lento akusinyona ukudlala* (Gentlemen, this is no playing matter)', (122) and asked what was the matter with Natal that it did not follow the example of the other colonies in arranging to send delegates to Bloemfontein.

The Congress was slow in responding. Only on 19 March did it issue a notice proclaiming a 'Great Meeting' of the whole of Zululand and Natal to discuss the draft constitution and to find means of co-operating with Africans in other colonies. The meeting was set for Pietermaritzburg on 1 April. (123) Meanwhile, the Chairman of the Congress, Simeon Kambule, and Dube himself would represent Natal at the Convention in Bloemfontein a few days hence. (124)

## The South African Native Convention

The South African Native Convention (SANC) met in a school-room in the Waaihoek township in Bloemfontein from 24 to 26 March 1909. It is a seminal event in the history of African political activity in South Africa. It was the first occasion on which African political leaders and the fledgling political associations in the various colonies co-operated formally. The meeting was a major step towards the formation of a permanent national African political organisation.

The Convention began at 3 p.m. on Wednesday 24 March. Not all the delegates had yet arrived, but this did not hamper proceedings as the agenda for the first day's activity was restricted to the formal opening. In addition to the delegates proper, a large group of local blacks were in attendance to witness the occasion. (125)

There were thirty-eight delegates from the four colonies. The Cape was represented by Walter Rubusana and A. K. Soga (South African Native Congress), Natal by Simeon Kambule and John Dube (Natal Native Congress), and the Transvaal by Z. More and E. T. Moeletsi (Transvaal Native Union, the latter also Transvaal Basotho Committee), (126) and A. Mpinda, S. Ndima and J. Ndaba (affiliations unknown).

The host Orange River Colony was especially well represented. Deputations from all the political organisations for blacks attended. The biggest of these was from the body that had organised the Convention, the Orange River Colony Native Congress. It included the President, John Mocher, the Vice-president and Treasurer, Henry Poho, the Secretary, Thomas Mtobi Mapikela, and politicians such as J. B. Twayi and Peter Phatlane, who had been involved in organised politics since the war. Most members of the executive were also present. (127) Joel Goronyane headed the deputation of the Becoana Mutual Improvement Association, other members of which were John Mokitlane Nyokong and Jeremiah Makgothi.

The maverick Eastern Native Vigilance Association from Bethlehem was also in attendance. It was represented by its President, Obed Mokhosi, S. Tshabalala, Nehemiah Serebatsi and A. R. Goliath Rakhatoe. Formerly the Bethlehem branch of the ORCNC, this group had formed itself into a semi-independent body around 1908, after it had lost contact with the mother body, and began forwarding resolutions directly to the government instead of working through the executive of the Congress. Neither the government nor the Congress recognised the body as a separate organisation. Although its leaders later reaffirmed their loyalty to the Congress, saying that the break had been the outcome of misunderstanding and lack of communication, (128) they continued to approach the government separately until after Union. (129) The Association claimed franchise rights based on the Cape system and said all Africans were fit for the franchise. At the same time it wanted Africans settled on reserves like the one at Witsieshoek, where fixed tenure and farming land could be provided. It was particularly concerned with the position of Africans working on white-owned farms. It called for the protection of farm labourers against ill-treatment, fair wages for children working on farms, and legal recognition of half-share agreements, as farmers sometimes did not honour their commitments and Africans were powerless to do anything about this. (130)

The members of the executive committee of the Orange River Colony affiliate of the African Political Organisation (for coloured people) also attended the Convention. (131) They did so with the full blessing of their President, Abdullah Abdurahman. He informed the organisers that he had advised APO branches that they could attend if they wished, 'for it matters not who initiates the movement as long as we attain our object'. (132) This important move was in keeping with the increasing contact between African and coloured politicians since the 1907 Queenstown Conference. The APO delegates were N. J. Daly, A. J. Maasdorp, G. Crowder, R. Symmons and B. Vorster.

Despite the appeal by the Convention's organiser, Thomas Mtobi Mapikela, for chiefs from all the British territories to attend, the response by traditional leaders was poor. The only chiefs present were Lekoko Montsioa and Silas Molema from British Bechuanaland. (133) The editor of the *Naledi ea Lesotho*, S. M. Phamotse, and a Mr Makepe had set out to represent Basutoland at the meeting, but the Paramount Chief Letsie Moshweshwe dissuaded them from attending when they stopped over to see him on the way to Bloemfontein. He did so in view of a pending important *Pitso* to be held in Maseru on the question of union. (134) Clearly the Basotho Paramount had no intention of upsetting the Imperial authorities at this delicate stage in the deliberations on the protectorate's future by getting involved in wider issues.

The most notable absentee was John Tengo Jabavu, whose disdain for the Convention was exemplified by his *Imvo*'s one scanty report (135) (in contrast to the wide coverage of many other newspapers). (136) Several messages of support were received. From Natal, the Umzimkulu Native Farmers' and Teachers' Association wired, 'We uphold whatever results the meeting may determine.' The *Iliso Lomzi* in Bulawayo in Southern Rhodesia offered its best wishes to the delegates and prayed for God's blessing over them. (The politically active Africans in Southern Rhodesia at the time were South African 'settlers', so it is not surprising that the Convention was being followed with interest in that territory as well.) (137) Theophilus Schreiner's message was that the paramount duty at the time was to bring about black unity so that the blacks could then press their views and claims constitutionally with all the force of a united people. Messages were also received from individuals in Johannesburg, Rustenburg, Ladybrand and Bethulie. In wishing the Convention God's guidance, S. S. Mahonke from Bethulie said it must remember that although the delegates were few they represented millions of African and coloured people throughout South Africa. (138)

The chairman of the Convention was Joel Goronyane of the Becoana Mutual Improvement Association. After he had briefly sketched the aims of the meeting he introduced Dewdney Drew, member of the Legislative Council of the Orange River Colony, representing African interests, who had been asked by the organising committee officially to open the convention. (139) Drew had been editor of the Bloemfontein newspaper *The Friend* from 1904 to 1908. During this term of office he had earned a reputation for his pro-African sympathies, and it was on this basis that he had become a member of the Legislative Council in 1907. (140)

In his speech Drew adopted a cautionary tone. Although he recognised that the draft Act fell short of 'equal rights for all civilised men' and limited representation for every one else, he felt that any serious attempt to bring about amendments would only worsen the position. To substantiate his point he quoted Lord de Villiers, who had said at Paarl that if the Cape proposed any amendments to the compromise agreement this would invite counter-proposals from the north, and vice versa. Drew himself had seen this happen at a recent conference of the closer union societies in Johannesburg. When the Cape delegates had attempted to entrench the non-racial franchise, the Transvaal delegates had done the same to prevent the vote for blacks being extended to the north. Both parties had then been forced finally to support the compromise agreement embodied in the draft constitution. Drew regretted the insistence of the northern colonies to bar blacks from parliament. He said there were already some Africans qualified to become members. In time the numbers would grow. Their presence there would do more good than harm. It would provide the vital contact between black and white that was necessary at the highest level. The tragedy was that intercourse mostly took place amongst the lowest classes of both races. The part played by Africans at church conferences and the trouble-free presence of Maoris in the New Zealand legislature showed that the natives of the country were fit to sit in parliament.

However, despite the fact that the draft constitution deprived Cape Africans of the right to sit in parliament and failed to extend the franchise to Africans in the other colonies, Drew expressed the opinion that Africans had on the whole gained substantially from the draft Act. He listed four points to support his contention:

1 For the first time some Africans were going to be accepted by the Afrikaners in the northern colonies as fellow voters on equal terms. He saw this as an important concession.

2 In twenty or thirty Cape constituencies members of parliament would have to take note of African grievances or else face the risk of losing their substantial vote. Therefore, Africans were sure to have their interests attended to in parliament. This applied to all Africans, not just those in the Cape, as Africans had developed a 'oneness of feeling' and the latter would highlight general grievances and speak for the rest as well. Drew felt that the airing of African grievances in parliament in this way would create a greater awareness of native affairs on the part of northern members and lead to deeper concern on their part. His opinion was that the northerners were fair-minded men who would be disposed to do justice to the reasonable complaints of Africans. Present grievances were caused more by the ignorance than the intention of the white governments in those colonies. This view, of course, contrasted sharply with those held by John Dube and other leaders of African opinion.

3 While the minority of Africans (those in the Cape) would lose a right they had never exercised, the great majority would through the four 'native representatives' in the Senate have 'a real and substantial measure of representation in the sovereign Parliament'. This was something they had never previously enjoyed. They would find that this representation would remove most of their practical grievances. Their representatives in the national parliament would redress any injustice done them by provincial councils or

municipalities.

4 A final advantage for Africans under union would be a settled and uniform native policy applicable to them all. This would put an end to the fragmentation and differentiation which had always existed in native affairs. He was confident that the two-thirds majority provision would not be used to the detriment of Africans, as many believed.

After this Drew went on to discuss prevailing opinions amongst whites on the so-called native problem. He contrasted the liberal, accommodatory school of thought, which favoured giving all 'civilised' Africans exactly the same privileges as whites, with the exclusivist group which saw Africans as a threat to white privilege and wished to subordinate and segregate them. The chief spokesmen of these two schools, he said, were Lord Selborne and W. J. Wybergh (a member of the Transvaal Legislative Assembly), respectively. It was important for Africans to be aware of the different viewpoints held by whites. Although he favoured justice towards Africans, Drew himself thought the segregation plan, if practicable, to be ideal.

He concluded his speech by posing the question: What was the attitude of the Africans to be? His advice was, 'Don't compromise your principles; you are bound to ask for equal rights, but take from time to time any privileges the Government offers you, and use those privileges so as to prove yourselves fit for more.' Whether they were separated territorially, given the vote or no more than councils in townships, Africans should accept this. He warned them: 'Don't expect to go very far in a short time.' As Lord Selborne had pointed out, Africans had been in touch with civilisation for only a hundred years, whereas Europeans had two thousand years of civilisation behind them. While they should not lose sight of the goal of equal rights which they would ultimately gain, the immediate emphasis should be on toil and self-improvement. Africans should learn to labour and to wait. (141)

Drew's speech was in discord with the mood of the Convention. His paternalistic assumptions were immediately challenged. A. K. Soga declared that the delegates should consider Mr Drew's words carefully, but not necessarily accept as the truth what he had said. Soga said he rejected the principle of 'accepting the half loaf'. He continued, '[Africans] could not wait for the white man to release them from their troubles. They should struggle—constitutionally I mean. They would not get any political privileges without a struggle. If they waited as Mr Drew suggested, they would get no further. .... They found that, after the trouble and expense of educating themselves and their children, the white man said "thus far and no further". Not to use their constitutional privileges to secure their rights would be a fatal mistake.' According to Soga the draft Act represented the interests of the capitalists and the landed section. (142)

Soga was supported by the chairman, Joel Goronyane. He also encouraged Africans to keep on struggling for their rights in a constitutional manner. Segregation would lead to serious trouble and stir up race hatred. White and black should work together, as they did 'in the Cape, where there has never been any trouble'. (143)

Drew then said he had not expected the delegates to accept the draft Act as satisfying all their wishes. However, he did feel that the concessions Africans had been granted were an important step. (144)

The proceedings for the opening day were then closed.

Using the procedures followed at the National Convention as a guideline, the delegates spent most of the next two days behind closed doors discussing the draft Act and how it affected Africans. Their decisions were to be made public at a meeting on the final evening on 26 March.

The discussions proper began at 10.45 a.m. on Thursday 25 March. Joel Goronyane's position as Chairman was confirmed by the meeting and Goliath Rakhatoe of the Eastern Native Vigilance Society was elected as Secretary. Then the minutes of the previous day were read and confirmed and the list of delegates was submitted. Then the resolutions adopted by the various regional conferences were read. Resolutions were submitted by the South African Native Congress, the Transvaal Native Union, the Becoana Mutual Improvement Association, the Orange River Colony Native Congress and the African Political Organisation in that colony. (145)

John Dube regretted that Natal did not have resolutions written out, but said that Africans in that colony were greatly dissatisfied with the draft constitution. Just as in the case of the United States some years earlier, the cry they had adopted was 'No representation, no taxation'. As British subjects they wanted freedom. No civilised man should be debarred from the vote. Dube then spoke at length on the Franchise and Exemption Laws in Natal. (146)

In the afternoon session Chief Silas Molema put British Bechuanaland's views. He dealt with the conditions under which the territory had been annexed to the Cape and laid the resolutions of the meeting in Mafeking in February before the Convention. (147)

Discussions ensued on the various sections of the draft Act (25c, 33, 44d and 153) that offended Africans. Clause 153, which embodied the provision for the disqualification of African voters in the Cape by a two-thirds majority decision of both houses of Parliament, was the main focus of attention. A long discussion took place on this issue. The other three sections were the colour bar clauses referring to 'European descen.'. (148)

That afternoon it was also decided to send an invitation to the delegates to a big church conference that was being held in Bloemfotein at the same time to attend the concluding meeting of the Convention on the Friday evening. (149) The church meeting was discussing the union of the Baptist, Congregational, Presbyterian and Wesleyan Methodist churches, and was attended by leading representatives from all these denominations. (150)

A telegram from John Knox Bokwe, in which he praised the Conference both for its temperate language and for its unmistakably clear and respectful protest (151) was also read. (152) Although not an active politician, Bokwe was an enormously respected African of that time. Like his contemporaries, Pambani Mzimba and Elijah Makiwane, he had been attached to Lovedale for many years. After a quarter of a century there, he became a partner with Jabavu in the *Imvo Zabantsundu* in 1898. This was prompted by his desire to heal the ethnic split which had opened in the Cape between the Mfengus under Jabavu and the Xhosa and Thembu leaders such as Rubusana and Soga. Soon afterwards he became a minister and was posted to Ugie. He became one of the most influential men in that town, winning the confidence of the white, African and coloured populations. Among other things, he negotiated with the Cape Education Department for a school for whites, held services for them at their own request, and virtually became Town Clerk. Known as *Umdengentonga* ('the little man with a big mind'), he was also a composer. (153)

Bokwe's assessment of the tone of the Convention was accurate and reflected the whole approach of that generation of African politicians. Their protests were respectful and temperate and framed according to the religious and humanitarian values of the missionary and other western agencies that had influenced them. They went to great lengths to prove their loyalty and their suitability to participate in politics.

Nothing demonstrated this more than the speeches and resolutions at the Convention, and the procedure that was followed.

Proceedings were started with prayers. (154) The Prime Minister of the host colony was formally thanked for giving the delegates the opportunity of holding a public meeting and exercising freedom of speech. He was asked to convey expressions of loyalty to the Governor. (155) Respectful greetings were sent to the High Commissioner, who was asked to convey the Convention's loyalty to the King. (156)

On Friday afternoon the Convention had finalised two sets of resolutions on the draft constitution, which summed up the general feeling of Africans in South Africa towards union. The first, embodying nine points, was concerned with the rights of Africans in the South African colonies. It criticised the decisions of the National Convention and suggested several amendments to the draft Act. The other focused on the future relationship between the protectorates and the union. In referring to the protectorates separately, the example was followed of the National Convention, which had dealt with these territories in a schedule attached to the draft constitution.

In the first resolution of the first set, the Convention recognised that union was 'essential, necessary and inevitable', but said it should promote the progress and welfare of all British subjects in South Africa. The draft Act did not do this. The colour bar constituted a fundamental wrong and injustice. It was deprecated that the proved franchise system of the Cape had not been extended to the northern colonies and that the principle of equal rights, which many leading statesmen had supported down the years, had been ignored. Instead, a clause should be inserted in the constitution which provided for all persons in the union to have 'full and equal rights and privileges, subject only to the conditions and limitations established by law and applicable alike to all citizens without distinction of class, colour or creed'. The Imperial government, to which blacks owed their loyalty, was bound by both fundamental and specific obligations to see that this happened. It should extend to the African and coloured people the same rights that were enjoyed by those of European descent under the law. If the Imperial authorities did not fulfil this obligation then the good and just government which the King and Empire owed to every class of their subjects would not be realised. By being deprived of the right of equal representation blacks would be left to the mercy of the ruling class.

In its deliberations on the responsibilities of the Imperial authorities, the Convention paid particular attention to the terms of the Vereeniging peace treaty. It was stated that this treaty did not abrogate the pre-war promises made by the British government to alleviate the position of blacks in the republics and to grant them the same rights as those enjoyed by their counterparts in the Cape. The eighth clause of the peace treat was interpreted as having left an 'open door' for the enfranchisement of blacks in the Transvaal and the Orange River Colony after the coming of responsible government. However, while the Imperial government had honoured its promises to those states by granting them responsible government, it had not treated blacks in the same liberal and generous way. On the contrary, it had both denied them any participation in the franchise and municipal rights, and had made their position even more difficult by granting these colonies charters which made provision for manhood suffrage for whites only. In the light of this, the Convention resolved that '. . . the Eighth Article of the Peace Treaty therefore demands to be fulfilled in the most liberal sense in relation to His Majesty's native and coloured subjects in the Transvaal and Orange River Colony, and those Colonies should be required to conform to the system of the Cape Colony with regard to the principles of the franchise as far as the native and coloured people are concerned.'

Referring to Natal, it was pointed out that after the annexation the Crown had promulgated a non-discriminatory constitution, but in practice this had not been implemented, placing exceptional difficulties in the way of Africans wishing to obtain the franchise. Thus the absurd state of affairs existed that out of a million Africans in Natal and Zululand the South African Native Affairs Commission had reported that there were only two African voters in Natal. Both these people were reported to be dead.

The last four of the nine resolutions in the first set all suggested amendments to certain sections of the draft Act. In sections 25 and 44, which dealt with the qualification of senators and members of the House of Assembly respectively, the Convention wanted the colour bar removed by the deletion of the words 'of European descent'. In section 33, which provided for increases in the size of the House of Assembly in proportion to the number of male adults in each province, it wanted the words 'and native and coloured voters' added to the existing 'European male adults' provision. With regard to section 35, it proposed that the franchise regulations which allowed Africans in the Cape to vote should be permanently entrenched and made unalterable. This new condition should also be written into section 153 which dealt with amendments to the constitution.

The second set of resolutions concerned the future position of the protectorates. It is an indication of the recognition by Africans of the need to harmonise their interests and to view matters affecting them along national rather than parochial lines that a stand was made on this issue, even though the protectorates were unrepresented at the Convention.

Delegates expressed anxiety at the lot of their 'fellow countrymen' in the protectorates under union. The past record of the three northern colonies in the administration of Africans gave no reason for them to believe that the protectorates would be wisely or sympathetically governed in the event of their incorporation into a union of South Africa. The numerous restrictions under which Africans lived in these colonies were listed, and it was noted that there was little prospect of a change for the better as public opinion overwhelmingly supported the retention of the status quo. Therefore, it would be preferable for the protectorates to remain under the direct control of the Imperial government, which had hitherto governed the territories according to the best interests of the inhabitants. Under the paternal rule of the Crown, they had progressed rapidly in respect of education, industry and religion and had enjoyed peace and security, 'together with the preservation of their land, their tribal existence and their inherited modes of self-government'. Incorporation would be especially harsh on the protectorates as they had come voluntarily under British rule.

However, if the British government decided it would be to the advantage of the protectorates to transfer them, the Convention would 'loyally acquiesce'. But certain conditions should first be met. First, the chiefs should be satisfied with the conditions of transfer. Secondly, the conditions should be fixed before the draft Act became law. Thirdly, the transfer should not take place until the union had adopted a native policy which accorded with Imperial traditions.

On the whole the Convention was satisfied with the terms of the Schedule to the draft constitution, but it felt that some of the conditions should be more fully and strictly stated so as to prevent the Schedule from later being bent to the detriment of Africans in the protectorates. The desired amendments were: the liquor prohibition should be tightened; the National Council should ultimately be allowed to become a representative Parliament on the European model; the proposed Commission and its members should be accorded greater powers and protection.

The Convention also expressed its deep appreciation to Lord Selborne for the statesmanlike manner in which he had represented the people of the protectorates in his negotiations with the National Convention. (157)

In addition to the formulation of these lengthy resolutions for submission to the Imperial and colonial governments, the press and the National Convention, the South African Native Convention also made tentative moves to form itself into a permanent organisation. A President and executive were elected 'to watch the draft Act, to promote organisation, and to defend the interests of the Natives'. (158) If the draft Act was not amended by the National Convention in the direction desired by the Africans, the executive was to meet to organise a deputation, and to choose the delegates, to proceed to Britain to lay the case of the Africans before the Imperial authorities. It was decided to ask W. P. Schreiner to assist them if this became necessary. (159)

The elected officials were: Walter Rubusana of the South African Native Congress (President), John Dube of the Natal Native Congress (Vice-president), A. K. Soga of the South African Native Congress (Secretary), Jeremiah Makgothi of the Becoana Mutual Improvement Association (Assistant Secretary), Joel Goronyane of the Becoana Mutual Improvement Association (Treasurer). The rest of the executive was: John Mocher, T. Mtobi Mapikela, N. J. Daly, J. B. Nyokong, P. K. Motiyane and H. S. Poho (all from the Orange River Colony), Chief Silas Molema (Bechuanaland), Z. More (Transvaal Native Union) and Simeon Kambule (Natal Native Congress). (160)

The decisions of the Convention were made public at a packed meeting on the Friday night after deliberations had been concluded. (161) Conspicuous by their absence were the delegates to the church union conference who had accepted the Convention's invitation to attend but did not arrive. (162) Joel Goronyane, who was in the chair, expressed pleasure at the large attendance. He stressed the importance of co-operation among blacks. This was echoed by succeeding speakers. Z. More said that Africans had assembled there from various areas to make each other's acquaintance and to roll away the stone of past differences. They had turned the firearms into ploughs. 'When we meet together,' he concluded, 'we learn to know each other and can talk over our differences like brothers.' (163)

After A. K. Soga had read the first set of resolutions, Dr Rubusana moved that they be passed by the meeting. He stated that

Africans had not come to Bloemfontein to act the part of political adventurers, but had been drawn by the vagaries of the time to obtain their just rights in a constitutional manner. They were loyal citizens and wished to live in peace, side by side, with the white man. John Dube seconded the motion. He also emphasised the need for black unity. The purpose of the meeting had been to bring about amendments which would benefit them and their children. After the hardships undergone by the Zulus in the past few years, he hoped that union would improve their position. The motion was adopted unanimously. (164)

Rubusana then read the resolutions concerning the protectorates, and Soga proposed that they be adopted, (165) saying that Africans were unquestionably loyal, that despite their grievances they still believed the British government was the best to rule over them. Rumours of a rising on the part of Africans were ludicrous. Africans had not yet developed enough to govern themselves; they still had a long way to go before they were ready for this; they would have to advance educationally, acquire a 'higher civilisation', and improve their organisations. At present the people did not support their newspapers and were hardly aware of what the leaders were doing. They would have to accept responsibilities if they wished to advance. (166) Soga's statement about the lack of support for the vernacular newspapers can be seen in the light of the imminent collapse of his own newspaper, the *Izwi Labantu*. After the Convention, only one more issue of the *Izwi*–a 'Special Convention Number'–appeared before it was forced out of circulation by financial problems. (167)

While Soga recognised, in continuing his speech, that the bulk of Africans still had a long way to go before they could participate on an equal footing with Europeans, he was scathing in his condemnation of the colour bar. It would not last long. Africans would continue to agitate constitutionally until it was removed. (168) As the son of an Englishwoman and a refined African theologian, Soga could not accept the logic of, and felt personally insulted by, the 'of European descent' clauses, which relegated him to an inferior position regardless of his physical, intellectual and moral capabilities. (169)

Soga's motion was seconded by Chief Silas Molema, who felt the colour bar offended his dignity and religious values. 'The natives are human, created by God, and their rights should not be taken from them.' (170) The motion was passed with acclamation by the meeting. (171)

Thus ended this highly important event in the course of black South African politics. Not only had blacks from all four colonies co-operated for the first time and formed an umbrella organisation, but they had also clearly spelled out their opposition to certain terms of the proposed union and stipulated the conditions which would have to be met to make these acceptable.

# 8 The struggle continues as the draft Act is approved

In the month after the meeting at Bloemfontein at the end of March, the draft South Africa Act came before the four colonial parliaments for amendment or ratification, and was then referred back to the National Convention at the beginning of May.

Meanwhile, Africans continued to oppose the draft Act right up to the final session of the Convention, and began to prepare themselves for further steps if their grievances were not redressed in the revised draft Act. Two further conferences were held, one by John Tengo Jabavu in the eastern Cape, the other by the coloured APO in Cape Town.

## Jabavu's Cape Native Convention
The meeting organised by Jabavu, styled the Cape Native Convention, met in King William's Town on 7 and 8 April 1909. Forty-one delegates from seventeen eastern Cape centres were present. The centres were: Cradock, Dordrecht, Glen Grey, Herschel, Keiskamma Hoek, King William's Town, Middledrift, Mount Ayliff, Nqamakwe, Peddie, Queenstown, Somerset East, Stutterheim, Tsomo, Victoria East, Whittlesea and Xalanga. The delegates had been elected at public meetings in the respective districts. A further fifteen people who had been elected as area delegates at these meetings should have attended but failed to make an appearance. None of the main Cape urban centres—Cape Town, Kimberley, Port Elizabeth and East London—was represented. A delegate from Kimberley arrived after the conclusion of the meeting, and apologies were received from Port Elizabeth, but Cape Town's non-representation was against the expectation of the organisers. (1)

Jabavu was unanimously elected president, with E. J. Mqoboli of Cradock as vice-president. The secretaries were S. Mloba of King William's Town and S. Milton Ntloko of Tsomo. Mqoboli was also appointed chairman of a committee to draw together the views expressed in the resolutions submitted by the various districts and in the discussions on the first evening. (2)

In his presidential address Jabavu explained how the draft Act's unexpected infringement of the rights of Cape Africans had necessitated a conference in King William's Town rather than at the originally agreed venue of Bloemfontein. Once the terms of union had become clear, it was 'a question of the Cape natives doing what they could to protect their own freedom which had been attacked'. (3)

Jabavu then went on to point out that the much treasured connection between Africans in South Africa and the Imperial government would be severed by union. The British government and parliament could no longer ask questions about internal affairs in South Africa. The Union parliament would stand in the position of the British parliament and Africans would no longer be in a position to appeal to the Sovereign. Therefore Africans should scrutinise the draft constitution carefully now and make representations, or forever hold their peace. He said, however, that Africans were not opposed to the principle of union. All they were concerned with was that the political rights and privileges given to them by the British government should not be tampered with. He then described how Africans had acquired these rights. In doing so, he quoted at length from the instructions sent to the Cape Governor, Sir George Grey, by the British government when the Cape was granted representative government in 1853:

Her Majesty's Government have come to the conclusion that in conferring upon the Colony the boon of a representative constitution, it is exceedingly undesirable that the franchise should be so restricted as to leave those of the coloured classes who, in point of intelligence, are qualified for the exercise of political power, practically unrepresented, and that any particular portion of the community should be deprived of its share of the management of its local affairs by restrictions which, so far as the imperfect statistics in our possession authorise the forming a judgment, it would, it is to be feared, establish too great a political preponderance in one class of the population. It is the earnest desire of Her Majesty's Government that all her subjects at the Cape, without distinction of class or colour, should be united by one bond of loyalty and a common interest, and we believe that the exercise of political rights enjoyed by all alike will prove one of the best methods of attaining this object. (4)

Jabavu said that these words, 'from the lips of Her Majesty were the charter of the rights and liberties of Cape Africans'. The introduction of the colour line in the new constitution was a flagrant breach of this royal charter. Those who sought to dispossess Africans should consider carefully their actions in going against it.

The only precedent that he could think of for the constitutional discrimination embodied in the draft Act was that of the ex-republics, and perhaps their fate had shown it did not work. Even native chiefs in their primaeval rule never dreamt of discriminating among their subjects. Why now ask the King to go back on the words of his mother? Africans were not asking for anything new. All they wanted was that the spirit and letter in which Africans had been given political rights more than fifty years ago should be retained in the new constitution. (5) He was mystified that the colour clauses could have crept into the constitution when the Cape delegates had been adamant in saying they would not depart from the Cape system, and influential northerners like Steyn, Botha and Farrar had said they had no thought of depriving Cape Africans of existing rights. It was questions such as these that the conference had to discuss and resolve. (6)

After the meeting had discussed the matter of union, it passed a twelve-point resolution put forward by Mqoboli's committee, summing up the attitudes of the delegates. Although it resolved only to discuss union in so far as it directly affected Africans, it expressed approval of the general principle of union. It declared that it was not prepared to oppose unification because it was convinced that 'much good and many advantages would accrue thereby'. However, the discriminatory clauses of the draft Constitution were condemned.

The introduction of the colour line into the draft South Africa Act is unjust to the aborigines and coloured people, is unprecedented in the annals of the British Empire, is moreover, in the opinion of this Conference, a grave reflection upon God who made these people, and is therefore calculated to create discontent among them, and . . . disturb the harmony and happiness of the people of South Africa.

The meeting deprecated the intended restriction of the political privileges which Africans in the Cape had hitherto enjoyed, and expressed regret that the National Convention had not devised some scheme whereby African taxpayers in the other colonies could have a degree of representation in the institutions which disposed of their taxes. (7) It acknowledged the stand taken by white sympathisers on behalf of Africans at this time. It thanked the Cape delegates to the National Convention for their efforts to maintain the rights and liberties of Cape Africans, and asked them to continue along those lines. It thanked J. H. Hofmeyr, the Schreiner brothers, the white missionaries and 'other white friends of the Natives' who had opposed the draft Act.

The meeting decided on three courses of action to fight 'to the end' the deprivation of rights that had been constitutionally conceded to Cape Africans. First, it would forward a petition embodying the meeting's decisions to the Cape parliament, which had assembled to discuss the draft Act, as well as to the National Convention when that body reassembled in Bloemfontein. Further, should such a step be necessary, a second petition would be sent to the Cape parliament when it met to approve the final Constitution.

Secondly, it resolved to establish a Native Rights Protection Fund. Districts were to forward one guinea to the Central Executive to enable it to carry out its work.

Thirdly, and significantly, it decided to transmit its resolutions to the executive of 'other native conferences' concerned with defending African interests, and to appoint twelve delegates to meet delegates of other conferences 'for concerted action in the prosecution of the cause'. (8) This was a clear sign that, even if Jabavu himself did not, the meeting recognised the importance of the South African Native Convention and the need for African unity.

**Other protest activities**
On the same day that Jabavu's Cape Native Convention ended, another meeting of prominent eastern Cape Africans started in nearby East London. Though not a political gathering, it discussed the draft constitution, deprecated its colour bar clauses and drew up a petition to the British government on the matter. The meeting in question was the annual conference of the Eastern Grand Temple of the Order of True Templars, the African section in the eastern Cape of the Independent Order of True Templars. This body had about 2 000 members, many of whom were registered voters. Its aim was to promote the cause of temperance, particularly by opposing the spread of liquor amongst Africans. Among the delegates from throughout the eastern Cape at the four-day meeting were well-known political figures like John Knox Bokwe, Elijah Makiwane (a one-time President of the pioneering Native Educational Association, who was the Grand True Templar of the Order), Isaac Wauchope, Walter Rubusana, Mesach Pelem and R. B. Milwana. (9) Jabavu did not attend because he was in Pietermaritzburg for a Wesleyan church conference. (10)

In line with the general pattern of protest, the Templars expressed anxiety at clauses 15, 33, 35 and 44 of the draft Act. They said these clauses aimed to take away from civilised and educated blacks rights which they had long enjoyed and never abused. If these provisions became law, the effect would be to alienate blacks from whites instead of fostering a feeling of mutual trust. In their petition, they asked the House of Commons to take these points into consideration when the draft constitution was laid before it. (11)

Templars like Rubusana, Bokwe and Pelem were not the only supporters of the South African Native Convention who continued to work against the draft Act after the meeting in Bloemfontein. The Natal delegates, John Dube and Simeon Kambule, returned home via Johannesburg, where they addressed a large meeting of Zulu migrants on 30 March. The two men were received with enthusiasm; the venue in Doornfontein was packed to overflowing. After they had explained the whole issue of union and reported on the Bloemfontein meeting, a collection was taken and they were presented with a gift of £2 16s 9d each. The meeting resolved that all Zulus in Johannesburg should subscribe monthly to a fund to send delegates abroad to bring African disabilities under the new constitution to the attention of the Imperial authorities. (12)

Another matter which came to light at this meeting was the dissatisfaction of the Zulus on the Witwatersrand with the ineffectiveness of the Natal Native Congress. They complained that while they were 'alive to all matters of the black race', they received no encouragement from Natal. They said they responded to matters raised in the *Ilanga lase Natal*, but they felt the people in Natal had 'given up'. This disheartened them. The meeting was critical of certain people—unnamed in the report—who undermined the effectiveness of 'native meetings'. It wanted the NNC to ensure that it elected men to office who were committed to the African cause. (13)

There appears to have been some validity in the criticism of the NNC. Not only was it the only black colonial organisation not to repond to the exhortations to meet before the Bloemfontein Convention assembled, but the meeting which was subsequently held to discuss union also proved unsuccessful and the issue was only briefly aired. A picture of internal division, lack of communication and government harassment emerges from reports of the meeting. Although it had been postponed from 1 to 8 April to enable Dube and Kambule to attend after returning from Bloemfontein, (14) neither was present. They and other leading men excused themselves on the grounds of illness, a transparent excuse which moved the convener, Mark Radebe, to lament, 'Does the meeting to which all of us have come today cause illness? We natives are simply injuring our cause by behaving in this way.' (15)

The position was further complicated by the interference of the Natal government, which actively discouraged chiefs and headmen from attending. The Minister of Native Affairs, F. R. Moor, had acted as early as 22 March, only three days after the NNC had given notice of a meeting. In a circular telegram to all magistrates, Moor informed them of the notice in the *Ilanga lase Natal* and instructed them to inform any Africans who made enquiries that neither permission nor authority had been obtained from the government for the holding of the meeting. Moreover, chiefs and headmen were not to leave their tribes without first obtaining leave from the authorities to do so. (16) This step was not without effect. The *Ilanga lase Natal* complained that because of magisterial pressure many people had been frightened from attending the meeting. (17) When Chief Mandhlakayise from Verulam asked for permission to attend the meeting, the Under-Secretary for Native Affairs instructed the local magistrate not to grant him permission on the grounds that as a chief, and therefore a government servant, he was not permitted to attend a political meeting. (18) Therefore, although Moor rescinded this decision at the last moment, Mandhlakayise stayed put. (19) On the morning of the meeting several Africans who had travelled to Pietermaritzburg from other districts decided first to report to the Native Affairs Department for fear of 'going behind the authorities'. They were persuaded to return home without attending the meeting. (20) The government also saw to it that an *umsetshane* (a derogatory word by which government informers were known) infiltrated the meeting.

During the course of the morning the delegates arrived at the venue which had been hired for the meeting, but the opening of the proceedings was delayed because the convener and NNC Secretary, Mark Radebe, was meeting the *Inkosi* (the Minister or his Under-Secretary). Radebe eventually arrived at midday and advised the gathering to reassemble at two o'clock.

Forty people attended, all *Kolwas*. No chiefs were present. In his introductory speech, Mark Radebe explained that the meeting had been called to discuss the draft constitution, an agreement which had taken place between the white people of South Africa. The Africans had not been provided for in the draft constitution. They had been differentially treated. Therefore, they wished to ask the authorities not to exclude them as the draft Act proposed to do. Africans wished to be placed 'on a proper basis at the outset, [so that] the present tendency to regard them with suspicion, as the Europeans of Natal did, would be broken down. It was only right that all races should unite if there was to be Union, not only particular ones.' (21)

One of the purposes of the meeting, Radebe said, was to compare their position in Natal under the draft Act with that of Africans elsewhere in South Africa, and to press for 'equally favourable treatment' for Natal Africans. In this respect he was probably referring to the guarantees provided for Africans in the Cape Colony and the protectorates.

The speaker after Radebe asked how the meeting could enter into a discussion of union seeing that so few people were present and that the leading men were absent. Moreover, there was not even a chairman. When a delegate was invited to take the chair, he refused and questioned the legality and desirability of the meeting. Why was it, he asked, that the leading men were not present? They must have received information which raised their suspicions and made them doubt the propriety of holding the meeting. Those present could not discuss the mode of government in the Cape if members of the delegation—M. Lutuli, P. J. Gumede and F. B. Bridgman—that had recently reported on the system of administration in operation there were not present to advise them. The speaker felt that the meeting should be terminated and followed shortly by another where the above could be consulted on the question.

Succeeding speakers also spoke along these lines. Most delegates favoured holding another meeting after the views of prominent men who were not present had been ascertained. Some even expressed misgivings about discussing at all the 'agreement between the European peoples' (draft Act). As a result, the meeting ended, only one and half hours after it had started, without having passed any resolutions on the subject of union. (22)

In British Bechuanaland, Sol Plaatje wrote to W. P. Schreiner on 13 April asking him to publicise Baralong opposition to the draft Act. He said that in this regard letters had been forwarded to the Cape Town newspapers. On behalf of the chiefs and all 'their people', Plaatjie sent the greetings of the Baralong to 'the defender of Dinizulu' and thanked him for his fearless championing of the African cause. (23)

In the Transvaal, on 15 April Sefaka Mapogo Makgatho, the Pretoria-based President of the African National Political Union, wrote to the authorities in Pietersburg requesting permission to hold a meeting with the local chiefs, whom he wished to consult on the decisions taken by the Bloemfontein meeting. (24) The Sub-Native-Commissioner of Pietersburg passed Makgatho's request on to the Minister for Native Affairs, who without giving reasons informed Makgatho that he was not prepared to authorise the meeting. He instructed the Native Commissioner to ensure that the meeting did not take place. (25)

The Transvaal Native Union executive was also active. On 19 April it convened a meeting at Nancefield where the Bloemfontein delegates gave an account of the proceedings and decisions of the Convention, and the question of raising funds for a delegation to Britain was raised. (26) Later in the month, at the insistence of the Transvaal government, (27) the TNU executive made a few alterations to the submission of the previous month informing the authorities about the first Nancefield meeting (8 March) and its resolutions, before it was returned in the form of a petition to the Native Affairs Department for forwarding to the Imperial government. (28)

In the Orange River Colony, the Becoana Mutual Improvement Association convened a mass meeting of the African and coloured people in the Thaba Nchu district on 28 April, only days before the National Convention was due to reassemble in Bloemfontein. The same resolutions which the Association had taken the previous month and submitted to the South African Native Convention were put to the meeting, unanimously passed and forwarded to the National Convention for consideration. (29)

Thomas Mtobi Mapikela, the organiser of the Native Convention and the driving force behind the Orange River Colony Native Congress, was also active at this time. Towards the end of April he and Isaiah Bud Mbelle, a brother-in-law of Sol Plaatje, visited John Dube at the latter's Ohlange Institute in Natal. (30) Unfortunately no details of the visit were reported, but one may surmise that they discussed developments regarding union.

Thus it is clear from the resolutions of the Native Conventions of Bloemfontein and King William's Town, from the meetings that were held in various areas subsequently, and from the attempts to collect funds in the Cape and Natal, (31) that Africans were not prepared to accept passively a final unfavourable decision from the National Convention. They continued to oppose the draft Act right up to the final session of this body and prepared themselves for further steps if their grievances were not redressed.

**African and coloured groups move closer together**

By now the Africans and the coloured population, who too had launched a large-scale agitation against the draft South Africa Act, were moving closer together in consequence of their shared, fierce opposition to the terms of union.

After the draft Act had been made public, the coloured people organised meetings throughout the various colonies to protest against its provisions. Dr Abdurahman's African Political Organisation was at the helm of the protests. No less than sixty APO meetings were reported to have been held by mid-April, when the APO convened its Annual General Meeting in Cape Town. (32) As we have already seen, Africans were present at some of the APO meetings, (33) while Dr Abdurahman allowed APO members to attend the South African Native Convention for 'it matters not who initiates the movement as long as we attain our objective'. (34) The interests of the African and coloured people had become fused. Both groups used the terms 'Native' and 'Coloured' interchangeably. In their respective protests no difference was made between the political rights of the two groups.

This point is forcefully demonstrated by the resolutions of the APO conference in Cape Town, which lasted from 13–17 April and was attended by eighty-nine delegates from more than fifty centres in the Cape, the Transvaal and the Orange River Colony. It criticised the draft Act in terms similar to those of the African conferences, expressed a willingness to co-operate more closely with its African counterparts, and also began to make preparations to send a delegation to Britain to appeal directly to the Imperial government. (35) It criticised the colour bar and called for clauses 25 and 44 to be deleted. It declared further that clause 35 did not sufficiently protect the Cape franchise. Not only should the black franchise in the Cape be permanently protected, but provision should be made to extend it to all qualified people in the contemplated union. It also protested against clause 33 which based representation in the Union Parliament on the European male adult population and not on the voters' list. Moreover, 'the native territories should not be transferred to the Union except upon conditions satisfactory to the Chiefs and Councillors'. (36)

The APO also gave its approval to the activities of the South African Native Convention in Bloemfontein and the conference organised by Jabavu in King William's Town, and expressed its desire to form a united front with these groups. It declared that 'the time has arrived for the co-operation of the coloured races in British South Africa.' The APO executive was instructed to liaise with the executives of the African organisations to bring this about. (37)

In addition, it was decided to start an APO newspaper to counteract what it felt was the bias of the colonial press, and to send a delegation to Britain to protest against the draft constitution. For this purpose, a 'Draft Constitution Fund' was set up. (38)

By making these preparations the APO manifestly was not anticipating any fundamental changes from the final session of the National Convention. Jabavu criticised the APO for not waiting for the final Convention report before making the decision to send a delegation. He felt no such action should be taken until every effort had been made to remove the colour bar in South Africa itself. (39) Understandably cautious because of his relationship with the Cape politicians, Jabavu was really making an unnecessary fuss. It was obvious by that stage that a large majority of whites in the various colonies were in favour of the draft Act with its colour bar provisions, a fact supported by the discussions on the draft constitution in the colonial parliaments during April.

## Discussions in the colonial parliaments

All four colonial parliaments confirmed the proposals of the National Convention regarding the franchise provisions for Africans. Not one of them called for amendments to the colour bar sections in the draft Act or for a tightening of the two-thirds safeguard for the franchise for blacks in the Cape. (40)

When the Legislative Assembly of the Orange River Colony met on 30 March, only days after the South African Native Convention had concluded its deliberations in Bloemfontein, a petition embodying the resolutions of the SANC was put before the Assembly by Prime Minister Fischer. (41) Fischer spoke at length on the so-called 'native problem'. In the course of his speech, he criticised the SANC in scathing terms. He said that at the Native Convention the African leaders had refused to take the advice of Dewdney Drew, who was supposed to be trusted by them. He asked, 'How then could it be expected that they would listen to and follow other white men?' (42) Fischer declared that the type of demands made by the SANC were the work of white agitators—'theorists and faddists and easychair negrophilists'—who instilled into the minds of Africans ideas they never would have thought of themselves. These people complicated the existence of the white races in South Africa. While accepting the necessity of the compromise with the Cape, Fischer strongly opposed giving Africans the franchise. Just because some Africans had a veneer of civilisation, it could not be claimed that Africans on the whole were ripe for equality. The white man had no intention of acknowledging the black man's equality or of giving him the same rights. 'The law of self-preservation' was stronger than any other. (43)

Fischer's speech was punctuated by cheers from the Assembly benches. (44) He carried the acceptance of the National Convention's decisions on the colour bar without any trouble. And both the Transvaal parliament, which confirmed the draft Act in its entirety, and the Natal House of Assembly similarly had no compunction about accepting the colour bar. (45) After all, it accorded with traditional practice in the three northern colonies.

The proceedings in the Cape parliament were a different matter. A whole line of speakers sympathised with the aspirations of the black population and opposed any tampering with the Cape franchise system. (46) Even the Cape delegates to the National Convention and others who were opposed to amending the draft constitution emphasised that they supported the Cape franchise system in principle. People like Merriman, (47) Jameson (48) and Sauer (49) stated that they were opposed to the exclusion of black people from parliament, but it was necessary to make this concession to preserve the union. They argued that there was no danger to the franchise rights of blacks in the Cape. On the contrary, they envisaged the spread of Cape liberality to the other colonies after union.

This argument was accepted by most members, but it failed to pacify W. P. Schreiner, one of the strongest critics of the colour clauses. On entering the debate Schreiner said he would be failing in his duty if he did not refer to the 'blot' on the constitution. He said the Cape Colony with its long non-racial tradition was in the position of trustee:

The rights of the coloured people should not be bartered away from any benefit which the Europeans should get. Union with honour before all things. There was something pathetic in it that they should take the rights of others away, and make them a matter of bargaining, and say, 'If you do not give them up there will be no Union. . . .' He would stand out of Union rather than give up his trust in the matter. Federation, Unification etc. were questions of detail; but that question stood out as an absolutely essential one. . . . We must recognise our trust, and they [the other colonies] must see that they could not ask us to break it, and build Union on a treacherous foundation of sand, because we would be treacherous in the truest sense of the term if we did not provide protection for the colonial native people. . . . General Smuts talked of the white nation; but did that not leave a bad taste in the mouth? Was fairness and equality only to be shown to the white races? . . . If a small number of Cape representatives in the Union Parliament were not true to their trust, and with others voted for the coloured franchise being removed, would not the rights of the native and coloured people vanish into thin air under Parliamentary sanction? . . . It was no use them saying that they were satisfied with a certain amount of protection; they must go further, and have absolute protection. . . . Union without honour . . . was the greatest danger any nation could incur. (50)

Throughout the session, which lasted eighteen days, Schreiner fought the colour bar point for point, introducing amendments at every opportunity. Although his arguments often evoked considerable sympathy, (51) he was unable to carry any amendments to the colour bar or to make the Cape franchise unalterable. Yet he persisted with his uncompromising defence of the non-racial Cape tradition to the end. By the time a harassed Merriman finally piloted the compromise through parliament on 15 April, Schreiner, he noted, had spoken no less than sixty-four times. (52)

While Schreiner and other sympathisers were fighting the colour bar in the Cape parliament, black groups also used the channels open to them in an effort to dissuade parliament from accepting the draft Act unamended. Jabavu's King William's Town conference, (53) the APO of Dr Abdurahman (54) and the Wynberg Coloured Men's Political Organisation (55) exerted their right of petition to protest against the draft Act. Dr Abdurahman also followed the debates from the public gallery and tried unsuccessfully to be heard at the Bar of the House of Assembly. (56) In a letter to her brother, the writer Olive Schreiner described the scene of Dr Abdurahman sitting on the outside watching the Cape parliament acquiesce in the restriction of the political rights of the black people:

It seemed as though the curse of the serpent has fallen on them all—on thy belly shalt thou crawl and dust shalt thou eat. I hardly know what was the most awful thing. Jameson's face, . . . or dear old Malan looking like a lost soul, . . . as they squirmed and lied, and each one gave the other away, and all gave away principle. All the while there was Abdurahman's drawn dark intellectual face looking down at them. Men selling their souls and the future —and fate watching them. (57)

During the sitting of the Cape parliament it was rumoured that 'a man of high position' would proceed to Britain to protest against the passing of the draft Act in the Imperial parliament if it was not amended. (58) Little imagination was needed to work out that the person in question was Schreiner. His trenchant resistance to the draft constitution in parliament had placed him firmly in the spotlight as the central figure of dissent against the terms of union.

The black (as well as white) protest movement now coalesced increasingly around Schreiner. Both major African conferences had expressed a willingness to work with Schreiner, Jabavu and his supporters sent their petition to him to put before the Cape parliament, African newspapers praised 'the noble Schreiner', (59) and described him as 'our South African Abe Lincoln', (60) individuals wrote to him expressing gratitude and support (61) and he was received with rapturous applause when he delivered an address at the opening of the annual conference of the APO, held during the parliamentary sitting. (62)

### The final session of the National Convention in Bloemfontein
The matter of black political rights received scant attention at the final session of the National Convention, which met in Bloemfontein on 3 May. None of the colonial parliaments had recommended changes in this respect, so the only time the matter arose was when petitions on the subject were tabled. There were representations from several quarters.

The only petition from an African organisation was that of the Becoana Mutual Improvement Association and the headmen of the Thaba Nchu district. This reiterated the decisions taken at the meetings in Thaba Nchu on 20 March and 28 April. (63)

Only one African sent an individual petition to the Convention. He was John Alfred Sishuba from Kamastone in the Queenstown district. Sishuba, a political colleague of Jabavu's, was influential in African politics in the Cape and had served for many years as an electoral agent for the South African Party. As we have seen, he had corresponded with F. S. Malan on the question of unification as early as October 1907, and the *Imvo Zabantsundu* had published their correspondence to refute rumours by the Progressives that the South African Party would use unification to disenfranchise Africans. (64)

Sishuba asked the Convention to expunge the colour bar clauses from the draft Act. He said these clauses did not adequately protect Cape Africans and caused great anxiety among people who were expected to repose their trust in the new union parliament.

'As anything based on colour can but lead to prejudice and injustice,' Sishuba said, Africans abhorred these clauses. He asked that the Cape system which had never made colour distinctions should be maintained. It had led to mutual trust and confidence between Africans and whites. These relations would be jeopardised if the draft constituion was passed in its present form. (65)

There was also a weighty petition from leading churchmen from various denominations asking the Convention to remove the colour restrictions from the draft Act. It was signed by the Anglican Archbishop of Cape Town, W. M. Carter, in his first public act since his enthronement, Dr J. J. McClure, ex-Moderator of the South African Presbyterian Church, E. Baker, President-elect of the Baptist Union of South Africa, and Ramsden Balmforth and George Robson, ministers of the Free Protestant (Unitarian) and Wesleyan Churches respectively. The clergymen stated that there was considerable dissatisfaction about the discriminatory clauses, especially in the Cape Colony, and not least among acculturated Africans. Some of these people were recognised as voters in the Cape, but not as real citizens of South Africa. The petitioners believed that the assertion of the principle of colour discrimination would inevitably divide the white and black people into opposite and hostile camps. They therefore asked that blacks who enjoyed political rights should be allowed to continue to do so undiminished, while the door of citizenship should not be closed on those who were advancing towards a standard of 'European Civilisation'. (66) The Revd Ernest Barratt from Tsomo in the Transkei submitted a similar petition. (67) He had earlier indicated his opposition to the way in which union was being achieved in a letter to an appreciative *Imvo Zabantsundu*. (68)

In addition to the above petitions there were representations for adequate political rights for black people from the active and efficient executive of Dr Abdurahman's African Political Organisation, (69) the coloured citizens and registered voters of Wellington (70) and the Wynberg Coloured Men's Political Organisation. (71) Like the APO, the last-mentioned body had already petitioned both the National Convention and the Cape parliament before. The APO document contained the resolutions passed at the annual conference of the organisation in Cape Town.

All the above were tabled, and the letter from the churchmen was read out on the instructions of Sir Henry de Villiers, but they made no impact whatsoever on the delegates. No discussion ensued, no amendments were moved and the sections in the draft

Act dealing with black political rights remained unaltered. (72)

After almost breaking up over the electoral issue of equal voting rights for town and country constituencies, (73) the Convention finally reached unanimous agreement, concluded its deliberations and issued its final report on 11 May. (74)

## The draft South Africa Act is approved

The revised draft South Africa Act received the overwhelming approval of the various colonies. In short sessions starting on 1 June, the Transvaal and the Orange River Colony parliaments unanimously passed resolutions supporting the draft Act. (75)

In the Cape parliament there were only two dissenting votes against a similar motion. (76) The earlier strong opposition waned. This was due mainly to the swing by J. H. Hofmeyr and his supporters in the Afrikaner Bond in favour of the draft Act. Merriman had persuaded Hofmeyr not only to support the Act but also to become a member of the official colonial delegation to finalise the transition to union with the Imperial authorities in Britain. (77)

However, W. P. Schreiner remained unswerving in his opposition to the colour bar. Immediately after the Prime Minister had moved that the Cape approve the draft Act in its revised form, (78) Schreiner made a final stand. He told the House that he could not accept what appeared to be a conspiracy of silence on the subject.

... there were remaining in the draft fundamental blots which, even if he stood alone, he could not hesitate to bring as clearly as possible to the notice of everybody throughout the Colony, the world, and the Parliament in England, by which means he hoped that even at the last moment some change could be effected. (79)

He said the new constitution should be one of the world's very greatest documents of liberty. Could they call this a great liberty document? Could they enthuse about this? Which member could deny that he had not through conviction or convenience assured those of another colour that under the free institutions of the Cape no political differentiation would be made against them? Were they now going to tamper with the rights that these people held so dearly? He foresaw that the Imperial government might intervene against the injustices of the constitution and said the House should now disapprove of these injustices so that forced amendments would not be necessary. He then moved as an amendment 'that this House accepts the draft Act of Union subject to the modifications necessary to safeguard the native and coloured inhabitants of this colony against discrimination on the grounds of race or colour in respect of political rights'. (80)

But the fight was lost. When Schreiner called for a division on his amendment two days later, it was defeated by ninety-six votes to two. Only another former Prime Minister, the octogenarian Sir Gordon Sprigg, in almost his last public act, voted with Schreiner for his amendment. (81) The Cape Parliament had agreed to abrogate its non-racial constitution for one which discriminated on grounds of colour.

The position in Natal was slightly different from that in the other colonies. Because of the strong fears about union in the colony, (82) the Natal parliament had decided in April to hold a referendum to test the feeling of the electorate after the National Convention had issued its final report. It was held on 10 June. Natal voted 11 121 to 3 701 to enter the union. (83) In a session between 16 and 18 June the Natal parliament endorsed the will of the electorate. (84)

Thus the draft South Africa Act received the support of a large majority of white South African colonists. Not only had every one of the thirty-three delegates to the National Convention concurred with the final report, but the voters or their representatives in each colony had resoundingly come out in favour of it. On the other hand, nearly all politically conscious members of the African and coloured communities, who were denied political rights in all the colonies except the Cape, were against the terms, though not the principle, of union.

Once the four colonies had drawn up and ratified the draft South Africa Act, the focus of the unification issue shifted from South Africa to Britain, where the draft constitution was to be submitted for assent to the Imperial parliament.

# 9 W. P. Schreiner and the 'Coloured and Native Delegation' to Britain

As soon as the final report of the National Convention had been released, arrangements began in earnest for W. P. Schreiner to lead a deputation to Britain to oppose the passage of the draft South Africa Act through the British parliament.

The centre of activity was in Cape Town where Dr Abdurahman and white opponents of the colour bar such as the Revd Ramsden Balmforth and Dr Robert Forsyth, a Cape Town councillor, had been working in close co-operation with Schreiner. (1) These people got in touch with interest groups elsewhere in the colonies, and such groups looking for a lead contacted Schreiner and his associates in Cape Town. To give an example, by 11 May Abdurahman had written to John Tengo Jabavu and A. K. Soga, and had received a reply from the latter saying a deputation to Britain was imperative. (2) Within a few weeks almost all the parties involved in protesting against the colour provisions of the new constitution had written to Schreiner asking him to act on their behalf in Britain or to work in co-operation with delegates they were sending: the African Political Organisation, (3) the South African Native Convention, (4) Orange River Colony Native Congress, (5) the Transvaal Native Union, (6) the Transvaal Native Congress, (7) Jabavu's Cape Native Convention (8) and the Paramount Chief (9) and other interested parties (10) in Basutoland. Schreiner had become the rallying point for the blacks who opposed the draft Act.

### Schreiner's preparations
Schreiner's campaign was launched in earnest on 14 May when he, Balmforth and other sympathisers drew up an 'Appeal to the Parliament and Government of Great Britain and Ireland'. This was intended to draw attention in Britain to what was seemingly now a lost cause in South Africa. They protested against the colour restrictions in the draft South Africa Act, as well as clause 35,

through which black voters could in future be disenfranchised. While they recognised the necessity of compromise in matters not involving fundamental principles in bringing about union, this was an entirely different matter. They were compelled to protest against provisions which jeopardised the essential principles of free government and contradicted the traditional policy of Great Britain when conceding popular government. To enshrine the denial of human rights in a constitution was a grave injustice which would 'eventually react with evil effect' on white South Africans. The 'civilised' black population was dismayed at the deliberate and formal introduction into the constitution of discrimination against them. It also felt humiliated that the 22 000 black voters (more, incidentally, than all the voters in Natal) had not been counted in allotting the proportion of Cape members in the South African Parliament. Similarly, the huge aboriginal populations of the native territories and the protectorates were apprehensive that their position would not be properly safeguarded under union. The appeal emphasised that the signatories were not asking for an extension of existing African constitutional rights, but merely the maintenance and protection of such rights. The Imperial power was the guardian of these rights. It had granted them. Only it could take them away. (11)

This was the line of argument opponents of the draft Act would adopt in the ensuing months as the focus of the unification issue shifted from South Africa to Whitehall. The appeal was eventually signed by twenty-two people. Among the signatories were churchmen of all denominations, leading Cape politicians and prominent local personalities. They included Sir Gordon Sprigg, Sir Bisset Berry (a former Speaker of the House of Assembly), five past and present Cape parliamentarians, Archbishop William Carter and Dr J. J. McClure (both of whom had also signed the petition by members of the clergy to the National Convention), C. Abercrombie Smith (a member of the Executive Council, Vice-Chancellor of the University of Cape Town and former Auditor-General) and the Vice-President of the Cape Town Chamber of Commerce. (12)

To prepare for his trip to Britain, Schreiner also made private approaches to well-placed sympathisers there like Sir Charles Dilke (13) and Ramsay MacDonald, the Labour parliamentary leader. (14) Since the publication of the draft Act, Dilke had already taken it upon himself to interview the Colonial Under-Secretary of State, J. E. B. Seely, and to lead a deputation of Liberal and Labour Members of Parliament to the Colonial Secretary,

Lord Crewe, asking them to protect the rights of blacks in South Africa. He also roused the Aborigines Protection Society to work towards this end. Dilke told Schreiner that his stand had not gone unnoticed in Britain. He said reports of Schreiner's views were eagerly read by the top Colonial Office officials and 'everything you do aids our cause powerfully'. (15)

Schreiner's preparations caused a worried reaction in the Cape and nervousness in official quarters. Anxious lest he should succeed in causing sufficient fuss to induce the British government into making amendments to the draft Act, Prime Minister Merriman took steps to forestall Schreiner's mission. First of all he persuaded Sir Henry de Villiers to forward his own travelling plans and leave for Britain on the same day as Schreiner. He said it was of the 'utmost importance' that De Villiers should keep an eye on Schreiner's 'mischief'. (16) Then on 16 June, the day Schreiner left for London, Merriman sent a memorandum to the Cape Governor, Sir Walter Hely-Hutchinson, putting the case against amendments and expressing the hope that the 'misguided' deputation would receive no encouragement from the British government. (17)

Merriman declared that 'no worse blow could have been struck between the races' than this attempt to induce the British government to override the 'almost unanimous wish of South Africa on a question of native policy'. If the deputation succeeded in its aims, it would wreck union, lead to bitter resentment towards the Imperial government and put the white population in the Cape 'on the same plane of intolerance' on the colour question as the people in the northern colonies. Even if it did not succeed, the 'agitation, and the unwise speaking and writing which is sure to accompany it, is bound to have an evil effect on the mind of the natives, who will be taught to read into the Act of Union an attack on their rights wholly contrary to the spirit in which the act is conceived.' (18) Merriman also claimed that the Schreiner deputation was unrepresentative. He said most Africans realised that they had secured more under the draft Act than they had dared hope for. The deputation represented 'some of the more educated natives, by no means the most substantial or well-to-do of their race', who had been politically exploited. (19)

As part of his plans to neutralise Schreiner, Merriman also asked Colonel Stanford, who was respected for his views on the so-called native question, to influence the Cape Governor against the Schreiner delegation. In an interview with Hely-Hutchinson on 28

June, Stanford said that although he shared Schreiner's objection to the 'blot' on the constitution, he was strongly of the opinon that the draft Act, which embodied the considered decisions of the Convention and the South African parliaments, should be accepted. His view was that amendments would later increase the danger of an attack on the Cape franchise. On the other hand, if the colour question was left to the people of South Africa it would be in the best long-term interests of the black population. From his experience at the National Convention, he felt assured that there was 'a growing feeling and intention amongst the leading politicians in South Africa in favour of promoting the real interests of the Natives'. (20)

Hely-Hutchinson supported these arguments enthusiastically. In commending them to the Colonial Secretary, he described Stanford as 'a lifelong friend of the Natives' and Merriman as a longtime defender of African rights who had encountered considerable opposition on this score from W. P. Schreiner himself. (21) Merriman's and Stanford's arguments made a significant impact. Their line of reasoning was to be used in Britain in arguing against amendments.

Fully aware that his stand was not supported by most whites, Schreiner offered to resign his seat in parliament before leaving for Britain. (22) However, as there would be only one more short session of the Cape parliament before union, his election committee in Queenstown persuaded him not to do so. (23) While the majority of his Queenstown constituents were probably against his mission, there is no doubt what the feelings of the local African voters were; they sent him a special message expressing their support, thanking him for his courageous stand and invoking 'Divine blessing on the work of the delegation'. (24)

And so, tailed by no less a person than the President of the National Convention, Schreiner sailed for Britain carrying the hopes of almost all politically conscious black people in South Africa with him. He was to be joined abroad by other African and coloured delegates.

### African preparations

While Schreiner had been busy making contacts in Britain and publicising the forthcoming visit of the delegation, the African groups who wished to send delegates to accompany him were occupied in trying either to raise the necessary funds from an impoverished constituency or to get the approval of the authorities for the trip. The financial aspect was an ever-present problem for these groups. They could barely collect enough money to run their organisations, let alone send representatives abroad. Nevertheless they showed pertinacity in getting down to the task.

For its delegation fund, the Orange River Colony Native Congress collected altogether just under £170. This money came from more than twenty towns throughout the colony. It was collected through local representatives, earning ten per cent commission on the amount obtained. Among the people who sent in money were Joel Goronyane of the Becoana Mutual Improvement Association in Thaba Nchu and A. R. Goliath Rakhatoe of the Eastern Native Vigilance Association in Bethlehem. Donations varied from the twenty pounds sent in from both Kroonstad and Winburg to sums of one pound (Springfontein, Reddersburg) and four shillings (Marquard). (25)

Not all this money had been collected by the time Thomas Mtobi Mapikela, the person chosen by the ORCNC executive to represent the colony on the delegation of the South African Native Convention, (26) left for Britain. Some of the money was merely pledged initially, and sent in later. It was then cabled through to Mapikela. At one stage of his overseas visit, he was short of funds and forced to ask Schreiner for a small loan to help him through. (27) This was repaid to Mapikela from the delegation fund after his return, (28) and he promptly reimbursed Schreiner. (29)

Once the ORCNC was satisfied that it had sufficient funds to send its chosen delegate to Britain, it began finalising arrangements for his trip. One of the first steps was for the executive to draw up a statement outlining the grievances Mapikela was to present to the Imperial authorities. The statement was submitted directly to the Colonial Secretary in the form of a petition to the King. This was an unusual procedure to follow, as representations to the Imperial government were normally first submitted to the colonial authorities for transmission to Whitehall. In the petition, the ORCNC declared that despite recognition by the Imperial government of the fairness of African demands for some form of representation in a similar petition at the time the question of responsible government for the Orange River Colony was being discussed in 1906, Africans were still without any kind of representation on local municipalities and in the government, although they were taxed and their welfare was at issue on both levels. This system of 'taxation without representation' was unjust: African grievances did not receive the consideration which their importance warranted. Under these circumstances, Africans had no other option than to appeal again to the King. The ORCNC asked the British government to insert a clause in the draft South Africa Act to provide for some form of representation for Africans, and said that the terms of the Treaty of Vereeniging, behind which the British government had sheltered in ignoring the ORCNC request of 1906, could no longer be considered as binding. (30) The ORCNC also called on their local Colonial Secretary's office in Bloemfontein (31) and met the Governor, who was asked to ensure that Mapikela was given the opportunity of presenting their views in Britain. (32) In another move, the executive wrote to Schreiner, begging for his co-operation and asking him to assist Mapikela if matters in the Orange River Colony were dealt with separately and he had to draw up a petition. (33) Lastly, it finalised Mapikela's travel arrangements. (34)

The South African Native Convention had hoped to send a delegation of twelve members, (35) but in the event there were only three: Dr Rubusana, Daniel Dwanya and Mapikela. (36) Dwanya, who had been chairman of the 1907 Queenstown Conference called by the *Izwi Labantu*, was sent as the representative of the Gqunukwebe tribe, (37) but, like Mapikela, he went under the mantle of the SANC.

It is not known who all the other members of the SANC delegation were intended to be. Joel Goronyane was thought by the ORCNC likely to be a member. (38) A. K. Soga, expected in some quarters to be a certain choice, (39) probably had to stand back for Dr Rubusana because of lack of funds. This led to a split between him and Rubusana, his close political ally for many years in the South African Native Congress. Soga accused Rubusana of 'self-appointment' to the delegation, and more than a year later he declared—in a letter criticising Rubusana's political activities—that this allegedly unilateral action was something he would always protest about. (40)

One of the people definitely selected as a member of the delegation was John L. Dube. On 9 June Dr Rubusana, the chief-coordinator, informed Dube that the delegation 'of which you are one' was leaving on the 23rd and that he should wire the money in Natal to him in East London. (41) Dube then replied to Rubusana stating simply, 'Cannot go as Deputation. My educational work debars me taking active part in politics.' (42) Nevertheless, Dube did go to Britain. He claimed his trip was solely for educational pur-

poses, and that he had decided to leave politics alone as he had
learned by 'sad experience' that politics injured his educational
work, to which he had devoted his life. He said that if he went
over at the same time as the deputation—in fact he did—it would
be merely for company. (43) This seems an unlikely explanation.

One suspects that Dube acted in the way he did to circumvent
the suspicious and disapproving Natal authorities, and that he did
in fact play a behind-the-scenes role in the activities of the delegation in London, in addition to raising funds for his Ohlange Institute. He had been politically very active in 1908 and in the early
months of 1909, and he did not retire from politics when he returned from overseas. He was present in London at the same time
as Schreiner's delegation, he attended at least one of its meetings,
and he was in contact with Schreiner. (45)

Why was it necessary for Dube to go to London by way of the
the back door? He lived in a colony where politically conscious
Africans were regarded with much suspicion by whites, and where
the government did not hesitate to exert pressure on them. As we
have seen, the government severely reprimanded Dube for remarks
he made during the 1906 disturbances, and also threatened him
with the closure of his newspaper, the *Ilanga lase Natal*. Because of
his role in the protests by Natal Africans against the three Native
Administration bills in 1908, Frederick Moor, the Natal Prime
Minister and Minister for Native Affairs, again warned Dube that
he was 'playing with fire', (45) and one of his white benefactors at
Ohlange, Marshall Campbell, urged him in a 'fatherly talk' to be
more moderate in his newspaper and to stop taking an active part
in politics. (46) Under this pressure, Dube took care to assure
Moor that he had no intention of leading a rumoured delegation
to Britain against the bills. (47) Now, a few months later, Dube was
again under pressure. Dr Rubusana told the *Cape Times* in an
interview that Dube had been made to understand that if he went
on the delegation the government subsidy to his Ohlange school
would be in jeopardy, and that as a recipient of government
funds he was expected not to 'interfere' in politics. (48) To reas-
sure the government, Dube sent Rubusana's telegram to the Native
Affairs Department as soon as he received it, together with his
reply, (49) and he also drew the attention of the Department to
the explanation for his new attitude in the *Ilanga*. (50) Thus, with
the authorities mollified, the way was clear for Dube to embark on
his trip abroad.

The Transvaal Native Union organised fairly extensively to send delegates, but at the last moment they were unable to go because of a lack of funds. (51) The TNU began its campaign in May when the executive committee sent out subscription lists for the 'Native Convention Delegation Fund' to representatives in the various districts. The executive encouraged them to call meetings at once for this purpose. It calculated that at least £750 was needed to defray the expenses of the five or six delegates the TNU wished to send to Britain. (52) Meetings were subsequently held at a number of different venues in the Transvaal: Johannesburg, Nancefield, Fordsburg, Jeppestown, New Doornfontein, Boksburg, Middelburg, Bethanie, Makapanstad, Phokeny, Hebron, Klerksdorp, Mabeskraal, Mabalstad, Saulspoort and Pretoria. (53) Members of the TNU also toured the various districts to collect funds. (54)

By the beginning of July the campaign had reached the stage where the TNU Chairman, William Letseleba, informed the government (55) that they had elected Chiefs J. O. More Mamogale, A. T. M. Makgatle and G. A. H. Mabala of the Bakwena tribe to go to lay the claims of Transvaal Africans before the British government. (56) The authorities did not interfere with the campaign. The Secretary for Native Affairs informed an enquiring Native Commissioner that it was not necessary to take any steps to prevent people from collecting funds for this purpose. (57) At the request of Letseleba (58) he also provided the delegates with a certificate confirming the purpose of their travels. (59) The organisers also tried to fix arrangements for the delegates in London. Both Letseleba and a white sympathiser, Edward Dallow, got in touch with Schreiner asking him to co-operate with the delegates, direct them to the other delegates and help them find accommodation. (60)

After a TNU committee meeting on 14 July, the departure date for the delegation was set for the 19th. (61) The delegates were due to sail from Cape Town on the *Walmer Castle* two days later. (62) However, even though everything seemed finalised—with the Administrator of the Transvaal wiring Lord Crewe (63) that the delegation had in fact sailed—the trip was abandoned and the delegates returned to their homes. (64) In a short letter, written a few weeks after the delegation should have left, the TNU's secretary, Z. More, informed the authorities that the trip was off and that the cancellation had been caused by a failure to raise enough money. (65)

The Transvaal Native Congress, which does not seem to have involved itself actively as an affiliate to the TNU, also took action to have its views on union heard in Whitehall. It did not attempt to send delegates of its own, but forwarded its opinions to Britain and asked South Africans studying abroad to act on its behalf. At its annual conference, held at Nancefield on 24 June, the TNC criticised the draft South African Act and vested Alfred Mangena and Pixley Ka Isaka Seme with a mandate to act on its behalf in London. The TNC instructed Mangena and Seme to work in co-operation with Schreiner, J. T. Jabavu, Mahatma Gandhi (who went to London on behalf of the Transvaal Indians) and other delegates. (66)

The TNC conference deprecated the draft Act because 'no provision had been made to safeguard the interests of the [Transvaal] natives'. They saw the terms of union, following on the Treaty of Vereeniging, as another step 'detrimental to our freedom'. It said the draft constitution departed in letter and spirit from the 1906 responsible government constitution which theoretically provided Imperial safeguards for Africans. It asked that these safeguards, embodied in paragraphs 13 and 21 of the Letters Patent of 1906, should be included in the draft constitution 'pending the extension of citizenship to the natives of the Colony'. The TNC also expressed its appreciation to Lord Selborne for his sympathetic statements and asked the British government 'to request him to grasp the reins of the Unified Government'. (67)

The fact that the TNC, in instructing Mangena and Seme to co-operate with Gandhi and other delegates, did not specifically mention the South African Native Convention or its delegates indicates that it stood aloof from the SANC, which the TNU supported, and the formal joint action it was trying to promote. An unsigned report about the TNU meeting of 19 April in Jabavu's *Imvo Zabantsundu* also points to divisions in Transvaal African politics. An unnamed correspondent complained that people who were not members of the TNU were not allowed to put questions, accused the TNU of falsely claiming to represent the Transvaal, and said people were against collecting money for a delegation to Britain because they did not trust the TNU. (68) The exact nature of these divisions is uncertain, but it is clear that the TNU was not fulfilling its aim of uniting all the Transvaal groups against the draft Act.

Meanwhile, John Tengo Jabavu, the only other African besides the three South African Native Convention delegates who was to go to London as a member of the joint 'Coloured and Native Delegation' under Schreiner, had also been preparing for his journey.

Originally Jabavu's *Imvo Zabantsundu* newspaper had greeted the final report of the National Convention with acclaim as it was under the misapprehension, from newspaper headlines and 'vague summaries of the amendments', that the Convention had decided to abolish the Europeans-only clauses and the provision stipulating the conditions for the disenfranchisement of Cape Africans. (69) The following week, however, the *Imvo* retracted its approval in an embarrassing about-face, and reiterated its strong opposition to the colour bar clauses. It said there now remained nothing for Africans and their sympathisers to do but don their armour and go on with the fight to the end. The feelings of Africans had not been heeded in their own country, so now they had to take the matter further. (70)

After the Cape parliament had given its final blessing to the draft constitution early in June, the committee chosen by the Cape Native Convention at the King William's Town conference met and elected W. P. Schreiner to represent them and Jabavu to accompany him if the necessary funds could be raised. (71) In the next few weeks the *Imvo* appealed to its readers in articles and prominent advertisements for support to send Jabavu to Britain. (72)

The response does not seem to have been very good. According to his son, Jabavu, who had been in financial difficulties ever since the closing down of the *Imvo* during the war, dug deep into his own pocket to finance his trip. In his father's biography, D. D. T. Jabavu blamed the 'heavy financial commitments' incurred by Jabavu on this and other 'national errands' for his subsequent decline into ill-health. (73)

Before Jabavu could join the delegation, he had to provide a bank guarantee of about £150 to finance the running of the *Imvo* during his absence. As he could not guarantee this money, he turned to 'friends of the cause' such as W. P. Schreiner and his brother Theophilus. Jabavu told them he would be able to repay the money as the *Imvo* was owed £4 000 in outstanding payments. (74) In an attempt to collect some of this total, he now placed several notices requesting debtors to settle their accounts promptly in each edition of the newspaper. (75) It is not clear how Jabavu met the financial poser facing him, but in any event he sailed early in July, with Daniel Dwanya as a fellow passenger, (76) hoping that he and the other delegates would make enough 'converts' to their views to force amendments to the constitution. (77)

Although he realised that the draft Act would probably be accepted by the British government, Jabavu was confident that the delegation would receive enough support to 'bring about trouble over the European descent clause'. (78) He warned in an *Imvo* editorial before he left that supporters of the draft Act should not be complacent because, it was rumoured, there were already about a hundred and fifty 'Schreinerites' in the British parliament. (79) African hopes that Britain might insist on amendments had also been raised by press reports that the Under-Secretary of State, Colonel Seely, had said in the House of Commons on 27 May that the proposed South Africa Act would have to be redrafted in Britain and that the Imperial government would propose amendments. (80)

Jabavu and Dwanya were the last of the African delegates to leave. They were preceded by Mapikela (23 June) and Rubusana (29 June). On the day he left, Rubusana emphasised that 'we are not going to England as agitators, but as humble citizens of His Majesty's Colony to plead—before Lord Crewe—for the deletion of those colour clauses in the Act which should never have been allowed in the Draft Constitution.' He said that Africans had exhausted every constitutional means to bring about amendments, they had been rebuffed all along the line. Therefore 'It now remains for us . . . to do all we can to get the Imperial Parliament to remove this blot and insult to the Native and Coloured races of this country from the Constitution. May God bless us in this.' (81)

### The petition of the Transkeian Territories General Council

In another important development during this period the seventh session of the Transkeian Territories General Council, which began on 14 June in Umtata, unanimously condemned the colour bar provisions in the draft constitution and forwarded a petition with the views of the Council to the Cape and British governments.

The subject of union was the first matter discussed at the two-week session. Enoch Mamba had tabled a late motion urgently requesting that the Council discuss the draft Act as it affected the Transkeian Territories before the other matters on the agenda were dealt with. (82) That this was agreed to is indicative of the seriousness with which the Councillors regarded the issue of union. In opening the discussions, Mamba (whom Walter Stanford had described as 'rather of the aggressive type of educated native whose attitude is not likely to help his people', (83) after a meeting on the draft Act a few months earlier) said that for the white people the benefits of union were obvious, but the same did not apply to Africans. The equal rights they had enjoyed with whites ever since they came under British rule were being tampered with. Using language calculated to appeal to the largely tribal audience, Mamba continued:

Before the Transkeian Territories were annexed there were many among the Natives who were anxious to fight for their freedom as a nation, but men of better understanding said, 'No! Do not take up arms. Go under British rule without fighting and you will receive those equal rights which have become traditional of Britain.' . . . Equal rights were emphasised. And now . . . they were not allowed to enter the Union Parliament, merely because of their colour. . . . The Government, who were their fathers, were sending this Draft Act to England . . . but it was a bad thing, not good even according to Christianity. (84)

Mamba said the King was the son of their 'late beloved' Queen Victoria and he had assured the Africans that he would rule them in the same way as his Mother. Now the King had before him a document which discriminated between black and white people and Mamba had read that it would become law. What had happened to the British sovereign, asked Mamba, that he should depart from the promises made to 'great nations' such as the Thembu, the Mfengu, the Pondo and the Baca when they came under British control. Mamba concluded that this was an important matter that the Council should not consider hastily and he therefore moved that a Committee be appointed to discuss it. (85)

Mamba's motion was seconded by Councillor S. Milton Ntloko of Tsomo (who had been one of the secretaries of Jabavu's King William's Town convention). Speaking as 'a true-born Britisher' who had been reared in the enjoyment of the rights of a British citizen, he rejected roundly the principle of racial distinction. If it was adopted in the South African constitution it would lead to enmity and could have serious consequences for the future. (86)

The matter was referred to a committee consisting of Chief Dalindyebo, Captain Veldtman, Councillors Shosho, Ntloko, Moshesh, P. Nkala, Bizweni, Mgudlwa, Gasa, Jamangile, Njikelana and Mamba with the Chief Magistrate of Umtata, W. T. Brownlee, as chairman. (87) The first two people mentioned were very influential figures in Transkeian affairs. Chief Dalindyebo was paramount chief of the Thembu for thirty-six years before his death in 1920, (88) and the eighty-eight year old Captain Veldtman was a leading Mfengu headman. He had earned his rank as Captain (and the present of a farm) for service in three Frontier Wars in the pro-government Fingo Levies. (89)

The committee met on 14 and 15 June. After considerable discussion, it resolved unanimously to recommend to the Council that in the interests of the Africans in the Transkeian Territories it was desirable that the draft South African Act should be amended in respect of the clauses referring to European descent. It recommended further that the resolutions be forwarded to the Prime Minister for submission to the Governor and King and that the Council appoint a committee to draft the petition. (90) This was agreed to. The Council appointed Councillors Silimela, Lehana, Ntloko, Moshesh, Mamba and Gasa, assisted by Brownlee, to draw up the petition. (91)

The petition drawn up by this committee was approved by the Council and sent to Prime Minister Merriman on 21 June. It followed the general pattern of petitions drawn up by African groups to protest against the draft Act. While reaffirming the loyalty of the petitioners, it expressed grave apprehension at the colour bar which threatened the cherished rights of equality before the law and the franchise that Africans had always enjoyed and never abused. It requested that the colour line be expunged from the draft Act. (92)

This petition was an important development in the whole campaign by Africans against the new constitution. The Council had a huge tribal constituency. It embraced sixteen Transkeian districts with an African population of more than 500 000. (93) One can reasonably infer that tribal opinion in these districts was reflected by this body. A visiting deputation acting on behalf of Natal Africans found that the majority of Councillors were 'red Kafir' representatives and that except for 'a few well-educated and able men . . . fully half of the representatives could not read or write.' (94) Most of the Councillors were headmen nominated from their own numbers. Locally, each District Council consisted of six members, four of whom were headmen chosen by the local headmen. District Councils in turn nominated two of the three delegates representing each district in the General Council. The other members in both cases were nominees of the Cape Governor. (95) Thus the General Council could claim with some justification to be representative.

## Attitudes in the protectorates
Africans in the protectorates continued to be apprehensive about union. The Paramount Chiefs of Basutoland, (96) Swaziland (97)

and Bechuanaland (98) were unhappy with the Schedule to the draft Act. They all expressed their opposition to being incorporated in the union. They wanted their territories to remain separate entities under the control of the Imperial government. If forced against their will into union, the protectorate tribes wished to be guaranteed the greatest degree of autonomy and freedom under such a dispensation.

As the time approached for the draft South Africa Act to be laid before the British parliament for approval, the Basotho and the Tswana made arrangements to be represented by delegates who were in Britain at the time. W. P. Schreiner was approached by the Basotho Paramount Chief Letsie, (99) S. M. Phamotse, the editor of the *Naledi ea Lesotho* and a member of the small educated class who had grouped themselves into the Basutoland Progressive Association, (100) and Edouard Jacottet, (101) a missionary of the Paris Evangelical Mission Society who worked tirelessly on behalf of the Basotho throughout the period that the negotiations on South African unification were taking place. (102) Although the above three people represented different groups, there was close cooperation between them. Paramount Chief Letsie had approached Schreiner to act 'as my advocate about the matter of Unification in England' after being prompted to do so by Phamotse; (103) Jacottet also kept in close touch with Letsie on the question of Union; (104) and Phamotse and Jacottet had been working together all along. Schreiner agreed to act on behalf of the Basotho. (105)

The tribes in the Bechuanaland Protectorate acted in a similar way. When Paramount Chief Bathoen of the Bangwaketse and Paramount Chief Sebele Sechele of the Bakwena heard that J. Gerrans, a 'friend for many years', was going to Britain for health reasons, they asked him to act on their behalf when the draft Act came before the Imperial authorities, to work as hard as he could to prevent Bechuanaland from being incorporated in the union, and to inform the British government that they wished to remain under its direct protection. (106) Gerrans then got in touch with Schreiner and became a member of the deputation in London.

### The preparations of Dr Abdurahman and the African Political Organisation

After the final session of the National Convention, the coloured people, who by now identified themselves completely with Africans in the fight against the colour bar in the draft Act, also orga-

nised on a large scale to send representatives on Schreiner's deputation. The APO was at the head of this activity.

There was a remarkable and immediate response to the APO
conference call for funds for a new newspaper and for the delegation to Britain. One thousand collection cards were sent out to the
various districts and fund-raising events such as tea meetings, concerts and dances were held. The organisers estimated that within
two months at least 12 000 people had contributed to the funds.
(107) Later they put the final cstimate at approximately 30 000.
(108) Collections were made in all four colonies and as far afield
as the Victoria Falls in Rhodesia. Over twenty new APO branches
were formed in this climate of enthusiasm. (109)

Just over a month after the APO conference, the organisation
brought out the first issue of its new newspaper. It was simply
named the *A.P.O.* The newspaper immediately entered the fray,
criticising the draft Act and exhorting coloured people (and
Africans) to respond to this threat to their interests. (110) It became the rallying point of the whole protest movement of the
coloured people. The rank and file were kept informed of developments as the newspaper printed letters from its readers and
reported meetings, resolutions and collections by the dozen.

Meanwhile, Dr Abdurahman started his campaign in Britain by
writing a letter to *The Times* on 19 May. He levelled the by now
familiar criticism against the 'Europeans only' clauses, and the provision providing for changes in the entrenched sections of the
constitution by a two-thirds majority. He declared that this clause
would lead to the eventual disenfranchisement of blacks in the
Cape. He quoted from speeches by prominent Transvaal politicians
like Botha, Smuts and Krause to back up his claim and show that
the opponents of the black franchise were determined to see it
restricted. He called on the Imperial government not to give its approval to the draft Act until the offending clauses were removed.
(111) *The Times* did not print his letter, but he later had printed
copies of it circulated privately in Britain. (112)

The next step was to finalise the delegates to represent the
coloured people in England. The APO executive decided formally to ask Schreiner to represent them and chose Dr Abdurahman,
D. J. Lenders and Matt J. Fredericks, the APO President, Vice-
President and General Secretary respectively, to accompany him.
(113) By now Schreiner was something of a hero. The APO newspaper referred to him in glowing terms (114) and at least fifty
meetings in the various colonies passed resolutions thanking him

for his stand and learning with 'inexpressible joy' that he had decided to proceed to Britain on their behalf. (115)

The APO enjoyed the overwhelming support of the coloured people for its campaign against the Act. However, some of Dr Abdurahman's political opponents opposed the idea of a delegation to Britain. The most notable members of this group were John Tobin and F. Z. S. Peregrino, neither of whom had an organisational base to compare with that of Dr Abdurahman. While favouring equal rights for coloured people, they contended that a deputation to Britain would damage their cause. Rather than appeal to the Imperial government to intervene, it would be better in the long run to depend on sympathetic whites at home. They claimed that the deputation would only lead to unnecessary expenses for an already impoverished coloured population. (116) In order to publicise their views and undermine Abdurahman's plans, Tobin and Peregrino wrote letters to the press (117) and made representations to the authorities. (118) In a further move, just before the departure of the government delegation for London to encourage the passage of the Act through parliament, they handed an address, embodying their views, to one of its members, J. H. Hofmeyr, for presentation to a suitable person in Britain. (119) In their campaign, Tobin and Peregrino claimed that their respective organisations, 'The Stone'—Tobin was supported only by a faction of this group—and the Coloured People's Vigilance Committee, were equal in stature to the APO. This was patently untrue. Of the two men, only Tobin, formerly a leading figure in the APO, had any formal support worth mentioning. Nevertheless, their claims were readily used by the government delegates as a counter to the APO delegation and their views were attended to by the British government. (120)

## Co-operation with South African Indians

The Indians in the Transvaal also sent a deputation to London at this time. Traditionally Indians had preferred to keep their own interests distinct from issues affecting blacks in general (121) and to work 'quietly along their own lines'. (122) In fact, for Indians to be classified and treated as Africans was a basic grievance they had against white law and custom. They saw themselves as sharing with Europeans ideas about the positive value of cultural and ethnic differences, and held themselves to be apart from and above Africans. (123) As early as the 1890s M. K. (Mahatma) Gandhi had drafted a petition to the British Colonial Secretary complaining that Indians were 'huddled together in the same compartment with Natives'. Indian leaders also endorsed a pass system for Africans and successfully demanded that the Natal authorities should provide three entrances instead of two in public buildings, so that Indians would not have to share entrances with Africans. (124) These views were still operative at the end of the first decade of the twentieth century. In 1909 one Kama, a well-known member of the Indian community, declared in court that he objected to carrying a pass 'in a civilised country as though he were a Kaffir'. (125) In the same year, a passive resister friend of Gandhi's wrote to him complaining about being 'locked up [in jail] with the Kaffirs'. (126) Gandhi's mouthpiece, the *Indian Opinion*, talked of Indians being 'degraded by commerce with Kaffirs'. (127)

Africans, for their part, also looked upon Indians with suspicion. An inspection of the columns of the *Izwi Labantu* between 1906 and 1909, a crucial period in the Indian struggle on the Rand, brings to light little more than a handful of references to this subject. One report said Africans could not be expected to regard the 'Indian question' with much sympathy: 'The countrymen of Gandhi are, like the Mohammedans and Malays, extremely self-centred, selfish and alien in feeling and outlook.' (128) A month later the *Izwi* placed without comment an extract from an American newspaper saying that the Africans in South Africa had not forgotten that Indians had volunteered to serve with 'the English savages of Natal who massacred thousands of Zulus in order to steal their lands'. (129) This report referred to an Indian volunteer group under Gandhi which had served as stretcher-bearers for the colonial forces during the 1906 disturbances. (130) Nevertheless, despite these feelings of mutual antipathy, recognition of a common lot did bring about a degree of solidarity between the African and Indian groups. The *Naledi ea Lesotho* for example expressed admiration for the passive resistance methods of the Transvaal Indians (131) and the *Indian Opinion* reciprocated by declaring that, 'Our sympathies go out to our oppressed fellow subjects who are made to suffer for the same cause that we suffer, viz., our slight pigment of skin.' (132) At another time the *Indian Opinion* warned that whites by discriminating against the various black groups were 'trying almost to compel them' into forming a united front. (133) This editorial was warmly welcomed by both the *Izwi Labantu* and the *Ilanga lase Natal*. (134) However, despite this growing recognition of joint disabilities, and although Indians foresaw that union would lead to a curtailment of the liberties of all 'non-whites' (135) and regarded it as 'a consummation devoutly to be deplored', (136) they did not join the African and coloured people in agitating against the draft Act. Their struggle throughout the period under review continued mainly to be focused on the past and present treatment of Indians, rather than on the wider issue of the future effects of union on the black population. This approach was based on the argument that while the indigenous coloured and African groups had a full right to demand political equality, the Indian settlers should not strive for political rights at this stage but should concentrate on their civil rights which were constantly in jeopardy. (137)

Even though the Indians did not launch a direct campaign against the draft Act, it is clear from newspaper comments that they were dissatisfied with the report of the National Convention. For several weeks running, the Natal-based *African Chronicle* criticised the draft Act in the strongest terms. (138) It said it was an unholy measure that restricted the rights of blacks and jeopardised the rights that remained. (139) The draft Act propagated union in theory, but would lead to disunion in practice. It was a union of the white people which ignored the majority of the population. (140) The newspaper urged Indians and other blacks to protest against the Act and to suggest amendments before it was laid before the British parliament. It suggested a 'South African Coloured People's Conference' for this purpose. (141) The *Indian Opinion* also reacted critically to the draft Act. It went so far as to say that the Act amounted to a declaration of war against the black population. Except for the practically worthless concession of senate representatives, the interests of blacks had been ignored. (142) The *Indian Opinion* declared that in the face of union it was the duty of Indians to banish religious and territorial differences and to maintain their self-respect, national honour and religious ideals against the united opposition of a future government of South Africa. (143)

In the meantime the Indian passive resistance struggle in the Transvaal had been proceeding. There was no sign to indicate an abatement in the harassment and deportation of Indians by the government. The Indian leaders, advised by white sympathisers, decided to take advantage of the presence in London, with the colonial government delegation, of the Transvaal leaders Botha and Smuts to petition the British government for a redress of their grievances. Two mass meetings of the British Indian Association in

June, attended by approximately 2 000 people in all, approved of the idea of simultaneous delegations to Britain and India, and nominated delegates for these. (144) Four of the seven prospective delegates were arrested by the government, which refused appeals for their release, (145) but two delegations went ahead. Gandhi and Haji Habib were to go to Britain and H. S. Polak to India.

The Indians in Natal decided, at a meeting in Durban on 7 July, to follow the example of their compatriots in the Transvaal and to send a delegation to take advantage of the concentration of South African and Imperial statesmen in London. The meeting appointed Abdul Kadir and M. C. Anglia, the Chairman and the Secretary of the Natal Indian Congress, and two Pietermaritzburg merchants, Amod Bayat and H. M. Badat, as the delegates. (146) The delegates would represent the Natal Indian Congress, the Natal Indian Patriotic Union, the Anjuman Islam Society of Durban, the Hindh Sudhar Sabha and the Catholic Indian Young Men's Society. A petition signed by 1 138 people was sent to Lord Crewe in support of the delegation, (147) which departed for London the day it was appointed. (148)

Gandhi and Habib had by then already left for Britain. After having been given a rousing send-off at the Johannesburg station by 800 cheering supporters, (149) they set sail from Cape Town on the *Kenilworth Castle* on 23 June. Their fellow passengers included John X. Merriman and several other members of the government delegation, and Dr Abdurahman and his APO co-delegates. (150) Dr Abdurahman and Gandhi were jointly seen off by a group of supporters that included W. P. Schreiner's sisters Olive Schreiner and Helena Stakesby-Lewis, both of whom had been active in opposing the Draft Act. (152) Before his departure, Gandhi said that although he was going to London in connection with the treatment of Indians in the Transvaal, he and Habib would interest themselves in the passage of the draft Act in Britain as well. (153) He said that Indians looked with despair upon the consummation of union, mainly because it was a union for whites only. He was opposed to the colour bar and noted that existing legislation concerning the movement of Indians in South Africa would remain unaltered until the union parliament chose to modify the laws. Gandhi had no doubt that when this time arrived matters would become worse for Indians rather than improve. The ideas of the Indophobe northern colonies would triumph over the comparatively liberal-minded attitudes in the Cape. He foresaw that a policy of artificial racial segregation would be implemented.

Under such a system, Indians would be confined to separate ghettos. (154)

There was, therefore, a degree of mutual sympathy and co-operation between the Indian delegation and the joint deputation that was protesting against the draft Act. This fellowship was to be extended when Gandhi met Schreiner in London.

## The delegation in Britain

The delegates from the various South African colonies who were proceeding to Britain to watch the progress of the draft South Africa Act through the British parliament arrived there by passenger ship at various intervals in July. By 17 July the full complement, no less than twenty-eight, was gathered. There were also other South Africans indirectly involved as advisers and supporters. (155)

The official government delegation were nineteen. They were Sir Henry de Villiers, John X. Merriman, J. W. Sauer, L. S. Jameson and J. H. Hofmeyr (Cape Colony); Louis Botha, J. C. Smuts, H. C. Hull, George Farrar and Sir Percy Fitzpatrick (Transvaal); Abraham Fischer, J. B. M. Hertzog, M. T. Steyn and A. Browne (Orange River Colony); and F. R. Moor, T. Hyslop, E. M. Greene, C. J. Smythe and T. Watt (Natal). All except one, Hofmeyr, had been members of the National Convention. Ranged against them were Schreiner and his Coloured and Native Delegation: Dr Abdurahman, Matt J. Fredericks, D. J. Lenders, Dr Rubusana, Thomas Mtobi Mapikela, Daniel Dwanya, John Tengo Jabavu and J. Gerrans.

Schreiner's delegation was in touch with Gandhi and Haji Habib, who were in London to protest against differential legislation applying to Indians in the Transvaal. Schreiner had discussions with Gandhi and corresponded with him. (156) In addition, the delegation received moral support from people like John Dube (157) and three aspirant young lawyers, Richard Msimang (158), Alfred Mangena (159) and Pixley Ka Isaka Seme, (160) who were to play an important role in the formation of the South African Native National Congress three years later. Mangena and Seme had been delegated by the Transvaal Native Congress to act on its behalf in Britain. Jabavu's son, Davison Don Tengo, who was to become an outstanding educationist and, like his father, a political leader, and Ismail, the younger brother of Dr Abdurahman, were also studying in London at the time and helped the delegates in their work. (161)

The delegation tried to win support for its cause by publicising its case in the press, co-operating with sympathetic groups, lobbying members of the British parliament and interviewing the Colonial Secretary. Schreiner started the campaign as soon as he arrived in England on Saturday 3 July. In a statement to the Reuters news agency, which appeared in the national press on the Monday, Schreiner stated that he had come to Britain

... to try to get the blots removed from the Act, which makes it no Act of Union, but rather an Act of Separation between the minority and the majority of the people of South Africa. True Union must consider all elements, but here the principal element is not merely not considered, but from our point of view is dealt with in an actually insulting way. The coloured inhabitants are barred from the opportunity to rise and evolve naturally, which is the right of every free man in a free country. We do not base our movement upon the doctrine of the equality of all men, but upon the doctrine of the right to freedom of opportunity— equality of opportunity. ... The principles of justice which are associated in our minds with Great Britain and her expansive policy are violated in the proposed Act of Union. We do not dream that Union is to be wrecked if Great Britain resolves that an injustice, which is apparent, is to be removed. We know that the incentives towards Union are so strong that none of the parties to the Convention would dream of rejecting it merely because the offensive exclusion of persons of non-European descent might be removed. (162)

The next day *The Times* published the full text of the 'Appeal to the Parliament and Government of Great Britain and Ireland' which Schreiner had brought from South Africa. (163) Later, accompanied by a letter with a special masthood of the delegation, and signed by Schreiner, Rubusana, Mapikela, Abdurahman, Lenders and Fredericks, (164) the Appeal was also circularised to 1 300 people, including all the members of the House of Commons and the House of Lords. (165)

As soon as he found his feet, Schreiner started putting out feelers at Westminster and Whitehall. He wrote to several people, including Lord Crewe, (166) asking for interviews and on Wednesday 7 July he began lobbying members in the Commons. (167) As a result of these endeavours, the delegation soon had the support of bodies such as the Anti-Slavery and Aborigines Protection Society, (168) the London Missionary Society, (169) the South African Native Races Committee (170) and the Personal Rights Association, (171) as well as Sir Charles Dilke, (172) the Labour Party leader Keir Hardie, (173) Ramsay MacDonald, Frederick MacKarness, G. P. Gooch, (174) Lord Courtney (175) and other parliamentarians. (176)

The delegates worked in co-ordination, particularly Schreiner and the APO and SANC representatives. They jointly signed letters and petitions, attended meetings, appointed a delegation secretary, Matt J. Fredericks, (177) and decided on specific tasks for certain people. Dr Abdurahman wrote of having been 'entrusted' with drawing up a petition to submit to parliament, (178) and having to negotiate this with Jabavu, Rubusana and Schreiner. (179) But it is clear that Schreiner was at the centre of these activities. As an established international statesman who commanded the respect and attention of British audiences, he assumed the dominant role in the delegation. He was usually the main speaker at meetings, invitations to his fellow delegates were extended through him (180) and he used his influence to arrange private interviews for them. (181)

However, while Schreiner was the outstanding figure and chief co-ordinator, the delegates also acted on their own initiative in bringing their grievances to the notice of the British public. They individually interviewed people, (182) addressed gatherings (183) and spoke to the press. They stayed at different addresses and were not always in close contact with each other. Schreiner and the APO representatives resided in different hotels in Trafalgar Square, but Jabavu, Rubusana, Dube and, most likely, the other African members, who probably could not afford the luxury of the Grand (APO delegates), Morley's (Schreiner) and Westminster Palace (Gandhi) hotels, were acommodated privately or in boarding houses. (184) Jabavu stayed with members of the Quaker movement for much of his stay in London, and became lastingly influenced by them. (185)

Despite the delegation's strenuous attempts to rally British public opinion in favour of amending the constitution, it was unable to do so. The British public and most parliamentarians showed little interest in its mission, or indeed in the whole draft Act. Of the major British daily newspapers, only the *Manchester Guardian* supported the delegation. (186) Next to Dilke its staunchest champion was W. T. Stead, the editor of the monthly *Review of Reviews*, who campaigned actively to have the discriminatory clauses removed from the constitution. (187)

The general apathy was due to the fact that public interest in Britain was concentrated on several other issues closer to home. These included German intervention in the deepening Balkan crisis, which threatened to precipitate a European war, the growing naval rivalry with Germany, the recent budget, serious friction between the Commons and Lords, and the worsening situation in Ireland. (188)

The presence of the official government delegation also helped draw attention away from Schreiner and his group. The government delegates received preferential treatment from the British government and press, and they provided Whitehall with convenient arguments for approving the draft constitution without unduly disturbing Britain's democratic conscience.

From the start the government delegates set out to discredit Schreiner and his co-delegates. Their line was that the Coloured and Native Delegation was doing more harm than good to blacks in South Africa, that it was not truly representative of the blacks, and that union would benefit, not harm, the blacks. (189)

The present agitation can have nothing but the worse possible effect. It will put the clock back and upset the very friendly liberal policy manifested by those states which do not adopt the Cape policy. I think Mr Schreiner's present mission is one of the most unkind things ever done to the natives. [Merriman]

I fear that the growing feeling in favour of liberality of treatment will be arrested because of the attempt, first, to obtain what is now impossible, namely equal rights, and secondly, because of the attempt to obtain interference from outside on a matter on which European people in South Africa are united. ... It is certain that if Mr Schreiner were to succeed, which I think is impossible, a strong reaction would set in against the continuance or extension of the liberal native policy in South Africa. [Sauer]

These arguments were largely successful, as people like Schreiner and Abdurahman conceded. The latter noted despairingly, 'Our own [i.e. Cape] delegates are our worst enemies.' (190)

The British government saw no necessity to change its policy of non-interference in the domestic affairs of the South African colonies or of disturbing what it perceived as a remarkable process of reconciliation between the Boer and Briton, with its concomitant advantages, political and economic, for the British Empire. Therefore, when the Colonial Secretary, Lord Crewe, met the government delegation in formal conference at the Foreign Office on 20 and 21 July, he made no attempt to induce them to accept any amendment to the colour bar provisions:

It is the fixed conviction of His Majesty's Government that these matters must be settled in South Africa itself. .... His Majesty's Government are prepared to see the Bill through as it stands both as to franchise and as to representation. (191)

He suggested only a few small amendments to the main body of the draft constitution. As none affected principles and most were purely verbal, they were accepted without objection. He did, however, inform the delegates that the Schedule, the section dealing with the protectorates, 'stood on a different footing' from the rest of the draft. He reiterated the view of the British government that as a specially obligated trustee of the people of Basutoland, Bechuanaland and Swaziland, who had come under British rule without being conquered, Britain could not hand over the trust without taking formal securities for its observance. Thus two main guarantees were insisted on for the protectorates: first, they would not be partitioned after their incorporation in the Union and secondly, they would receive the full protection of the Schedule when they were incorporated. These conditions caused some dissent among the official delegates, but they finally agreed to them. They also accepted smaller amendments to almost half the clauses of the Schedule.

The amendments in respect of the protectorates came as some consolation to the Coloured and Native Delegation and to sympathetic British groups, but their main point of concern, the colour bar in the constitution, remained. When Schreiner introduced Rubusana, Mapikela, Abdurahman, Lenders and Fredericks to Lord Crewe on the 22nd, the morning after he had finalised matters with the government delegates, he received them courteously and responded sympathetically to their representations, but he could not give them any assurance that the desired amendments would be made. (192)

On the same day, Lord Crewe moved the first reading of the South Africa Bill in the House of Lords. Five days later the Bill came up for the second reading in the Lords. The only debate on the draft constitution in the Lords took place on this occasion. After a further interval of a week, the Bill passed the third reading without further discussion and without any amendments having been pressed to a division. (193)

When the debate took place in the House of Lords on 27 July, all the South African delegates were in attendance. Exercising their right as Privy Councillors, De Villiers, Botha, Merriman and Moor sat in the chamber of the House, while the other government delegates looked on from the Official Gallery. Above, seated in the Strangers' Gallery, were Schreiner, Abdurahman, Gandhi, Jabavu 'sitting eagerly . . . with his head on the rails, watching with every nerve astrain the discussion of his people's rights' (194) and the other African and coloured delegates.

Only seven peers participated in the debate in the Lords, and of these, six (including Lord Crewe, Lord Northcote, Lord Curzon, the Marquis of Lansdowne and the Archbishop of Canterbury) were in favour of the Bill's being accepted without amendments. The Archbishop said in his speech that it was justifiable to impose on the black people in South Africa restrictions and limitations that 'correspond with those which we impose on our children', because the overwhelming majority of the South African population would for generations to come be quite unfit to share equal citizenship with whites. Dr Abdurahman especially singled out the Archbishop's speech as 'the most hypocritical piece of humbug I ever listened to'. (195) The only member of the House of Lords to speak against the Bill was Lord Courtney. (196)

In the time that the South Africa Bill was before the British parliament, the Coloured and Native Delegation and its British friends continued its fight, even though it was apparent that the Bill would be passed without the desired alterations.

On 27 July Schreiner, Abdurahman, Jabavu and Rubusana addressed a public breakfast organised by the Anti-Slavery and Aborigines Protection Society in honour of the delegates. In his speech, Jabavu said whites had not realised the depth and strength of feeling existing amongst Africans on the unification issue. He reflected sadly on his old South Africa Party political associates and recalled that only a few years ago the Afrikaner Bond had asked him to stand for parliament, but now this privilege was to be withdrawn. And on top of it all, Mr Merriman and Mr Sauer had also changed their views. Jabavu declared that the parting of the ways between the white and black races had now been reached. (197)

Speaking on the same occasion, Schreiner welcomed the amendments to the Schedule, but he said he still sought additional guarantees. He felt that the incorporation of the protectorates should be delayed and should take place only with the consent of the inhabitants. As a matter of course, he criticised the draft constitution which was 'rotten and unjust to the natives' and called on the Imperial parliament not to abdicate its responsibility to them. (198)

Among those present at this function were Alfred Mangena, who had been delegated by the Transvaal Native Congress to act on its behalf in Britain, and John Dube. (199)

Schreiner's speech was partly a reiteration of the views expressed in a long, column-length letter published in *The Times* that same morning. In the letter, Schreiner stated that within a few days the British parliament would be asked to enact the draft constitution, a measure of vast importance to the whole Empire. While not underrating the work of the National Convention and the colonial parliaments, he asked that the constitution should not be regarded as just a South African matter, and summarily passed. British principles were at stake—the majority of the population were being discriminated against 'solely on the grounds of prejudice'—and it was the duty of the British parliament to correct the violation of these principles. Schreiner listed four issues he wished to see resolved for the better: the limited guarantees for Africans in the Letters Patent of the ex-republics should be maintained and preserved under instructions to the Governor-General of South Africa; the 'European descent' clauses should be removed; the clause whereby Cape Africans could be disenfranchised, a provision that would be unique in British parliamentary history, should be refused; and guarantees for the protectorates should be improved. He concluded by saying that such moderate amendments would not 'wreck' union, but 'an easy downward step now taken may only be retraced, as it some day assuredly must be, with infinite labour, and at what cost?' (200)

On the following day, 28 July, *The Times* printed a letter from Dr Abdurahman. He called for the repeal of the colour clauses in sections 25, 35 and 44, and quoted speeches from Botha, Smuts and Krause in the Transvaal to show that South African statesmen were intent on depriving blacks in the Cape of existing political rights. (201) Of three letters from Abdurahman, this was the only one *The Times* actually published. The first letter, it will be recalled, was written on 19 May and the second, which suffered the same fate as the first, on 10 July. To ensure that Abdurahman's arguments were noted the delegation prepared printed copies of the first two letters for private circulation. Coincidentally they were sent out, under the signature of W. P. Schreiner, on the same day that *The Times* eventually published Abdurahman's views. (202) Like the delegation's 'Appeal' of 21 July, the circular of the 28th was sent to the more than one thousand members of the Commons and Lords. (203) In addition to Dr Abdurahman's printed letters, the document contained letters from Sir Harry Johnston and Sir Charles Bruce, which had appeared in *The Times*, and an article from the *Manchester Guardian* by J. A. Hobson. (204) Also on 28 July the *Morning Post* quoted Dr Rubusana as saying that South Africa's hope lay in levelling up to the Cape's standards, not levelling down to those of the north. (205)

On 29 July Ramsay MacDonald organised a meeting of Liberal and Labour members of the House of Commons to meet the delegates. The MPs agreed to move amendments when the Bill came before the Commons. They decided to call for the elimination of the 'European descent' qualification, suggesting that it be made applicable to the Transvaal and the Orange River Colony only, and to demand the deletion of the provision allowing a two-thirds majority of the union parliament to abolish the Cape franchise. (206) The following morning the delegates had another exchange with 'non-conformist' MPs at a private meeting held under the auspices of the London Missionary Society. (207)

In August, as the focus shifted to the impending debate in the House of Commons after the South Africa Bill had passed through the Lords, the delegates remained in touch with supporters like Dilke (208) and Keir Hardie (209), and continued to address themselves to MPs, even though they had already been warned by Dilke that no amendments would succeed in the Commons, and therefore 'what we move (if anything) depends on how it looks'. (210) The delegates received a boost when the Labour Party decided officially on 5 August to move amendments against colour restrictions in the South Africa Bill. (211) They had further rounds of meetings with MPs on 10 (212) and 11 August. (213)

Members of the black delegation also made several further representations to the Colonial Office in August. On the 6th, Jabavu and Daniel Dwanya, neither of whom had signed the 'Appeal' or accompanied Schreiner, Rubusana, Mapikela and the APO delegates to see Lord Crewe the previous month, were granted an interview with him at Schreiner's behest. (214) On 11 August, the delegation's secretary, Matt J. Fredericks, wrote to Lord Crewe bringing to his attention communications it had received from blacks in the Orange River Colony, and asking that existing safeguards in the ex-republics whereby Royal assent was needed for legislation directly applicable to blacks should be inserted in the new constitution. (215) Schreiner followed up the matter in another communication to the Colonial Office. (216)

Lord Crewe also received a separate representation from the Natal Native Congress, which was not officially represented in the black delegation at this time. In a brief telegram, the NNC requested him to do his utmost to safeguard Africans in Natal under union and expressed its full confidence in the British government. (217)

The debate on South African union in the House of Commons

took place on 16 and 19 August. When it started the House had before it a petition from the Coloured and Native Delegation. The petition repeated the whole range of grievances which had been expressed so often in numerous representations and meetings in the months since the release of the draft constitution in February:

The Bill now before the Parliament of Great Britain and Ireland for the purpose of enacting a Constitution to unite the self-governing British Colonies of South Africa into a legislative union under the Crown would for the first time in the history of the legislation of that Parliament by virtue of the phrase 'of European descent' . . . create a political discrimination against non-European subjects of His Majesty, and thus introduce for the first time since the establishment of representative institutions in the year 1852 into the Colony of the Cape of Good Hope a colour line in respect of political rights and privileges.

Your Petitioners are deeply disappointed at the non-extension of political and civil rights and privileges to the coloured people and the natives in the Transvaal and the Orange River Colony.

Your Petitioners feel aggrieved that solely on account of differences in race or colour it is contemplated by the proposed Constitution to deprive the coloured and native inhabitants of the colony of the Cape of Good Hope of their existing political rights and privileges. Your Petitioners fear that the franchise rights of the coloured people and natives of the Cape Colony are not adequately protected under the provisions of the proposed Constitution, but are indeed threatened by the provisions of Clause 35.

Your Petitioners apprehend that by the racial discrimination proposed in the aforesaid Bill as regards the qualification of members of the Union Parliament, the prejudice already existing in the Transvaal, the Orange River Colony and Natal, will be accentuated and increased; that the status of the coloured people and natives will be lowered, and that an injustice will be done to those who are the majority of the people in British South Africa, who have in the past shown their unswerving loyalty to the Crown, their attachment to British institutions, their submission to the laws of the land, and their capacity for exercising full civil and political rights. (218)

The petitioners said they fully approved of the principle of union, but 'the only practical and efficient means whereby fair and just administration and legislation can be attained, peace, harmony and contentment secured, is by granting equal political rights to qualified men irrespective of race, colour, or creed'. Therefore, they asked the House of Commons to make such amendments as would protect the existing rights held by African and coloured people, and to ensure that these rights were permanently safeguarded.

The petition ended with the request that Schreiner or one of the other delegates should be allowed to speak at the Bar of the House of Commons. The request was refused on the grounds that only the Lords Mayor of London and Dublin could be heard at the Bar on petition. (219)

All that now remained was for the members of the delegation to sit through the debates as the South Africa Bill passed through the House of Commons unamended. Even at this late stage the delegates did not accept the inevitable outcome lying down. When the Under-Secretary of State for the Colonies, supported by the Prime Minister, said in the debate on 16 August that if the union parliament decided to alter the Cape franchise by a two-thirds majority of both Houses sitting together, the measure would have to be reserved for the signification of His Majesty's pleasure, Schreiner wrote to *The Times* and the *Morning Post* pointing out that the statement gave rise to an erroneous impression. He said people were wrong in thinking the Crown would be in a position to prevent further and future injustice in South Africa after union. (220)

As the South Africa Bill came up for the third and final reading in the House of Commons on 19 August, John Tengo Jabavu made a last unusual appeal in *The Times*. In a letter to the newspaper on that day, he said he accepted that the colour bar would be implemented in South Africa, but he did not want it officially to 'sully' British statutes. Like Pontius Pilate, Britain should wash its hands of the matter by erasing colour clauses at present in the Bill but, at the same time, it should leave the way open for the South African parliament to reintroduce the clauses if it chose to do so. If Britain passed the constitution in its present form it would legitimise colour discrimination. 'What the Imperial Parliament is being asked to sanction will be used as a precedent in future legislation against all native advance, and the Parliament will be quoted for all time as having put its seal on discrimination.' (221)

The delegation failed to have the offending clauses in the constitution amended. The House of Commons passed the South Africa Bill on 19 August without a division. However, in moving the third reading of the Bill, Liberal Prime Minister Asquith said that although the Bill had been passed without amendment it would be totally false to say that members of the House wholeheartedly supported all the provisions. On the contrary, there was an 'absolute unanimity of opinion in the way of regret' that some of the clauses which dealt with the treatment of blacks and the access of

blacks to the legislature had been inserted. (222)
    Mr Asquith said further:

I wish before this Bill leaves the Imperial Parliament to make it perfectly clear
that we here have exercised, and I think wisely and legitimately exercised, not
only restraint of expression, but reserve of judgement in regard to matters of
this kind, simply because we desire this great experiment of the establishment
of complete self-government in South Africa to start on the lines and in
accordance with the ideas which our fellow citizens there have deliberately
and after long consideration come to. ... It is perfectly true, the Imperial
Parliament cannot divest itself of responsibility in the matters ... but if we
have yielded ... it has been because we have thought it undesirable at this
stage to put forward anything that would be an obstacle to the successful
working of the future. ... Speaking for myself and the Government, I venture
to express not only the hope but the expectation ... that the views which
have been so strongly given utterance to here will be sympathetically considered by our fellow citizens there. For my part I think, as I have said
throughout, that it would be far better that any relaxation of what many of
us, almost all of us, regard as unnecessary restrictions from the electoral
rights or rights of eligibility of our fellow subjects, should be carried out
spontaneously, and on the initiative of the South African Parliament, rather
than they should appear to be forced upon them by the Imperial Parliament
here. While we part from this measure without any ... Amendment, ... I
am sure our fellow subjects will not take it in bad part if we respectfully and
very earnestly beg them at the same time that they, in the exercise of their
undoubted and unfettered freedom, should find it possible sooner or later,
and sooner rather than later, to modify the provisions.

This was the line of argument that had generally been followed in
the debates. While most speakers expressed themselves against the
principle of the colour bar, they did not wish to endanger union or
retard the envisaged future spread of Cape liberality by interfering
in the domestic affairs of the South African colonies.

    The South Africa Bill nevertheless had a rougher passage in the
Commons than it had had in the Lords, where only Lord Courtney
had opposed it. A number of speakers in the Commons opposed
the constitutional colour bar and called for amendments. They
included Dilke, Keir Hardie and Ramsay MacDonald, trusted
friends of the black delegation, and other Liberal and Labour
members such as E. J. Griffiths, A. Lupton, G. H. Roberts, W. P.
Byles, H. F. Luttrell, C. Duncan, G. N. Barnes, R. W. Essex and B.
Greenwood. However, these MPs formed only a small minority.
Their opposition was overcome without much difficulty. Both the
Government and Opposition front benches were basically agreed

on the matter. (223)

Meanwhile, the Colonial Office had also drafted Letters Patent for the creation of the office of Governor-General and Commander-in-Chief of the new union, as well as Royal Instructions to these two officers, (224) and the government delegates had in conjunction with Lord Crewe agreed to 31 May 1910 as the date for the inauguration of the union. (225) Thus when the British Parliament passed the South Africa Bill the way was finally cleared for the unification of South Africa.

# 10 South African union consummated

## African responses to the South Africa Act

The political excitement that had existed for months in South African politics over union subsided once the Imperial parliament had sanctioned the new South African constitution. Although still dissatisfied with the terms of union, Africans now resigned themselves to the inevitability of a new dispensation based on discriminatory principles, and to their powerlessness to alter the situation. Faced with the reality of union, the political élite now began to look to see how it could best protect African interests in the future.

This new resolve was well reflected in the *Imvo Zabantsundu*'s editorial response to the passing of the South Africa Act by the British Parliament:

The blow has fallen, and the British Government and the House of Commons have passed the Union Constitution Act without the amendments we had hoped for. . . .

The Native and Coloured people must now realise that an entirely new chapter in South African history is opening, in which they will have to depend on themselves and their South African European friends for the securing and maintenance of their civil and political rights. They must become united politically and, refusing to cling to any of the present political parties, must work for the creation of a new political party in the State which will unite the religious and moral forces—European and Native—of South Africa upon lines of righteous legislation, justice and fairplay, irrespective of race or colour.

The Natives—men, women and children—must bend their energies to the advancement of themselves in all that civilisation and true Christianity means, so that their claims to equality of treatment for all civilised British subjects may be irresistible. (1)

The *Naledi ea Lesotho* responded in a similar manner:

The present was the occasion when she [i.e. Britain] should have shown the Natives that she really bore the responsibility for them. But what has she done? She has thrown them overboard to trust to chance. Thenceforward they will be like orphans who have lost both parents and are left in the care of a relentless guardian whose guardianship extends only as far as they administer to his wants and no further. . . .

What remains now for us, and for every Native organ and every freedom-loving Native to do, is to work for the consolidation of all blacks into one whole irrespective of nationality or creed, for we have seen, that 'Union is strength'. (2)

After the failure of the Coloured and Native Delegation, and all the earlier protests, to have the draft constitution amended, it might have been expected that politically conscious Africans would be discouraged and deflated, but this was not the case. The fact that Africans had mobilised on an unprecedented scale to protest against the draft Act had instilled confidence into them.

'Had the natives remained silent and allowed the draft Act to be passed without them uttering their word of dissent,' the *Imvo* declared, then 'they would not have been worthy of their race, and deserved to be treated as children.' (3) But Africans felt they had done their utmost to protect their interests.

Far from returning home to a climate of defeatist apathy, the delegates were received with acclamation when they arrived back. They were specially welcomed at the docks, treated to banquets, praised in the African newspapers and thanked for their endeavours by appreciative audiences at report-back meetings.

When Schreiner, Abdurahman, Fredericks, Lenders, Rubusana, Mapikela and Dwanya arrived in Cape Town on 21 September they were welcomed by a 'Coloured Reception Committee' which included the remaining APO executive members and the Revd F. M. Gow, a leading member of the AME Church. In an address of welcome to the delegates, the Committee declared that although the mission was regarded as a failure in some quarters 'we feel that it has been a glorious success' that would inspire blacks to continue fighting until justice prevailed, as it one day surely would. Telegrams of appreciation from various centres were also read. (4)

Two days later the Committee organised a reception for over two hundred people in the Cape Town City Hall and the delegates were welcomed by an orchestra playing 'The Gladiator's Return' and presented with silverware gifts. The money for this welcome came from a reception fund initiated by the APO newspaper to which thousands of people throughout South Africa had subscribed. (5) Rubusana, Mapikela and Dwanya were also welcomed by members of the Cape Town African community at a meeting in

Ndabeni. (6) When Jabavu, who had remained behind in Britain on 'business matters', which included collecting funds, returned later he was given a similar reception. (8)

In the months after the delegates arrived back in South Africa more receptions and meetings were organised in the various colonies to honour the delegates and to hear about their activities in Britain. D. J. Lenders reported back in Kimberley; (9) Jabavu spoke at a meeting in Port Elizabeth on his way home to King William's Town; (10) Mapikela toured the Orange River Colony; (11) Dr Rubusana reported back in East London and then travelled to Bloemfontein, Thaba Nchu, the Witwatersrand and Kimberley for the same purpose; (12) the African women of King William's Town (December 1909) (13) and Queenstown (March 1910) (14) held banquets for the delegates; the APO convened another meeting in Cape Town publicly to honour W. P. Schreiner; (15) and, when Schreiner went to take leave of his Queenstown constituency in January 1910, the coloured and African people there presented him with an address of appreciation for his efforts in Britain at a meeting in his honour. (16)

By then Schreiner's reputation among blacks had come to acquire almost heroic proportions. His name was mentioned in the same breath as those of Glanville, Sharpe and Wilberforce, (17) and although he insisted that his co-delegates deserved an equal share of the acclaim, (18) they themselves singled out Schreiner for his sacrifice and work. Dr Abdurahman said every house should have in it a photograph of Schreiner next to that of the Queen. (19) Mapikela wrote that the Africans in the Orange River Colony wanted him to know that 'they shall never forget your name in their homes'. (20) Jabavu told Schreiner that no greater work had been done on behalf of the people of South Africa (21) and 'all the honours of the fight are yours'. (22) The *A.P.O.* carried a special Christmas message headed 'Forward!' from Schreiner (23) and both the APO paper and the *Imvo* published souvenir photographs of the Coloured and Native Delegation. (24)

This was hardly the response that a failed mission would have evoked. Clearly the politically conscious blacks in South Africa saw the delegation as a milestone in the history of black politics and regarded it as a successful demonstration of protest against union. This was also the feeling of the delegates. The line they took in the series of meetings after their return was that the mission had been a success because it raised the question of black political rights to a priority topic in the whole unification issue.

Instead of the matter being quietly glossed over in Britain, the activities of the delegates had led the Imperial government and parliament to register their disapproval of the colour discrimination in the new constitution, and this in turn had forced the South African government delegates to deny that they intended to restrict the rights of black people in the forthcoming union. The delegates argued that the considerable attention they had caused to be focused on the issue would help in the struggle for political equality that lay ahead in South Africa. (25)

### Attempts to consolidate the South African Native Convention
The most significant developments in African politics in the aftermath of the black delegation to Britain were the attempts by Rubusana, Mapikela and others to consolidate the South African Native Convention into a permanent national organisation. Hitherto scholars have failed to establish that the SANC actually functioned as an organisation, but there is definite proof that it did.

At the meeting in Bloemfontein of March 1909 the SANC had taken tentative steps to form itself into a permanent organisation by electing an executive 'to watch the draft Act, to promote organisation and to defend the interests of the Natives', and it subsequently had sent Rubusana, Mapikela and Dwanya as delegates to Britain with Schreiner. While in London, the delegates had had discussions with Pixley Ka Isaka Seme (and probably others like Alfred Mangena and Richard Msimang who were also studying abroad and had made contact with the delegation) about the formation of a national political organisation for Africans in South Africa. More than a quarter of a century later, at the time of Dr Rubusana's death, Mapikela declared that 'the conversations which took place then had reference to the starting of the great African National Congress'. (26)

After their return, Rubusana, the SANC President, and Mapikela, who had been the chief organiser of the meeting in Bloemfontein, were politically active on SANC business. They reported back as SANC delegates to meetings in the various colonies, made attempts to organise local and regional groups under the SANC, organised the second SANC annual congress, and made representations to the colonial governments and subsequently the Union government. The aim was for the SANC to open channels of communication with government and to represent the interests of the African out-group to the authorities.

Within a fortnight of Rubusana returning to the eastern Cape

he travelled to Bloemfontein, where on 11 October he and Mapikela interviewed the Governor and Prime Minister and requested
permission to hold a political meeting they had arranged. Prime
Minister Fischer was reluctant to accede to the request, as he regarded Rubusana as 'exactly the class of gentry that I would debar
from coming into this Colony to start agitations when our own natives do not require or do not understand what, under agitators,
they are made to demand', but he eventually did so because
Governor Goold-Adams was in favour. (27) The meeting was held
that same evening in the AME church hall. On this occasion,
Rubusana, who spoke for more than two hours, and Mapikela reported back in detail to the Orange River Colony Native Congress
about their visit to Britain. (28)

They then arranged a similar meeting in Thaba Nchu, where the
Becoana Mutual Improvement Society operated. (29) The President
of the BMIA, Joel Goronyane, it will be recalled, had chaired the
meeting in Bloemfontein, and Jeremiah Makgothi, another BMIA
member, had been elected as the SANC's General Secretary. The
BMIA had also seen to it that its views were forwarded to Schreiner
and Mapikela when the delegation was in London. (30)

After the Thaba Nchu meeting, Rubusana went on to the Transvaal where meetings had been arranged for him, (31) while Mapikela visited the various districts in the Orange River Colony explain-
ing the results of the mission to Britain and organising support on
a local basis for the Orange River Colony Native Congress and the
SANC, the related regional and national bodies. Among the places
Mapikela visited, in a heavy schedule that moved him to complain
to Schreiner that he had not had time to rest with his family since
his arrival, were Winburg, Kroonstad, Heilbron, Viljoensdrift,
Vrede, Parys, Bethlehem and Harrismith. (32) At well-attended
meetings he encouraged the local groups to submit statements to
the ORCNC on any matters which they wished to have raised. He
said these matters would then be discussed at the annual congress
of the ORCNC in January and probably also at the next SANC
meeting before being submitted to the government. (33)

When Rubusana returned to the Orange River Colony late in
November, he, John Mocher and Mapikela petitioned the government on behalf of the SANC and the ORCNC on the question of
compulsory passes for African women in municipal townships.
The petitioners said that the degrading regulations compelling
African women in the Orange River Colony to carry passes in
municipal areas constituted a long-standing and deep-rooted grie-

vance. They asked that, particularly in view of the approaching union, the government should abolish or suspend these regulations during the last session of parliament, which was then sitting. (34) After a trip to Kimberley, (35) Rubusana was back in Bloemfontein again in mid-December to make further representations with Mapikela on the matter of passes for women. (36)

The outcome of all these activities was that Jeremiah Makgothi, the Thaba Nchu-based SANC Assistant General Secretary, issued a notice in February 1910 convening the second annual congress of the South African Native Convention in Bloemfontein in March. The purpose of the meeting was for Africans to formulate and submit to the new union parliament their views on important matters which would be discussed by that body. (37) In this way they hoped to exercise an indirect influence on the legislative process.

The second annual congress of the South African Native Convention took place on 23 and 24 March and was attended by delegates from the Orange River Colony, the Transvaal, the Cape and Bechuanaland. No people from Natal were present. As the newspaper report of the meeting suggests, this could have been because of the Natal Government's proclamation in February 1910 prohibiting all chiefs and exempted Africans from attending political gatherings without the permission of the Secretary for Native Affairs. (39) This was a step the Natal authorities had long threatened to take. John Dube, the SANC Vice-president, could not attend the meeting as he was still abroad.

Newspaper reports of the meeting do not provide a complete list of the delegates, but it is clear that, as in the previous year, the overwhelming number of delegates were from the Orange River Colony. The only names mentioned from outside the ORC were Dr Rubusana, Chief Silas Molema from Bechuanaland, J. S. Noah of the Transvaal Native Union and Sol Plaatje 'representing Johannesburg and Pretoria'. The ORCNC was represented by familiar figures such as Mapikela, Peter Phatlane, John Mocher, J. S. Mocher and J. B. Twayi, while the BMIA contingent included Jeremiah Makgothi and the Revd Gabashane. N. Daly of the APO branch in the ORC once again attended. (41)

The conference was opened for the second time by Dewdney Drew. He had stepped into the breach at the last moment after both Sir John Fraser and A. G. Barlow, also a member of the Legislative Assembly, had declined invitations to open the proceedings. (42) In his speech Drew said it might be well to review the progress of the 'cause' since the SANC last met. The most important event in that time had been the passing of the South Africa Act. He felt the Act would benefit Africans. In justifying this statement, Drew repeated many of his arguments of the previous year.

First, the Cape franchise had been secured and this meant that 'the natives in the other colonies were going to get representatives in the Assembly, because the Cape natives would only vote for men who would espouse the native cause throughout South Africa'. Secondly, the four native senators, if they were capable, should do much to protect Africans and bring to light local and provincial irregularities. A question he would ask if he were a senator, for example, was why there were no Natal delegates at the meeting. Drew supposed that it was because some officials were making threats which were quite *ultra vires*. He believed 'tyranny of that sort' would not last long after being exposed in a national parliament. A third factor in the Act's favour was the protection given to the protectorates by the Schedule. (43)

With the African vote untouched in the Cape and constitutional government taking root in the protectorates, Drew declared that the unenfranchised Africans in the other colonies were bound to find themselves in a better position under union. And another development which had set the African cause forward appreciably was the Coloured and Native Delegation, which had educated public opinion in Britain. (44) But there had been setbacks in the African cause in the past year, the chief one being the colour bar in the constitution. He said the National Convention had been 'deliberately looking for trouble' when it decided on a constitutional colour bar. He also singled out the continued unsatisfactory treatment of Africans in the ORC, particularly the law compelling African women in municipal areas to carry passes. (45) He ended his speech by saying Africans nevertheless were advancing in numbers, education and industrial capacity and he hoped their just demand for equal rights for all civilised men would be listened to with increasing favour in the new union parliament. (46)

The resolutions adopted this time around by the SANC reflected the change in emphasis in the approach of African political organisations after the passing of the South Africa Act. Instead of making lofty but futile moral statements on matters such as the franchise, the SANC concentrated on issues which affected the everyday welfare of Africans. It called for the statutory control of charges between attorneys and their clients, improvements in railway facilities, the easing of pass laws, the repeal of laws preventing

Africans in the ORC from buying land, and it laid down guidelines for a more just labour dispensation. The resolutions were sent to the government when the first session of the South African Parliament assembled in October 1910. (47)

On the level of national politics, the SANC sent a telegram to Lord Crewe informing him that they desired the appointment of Sir Bisset Berry (Cape), Dewdney Drew (Orange River Colony), William Hosken (Transvaal) and Sir David Hunter (Natal) as the native senators. (48) Crewe referred the telegram to the Officer administering the Cape who informed Rubusana that the appointments would be made on the recommendation of the first Union Ministry. (49)

The conference re-elected Dr Rubusana and John Dube as President and Vice-president. The rest of the new executive consisted of Moses Masisi (Treasurer) and Jeremiah Makgothi (Secretary), both of the BMIA, (50) and Sol Plaatje (Assistant Secretary). (51)

After the conference, Plaatje led a deputation to the Transvaal Prime Minister, Louis Botha, personally to hand him a copy of a SANC resolution thanking Botha for repatriating the Chinese laboureres who had been imported to work on the Transvaal mines. At the interview with Botha Plaatje pointed out that the repatriation of the Chinese had increased the availability of money to Africans. (52)

Rubusana did not accompany the deputation to Pretoria. He went straight from Bloemfontein to Port Elizabeth where he attended the APO annual conference, which was held there at the beginning of April. He was given a special welcome, and in turn conveyed the greetings of the SANC, saying that there should be more co-operation between the coloured and African people. His views were endorsed by Dr Abdurahman in a vote of thanks. When the conference later discussed the matter of closer co-operation with Africans, the idea received much support. (53)

During his visit to Port Elizabeth, Dr Rubusana was also involved in discussions with other leading Africans such as Messrs Mqhayi, Bopi, Mesach Pelem and W. W. Skweyiya of Cape Town about the possibility of founding another African newspaper, but nothing came of the idea. (54)

It is clear that from September 1909 strenuous attempts were made, particularly by Dr Rubusana, to organise and unite politically conscious Africans around the country in the face of impending union. The SANC was meant to play an important part in these plans. In attempting to get the local associations to amalga-

mate and then affiliate to the SANC, Sol Plaatje explained to two
meetings in Pretoria in April 1910 that the aim of the SANC was
'to combine all African organisations with a view to co-operation
with the officials who will be entrusted with the administration of
native affairs under the Union government'. (55) Clearly, therefore, the SANC was intended to be a permanent organisation to
represent Africans on a national basis under union; it was not
merely, as has been claimed, (56) an *ad hoc* body whose only
function had been to co-ordinate African opinion on the draft
South Africa Act in 1909. As this and the ensuing sections show,
the SANC went some way towards realising its aims.

### The inauguration of the Union of South Africa

On the broader political front, in the meantime, the British government had in December 1909 appointed a junior cabinet minister,
Lord Gladstone, as the first Governor-General of South Africa.
Gladstone, the son of a former British Prime Minister, was not in
the mould of a strong pro-consul like Milner, but this was pre-
cisely the reason why he was appointed, since basically the Governor-General was to have the constitutional function of assenting to
the decisions of the South African ministry. The time had now
passed when British colonial administrators could dictate to South
African statesmen. (57)

Although Africans would have preferred a familiar figure like
the respected Governor of Natal, Sir Mathew Nathan (58), or Lord
Selborne (59) to have filled the post, Gladstone's appointment
met with general approval. Referring to his political background,
the *Imvo Zabantsundu* expressed joy that 'a stalwart from liberal
stock' had been appointed, adding that he would have a heavy
responsibility towards the protectorates. (60) The *Ilanga lase Natal*
said it realised that the times had changed and that the Governor-
General would be working under difficult circumstances, but it
hoped Gladstone would be 'an up-to-date Sir George Grey' who
would do his best to repair the wrongs of the past. (61)

As the date for union approached, South African politics was
dominated by the questions of who would become first Prime
Minister, what the composition of his cabinet would be and on
what lines the first general election would be contested. The obvious contenders for the post of Prime Minister were John X.
Merriman of the Cape and Louis Botha of the Transvaal. Ex-
president Steyn of the Orange River Colony would normally also
have been a strong contender, but his deteriorating health forced

him out of the running. (62)

Africans were in no doubt as to which of the two candidates they favoured. For them there was no question but that Merriman was a better choice than Botha. Merriman was not only the Prime Minister of the Cape with its accomodatory political system, but he also had a good personal record on the question of African political rights. Botha on the other hand had been brought up in the tradition of republican white exclusivism. As the *Izwi Labantu*, the *Ilanga lase Natal*, the Coloured and Native Delegation and other antagonists of Botha had pointed out in the past, he had advocated the breaking up of African reserves for labour supplies and predicted the further restriction of African political rights after union. (63) The *Imvo Zabantsundu* summed up the feelings of most Africans on the matter when it declared:

Bitter indeed would the disappointment and dark and cheerless the prospect of Union to the millions of South African Natives, if at its beginning they did not have Mr Merriman as Prime Minister to inaugurate native administration on an enlightened and sympathetic basis such as has been associated with the Cape. (64)

But once again the tide of events moved against African public opinon. By the time Gladstone arrived in South Africa on 17 May 1910 Botha had become the overwhelming favourite to become Prime Minister. After discussions lasting several days with Lord Selborne and cabinet ministers from the various colonies, on 22 May Gladstone asked Botha to form the first union government. (65)

Africans were not happy with the news. The *Imvo* described Botha's appointment as a 'lamentable' beginning to union. (66) Immediately on hearing of it, John Tengo Jabavu wrote to his old political champion Merriman and said he had 'never felt so disappointed in politics' than when he read that Merriman had not been asked to assume office. (67) Merriman also received letters from the annual conference of the Ethiopian Church, meeting at Lindley in the Orange River Colony, which expressed its appreciation for his past services on behalf of Africans and said his non-appointment as Prime Minister was a 'serious blow' and a 'puzzle story', (68) and from John Alfred Sishuba who wrote that 'the natives are awaiting the union with a great deal of anxiety' and that he hoped Merriman would continue to exert his influence in the government or parliament. (69)

Far from causing offence, however, Botha's first acts as Prime Minister in respect of 'native affairs' met with approval from Africans, and raised hopes that their overall position would be improved under union. For example, under behind-the-scenes pressure, Botha appointed Henry Burton, an ex-Cabinet Minister in the Cape parliament as his Minister of Native Affairs. (70)

Burton was a strong supporter of the non-racial Cape system and had privately been 'ill at ease' about the colour bar which he regarded as a 'dreadful' and 'unnecessary' blot on the constitution. (71) In acknowledging the congratulations of his African constituents in Burgersdorp, Burton said, 'I hope I may be able to do some good.' (72) After his appointment, he continued to emphasise his good intentions as Minister of Native Affairs. During a visit to Dube's Ohlange Institute in Natal, he told the students:

I know you are anxious as to what the Union government is going to do with you. I want you to know that I represent the government, that I am in charge of all the Native work in South Africa. You need not be afraid that we shall oppress you; we shall do what we can to improve your conditions; we sympathise with you. (73)

Africans were pleased with Burton's appointment and hopes were now high that the administration of native affairs under union would be launched on the basis of the more accomodatory Cape model instead of those of the northern colonies. The appointment of another top Cape Native Affairs Department official, Edward Dower, as Secretary for Native Affairs in the union administration seemed to confirm this view. (74) African newspapers described the appointments of Burton and Dower as reassuring and favourable auguries for the position of Africans under union. (75)

Africans were also encouraged by the inclusion of three other Cape politicians–D. P. de Villiers Graaff (Minister of Public Works), J. W. Sauer (Minister of Railways and Harbours) and F. S. Malan (Minister of Education)–in the cabinet. The *Imvo Zabantsundu* was particularly pleased about the appointment of Sauer, 'Mr Merriman's *alter ego*' and another of Jabavu's long-standing political favourites. (76) Jabavu and other supporters of the South African Native College Scheme also saw F. S. Malan's appointment to the Education portfolio as a chance for the Scheme to be pushed through under the supervision of a minister who was an acknowledged supporter. (77)

The rest of the first Union of South Africa cabinet were J. C. Smuts, Minister of the Interior, Minister of Mines, and Minister of Defence; J. B. M. Hertzog, Minister of Justice; H. C. Hull, Minister of Finance; A. Fischer, Minister of Lands; F. R. Moor, Minister of Commerce and Industries. (78) Jabavu's *Imvo* regarded the Botha ministry on the whole as sound and better than any that could be raised by opponents of the governing parties, although it still continued to lament Merriman's non-appointment as Prime Minister. (79)

Almost the first act of the new ministry—on the day union was inaugurated on 31 May—was to authorise the release of the Zulu Paramount Chief Dinizulu from jail in Natal, where he was serving a sentence for complicity in the 1906 Bambata rebellion. (80) The release of Dinizulu, personally instigated by the Prime Minister, an old ally of the Zulu Paramount from the days of the South African Republic, received widespread approval amongst Africans and again raised hopes about their position in the new dispensation. John L. Dube, who had close connections with the Zulu Royal House, greeted the news of Dinizulu's release with delight from the United States, where he had been since his visit to Britain. (81) The *Ilanga lase Natal* (82) and white friends of Dinizulu such as Harriette Colenso (83) and W. P. Schreiner, (84) whose defence of Dinizulu had caused him to resign from the National Convention, also greeted the news with approval. In the Cape, the *Imvo Zaban-tsundu* commented that Dinizulu's release did the government great credit in the eyes not only of the African people, but of the world. (85) And indeed it did. The British government greeted the news with 'much satisfaction' (86) and the Anti-Slavery and Aborigines Protection Society (87) and other humanitarian bodies (88) wrote letters of appreciation to Botha.

The conditions of his release prohibited Dinizulu from returning to Natal or Zululand, but he was given a farm bought by the government at Middelburg in the Transvaal, and the pension of £500 per year formerly paid to him by the Natal government was restored. Several of his followers were allowed to live with him and the government erected suitable new buildings for his use and provided him with stock and farm implements. (89) Considering the position of prominence occupied by Dinizulu in African society by virtue of his paramountcy of the important Zulu people his release by the new government had an important psychological effect at an important time.

The inauguration of the Union of South Africa was to have been marked with pomp and jubilation but, owing to the death of King Edward VII on 6 May, there was a minimum of ceremony and festivity. The main ceremony was the swearing in of the Executive (Governor-General and Cabinet) and Judiciary in Pretoria. The administrators also officially assumed office in the provincial capitals and on a local level commemorative ceremonies took place. (90)

No Africans were included in the official national ceremonies. Locally, they either remained quietly aloof or, especially in the case of school-children, attended the ceremonies as a matter of formality. There was no orchestrated campaign of boycott or protest against the proceedings. The traditional bulk of the African population were hardly touched by Union Day, and were generally indifferent to the whole transition as it had no immediate effect on them. (91)

There was a more negative response from the coloured people. The APO decided to boycott any festivities and treated 31 May as a day of humiliation and prayer. (92) Dr Abdurahman said, 'No coloured man can feel happy; no coloured man, I hope, will sing "God save the King" on that day. I know I won't.' (93)

Although most politically conscious Africans shared this disquiet, and some announced that they would have nothing to do with the 'jollification', (94) Africans generally took up a less aggressive position towards Union Day. Enoch Mamba declared in the Transkeian Territories General Council that although Africans had made an unsuccessful appeal to the Crown to have the constitution changed 'their ardour was not dampened and [they] would like to join in the general rejoicings on this day'. (95) The *Imvo Zabantsundu* identified itself completely with the advice given to blacks on the matter by W. P. Schreiner at the request of the coloured people of Kimberley: (96)

As to the actual doings on May 31, I think that freedom of action according to sincere feeling should be left within the limits of the law and propriety to each individual. Those who feel that they can honestly rejoice should not be obliged insincerely to repress their sentiments. But I think that most Coloured people throughout the Colony will realise that the day is great and solemn, and will incline to possess their souls in patience. Many will be greatly helped to gain or maintain a spirit of faith and confidence in their future by treating that day as one for prayer and religious observation. Yet no attempt should be made to lay down a rule for all; let each follow the natural guidance of his views, and do within these limits what he sees to be right; neither pretending to be merry when he feels serious, nor assuming a sad demeanour when really he may have firm confidence in a bright future. (97)

Schreiner also said the discriminatory terms of union had given rise to conflicting feelings in many worthy and loyal citizens who were reluctant wholly to sever themselves from celebrating the great event, but who could not accept the status that had been accorded to blacks. He sympathised with them. He said, however, that blacks should be careful not to do anything ill-conceived that would increase the difficulties of those who were fighting for the maintenance and advancement of Cape principles. He recommended, particularly, that blacks should welcome the Prince of Wales who was to be the King's representative at the ceremonies.

Like the *Imvo*, the *Ilanga lase Natal* also made no objection to Africans participating in union ceremonies, but the newspaper criticised distinctions that were being drawn between black and white school children in Durban in the distribution of commemorative Union Memorial Medals. (98)

Several African groups sent messages of welcome to the new Governor-General. These included the Orange River Colony Native Congress, (99) the Transvaal Native Organisation, (100) the association representing the Mfengu on the Diamond Fields (101) and the Ethiopian Church. (102) The address from the latter body was overtly political:

We pray that your Excellency's interpretation of the Union Act in reference to the natives of South Africa may be a true, honest and liberal one; that your Excellency and his Council will show themselves strong and upright guardians of our people, especially in those provinces where we are taxed and yet have no representation in Parliament, and where laws which deal with us alone are passed by those who are not aware how they are pinching us—for, Your Excellency, the wearer of a shoe alone knows where it pinches. Such are many of the laws. ... the Pass laws which are even extended to women and girls of 16 years, Squatters and Location laws which keep us like fugitives and outcasts wandering from place to place; as well as the laws preventing us from purchasing land. (103)

Two of the signatories to the address were the Moderator of the Ethiopian Church, I. G. Sishuba, like his namesake, John Alfred Sishuba, from the Queenstown district and active in politics, and its Secretary, H. R. Ngcayiya, who was connected with the Orange River Colony and Transvaal Native Congresses, and subsequently also was to become active in the South African Native National Congress. Because of the political content of the message, the Church had difficulty getting it accepted for presentation to the Governor-General. (104)

The address from the Transvaal Native Organisation was the first by that body to the authorities. The TNO was an amalgamation of the most important Transvaal African organisations: the Transvaal Native Congress, the Transvaal Basotho Committee, the Transvaal Native Union, the 'Transvaal L. B. Committee' (prob-

ably the *Iliso Lomzi* of Edward Tsewu), 'The Vigilance, Pretoria'
and the African National Political Union. (105) It had come into
existence in May 1910, and its formation appears to have been inspired by the South African Native Convention. A report in the
*Pretoria News* early in April stated that Sol Plaatje, the SANC
Assistant Secretary, had informed meetings of the last two of the
above-mentioned affiliates that it was the aim of the SANC to
combine all African organisations, and that they had agreed in
principle to amalgamate and affiliate to the Convention. (106) The
first Chairman of the TNO was S. M. Makgatho, the President of
the African National Political Union since its formation in 1906.
The long-serving Transvaal Native Congress Secretary, Jesse Makhothe, became Secretary. (107) The Transvaal's Secretary of Native
Affairs said the TNO represented 'a considerable section of the
native population principally in Johannesburg and Pretoria'. (108)

The SANC itself also took further action at this time. A few
days after union, Dr Rubusana sent Louis Botha a letter of congratulation on behalf of the SANC, which, he said, represented
'the educated and leading natives' in South Africa, and informed
the Prime Minister that it was

... the earnest prayer and wish of the natives of this country that you and
your government may be wisely guided in the discharge of your onerous
duties of the State—by Him from which all true wisdom proceeds—so that you
may be able to govern the country in a way that will give some measure of
satisfaction to all alike without distinction of colour, class or creed, and thus
strive—in the treatment of natives especially—to maintain that righteousness
alone which exalteth a nation. (109)

## The first South African general election

After the inauguration of the Union attention turned towards the
September general election for the House of Assembly and the
Provincial Councils. The Executive and Judiciary had come into
being, but there still was no Legislature. Union would be properly
consummated only after the country had its own parliament.

The elections were fought between the governing parties in the
various colonies, a coalition loosely termed the Nationalists, who
supported the Botha administration, the Unionist Party, a coalition of the pro-British opposition parties under Dr Jameson, and
the South African Labour Party. There were also many Independent candidates standing. (110)

The so-called 'native question' was not an election issue. In his
election manifesto, released in Pretoria on 14 June, Botha stated

that one of the government's principles was 'the placing of the Native question above party politics, and the fair and sympathetic treatment of the coloured races in a broad and liberal treatment'. (111) He said the aim was to improve the conditions of Africans through a fair, non-party policy 'under the strong arm of protection'. (112)

The Unionists propagated 'a Native policy, admitting of the treatment of questions relating to Natives, in accordance with the degree of civilisation attained by them, and with the different and local conditions under which they live and work'. (113)

Neither of these election pledges indicated a definite intent on the part of the two major parties to pursue actively a new, more sympathetic line in South African 'native policy'. Although, with an eye on the black vote in the Cape, the 'native policy' sections were couched in vague and comforting language, both manifestos implicitly witnessed to the conceptions of an exclusive white nation held by most South African politicians and voters.

The Labour Party traded in no such ambiguities. Its manifesto advocated a hard line towards blacks: the African franchise should not be extended. 'Kafirs' should be segregated politically into a separate Advisory Council and territorially into reserves; and they should be prohibited from occupying or owning land in 'white' areas. (114)

A body of opinion headed by people like Rubusana (115) and A. K. Soga (116) believed that Cape Africans should depart from the old pattern of voting along party lines and back candidates who supported the 'native interest', regardless of party affiliation, but the black political élite in the Cape was again split along party lines.

John Tengo Jabavu now carried the election banner for the Botha government with as much uncritical gusto as he had done for the South African party. (117) His fierce disdain for the Cape Unionists reached a new intensity because Jameson had undermined Merriman's chances for the premiership by giving his support to Botha. Now, charged Jabavu, Jameson and his followers had raised the 'racial spectre' of anti-English 'Hertzogism', a word that would never be heard again after the election, and were opposing Botha. What kind of logic was that, Jabavu asked. (118) He had wanted the liberal Merriman as Prime Minister, but failing this he was convinced that Botha's 'best-man' government and 'fresh-start' policy, as exemplified in African affairs by the release of Dinizulu, the appointment of Burton and Dower to head the

Native Affairs Department and the Botha election pledge for a fair and liberal 'native policy', was infinitely better than any alternative offered by the bankrupt Unionists. (119) 'One swallow does not make a summer' was Jabavu's retort to Unionist reports of anti-African speeches by government members, and he countered by pointing to similar statements by Unionist leaders such as Sir George Farrar, and by arguing that the Unionists had no leg to stand on because they had supported a northerner as Prime Minister against a great liberal Cape statesman. He said Unionists like William Hosken in the Transvaal had exposed themselves by adopting a liberal stance towards African affairs on the grounds that any other policy might lose the Cape Unionists as many as sixteen seats. This was a typically Unionist approach, based on expediency rather than principle. (120)

Jabavu showed a particular interest in the election in Queenstown, one of only two frontier constituencies in the eastern Cape which were being contested by both the Nationalists and the Unionists. He gave his full support to Thomas Searle, who was standing as a Nationalist against the veteran Progressive politician, Sir Bisset Berry. He not only issued a special twenty-point call to the Queenstown African voters (121) and placed a huge advertisement supporting Searle's candidature in the *Imvo*, (122) but he also campaigned actively on Searle's behalf in the constituency. (123) The focus of his attention was the 360 Mfengu voters in the Kamastone location. They comprised about seventy-five per cent of the African vote in the constituency. (124) The two new South African cabinet ministers, Burton and Sauer, also took part in the campaign to have Searle elected. (125)

In contrast the newspaper of Dr Abdurahman's APO was outspoken in its support of the Unionists, pungently reflected in the tags used by the newspaper to describe candidates opposing Unionists: 'oft-rejected' Liberman, 'cynic' Sauer, 'fitful' Merriman, 'ex-Meat King' Graaff, 'Socialist' Noon, Beck the candidate famous for 'ill-written coloured leaflets' and 'wind-bag' O'Reilly. (126) The APO argued with passion that the Unionists were the only answer for the black people. (127) The two newspapers took turns in criticising the other side's leader. (128) Here were blacks, who a year earlier had been totally united in their actions against the terms of union, squabbling among themselves about the merits of the white politicians who meanwhile were generally in agreement about the union.

A. K. Soga, the former editor of the now extinct *Izwi Labantu* newspaper, wrote a long letter to the *Imvo* when the elections were over, and warned Jabavu and Abdurahman that the time had now come for blacks to become 'Race leaders', instead of subordinating their activities and interests to extreme loyalty towards white political parties. He said it was now time to build up black organisations and to put black interests first. The party posturing in the recent elections had not done the black people any good. Blacks should work on a non-party basis in the same way as the Coloured and Native Delegation had acted in Britain the previous year. (129)

Soga's approach was shared by Dr Rubusana and Sol Plaatje. Even though he was more inclined to the old Progressive view, Rubusana declined to back the Unionists in the election because there were candidates from the other provinces who did not support the Cape franchise. He preferred to adopt an independent line, supporting individual candidates with proved records of support for African political rights. (130) Plaatje encouraged Africans to vote for the Unionists, but his support too was not unconditional and he derived a great deal of satisfaction from the fact that a number of 'anti-native' candidates of both parties were defeated. (131)

The Nationalists won the election comfortably, gaining 67 of the 121 seats in the new parliament. The Unionists gained 39 seats, the Labour Party four and Independent candidates eleven. (132)

In the frontier constituencies of the eastern Cape, where the African voters were mainly concentrated, there were straight fights between Nationalists and Unionists in only two, Queenstown and Griqualand East. In East London, Colonel Crewe of the Unionists stood successfully against an Independent. Candidates were returned unopposed in Tembuland, Albany, King William's Town, Port Elizabeth South-West, Port Elizabeth Central (all Unionist), Aliwal North (Nationalist). (133) In Queenstown, the Nationalist Thomas Searle, who had been actively supported by Jabavu, lost by 942 votes to 1156 to the Unionist Sir Bisset Berry. A bitter Jabavu complained that the Unionists had won by raising the racial (i.e. Afrikaner versus English) bogey. He said the final voting figures coincided almost exactly with the division of English voters on the one hand and Afrikaner and African voters on the other. (134) And indeed the coincidence was close. In East Griqualand, where blacks comprised 20 per cent of the vote, the Unionist J. G. King was elected by 877 votes to the 675 of C. E. Todd, who stood as an Independent Nationalist. (135)

## Dr Rubusana and the Cape Provincial Council

An event which raised as much interest as any of the contests in the election for the House of Assembly was the candidature of Dr Walter Benson Rubusana in the Tembuland constituency in the election for the Cape Provincial Council. This was the first time that an African had stood for a legislative position in South Africa.

The first inkling that Rubusana might stand in Tembuland came early in August, when Theophilus Schreiner, who was contesting the Assembly seat in the constituency, sent a telegram to his brother, W. P., asking him for his opinion on whether an African voter was legally entitled for nomination for the Provincial Council, and whether he thought such a step would be advisable. (136) W. P. Schreiner replied that he saw no reason why an African should not stand. (137)

Dr Rubusana's decision to contest the seat was part of the whole campaign after the return of the delegates from Britain to mobilise Africans effectively in the face of union. It was taken mainly to further the 'native interest' and not, as some people hostile to Rubusana suggested, (138) to promote selfish personal prestige. He tried to get other Africans to stand in at least one other frontier constituency as well.

After visiting the Stockenström district, Rubusana called on Jabavu in King William's Town early in August and suggested that he stand for the Provincial Council in the Fort Beaufort constituency. He said that a large meeting of Africans, coloured people and a few Afrikaners in Stockenström, which fell in the Fort Beaufort constituency, had come out in favour of Jabavu as a candidate. Jabavu informed him that he had not thought of standing in the elections and that he could not do so without a more definite assurance, so Rubusana wrote to the people involved and Jabavu was promptly contacted 'on behalf of the native voters of Stockenström' to stand. But after further communications and a trip to Fort Beaufort, where he found the idea of his candidature was 'generally applauded', Jabavu finally decided against standing. (139)

Nothing could have demonstrated Rubusana's care for the 'native interest' more than this episode. Here was a 'crusted old Progressive', to use Jabavu's words, (140) trying to get his old South African Party adversary to stand in a constituency against two white candidates, both of whom sympathised with the Unionists.

There was also talk that a third 'native representative'—Dr Ab-durahman—might stand in the Provincial Council elections. (141) Although Dr Abdurahman decided not to stand, this indicated some kind of plan, at least between Rubusana and Abdurahman, to get the leaders of the three major black groupings in the Cape on to the highest representative body open to them. At its annual conference, the APO even decided to test the 'European descent' clause in the constitution by putting up a candidate of mixed descent in the House of Assembly elections, (142) but in the event no APO candidate stood for the House of Assembly or the Provincial Council.

When the nomination court met on 19 August, Rubusana was proposed as a Tembuland candidate for the Provincial Council by two of his African supporters. His opponents in the election were T. G. H. Gray, who supported the Unionists, and W. J. Clarke, an Independent Nationalist. (143)

Rubusana outlined his reasons for standing for the Provincial Council and his policy in a long speech after his nomination. He said he was aware that it was 'quite a novelty' for an African to stand for parliament in South Africa, and some might think him fit for a lunatic asylum for having done so, but he had considered this matter carefully and he appealed to those present as 'Britishers' to fight the campaign fairly, preserve good feeling and desist from mud-slinging.

He said that the open door policy at provincial council level in the Cape could not have been intended for whites only. Every voter could, and was expected, to participate. The country was not inhabited by white people only; the interests of Africans and whites were indivisible and 'they were all here to live together'. He said there was no reason why his candidature should raise hostile feelings and increase colour prejudice as some people had suggested. His answer to those who questioned the wisdom of Africans standing for parliament at that juncture was, 'If the native people waited five or ten years, would the colour question in the meantime have died a natural death?' He did not think so. The amicable co-operation between the Maoris and Europeans in the New Zealand parliament had shown that there was no need for race friction in the matter.

He appealed to the electors to throw the prejudices of the country aside: 'Let the people work hand in hand. The native recognised the superiority of the race of the white man, and all he asked for was equal opportunity and the open door.' He pledged that if he were returned he would work for all his constituents regardless of race, colour or creed and said a man would be lacking in his duty if he went to parliament to represent one section of the constituency only. His programme, however, shows that his main aim was to take up the cudgels of the African cause in the new institutions of state. He said he was confident that he would be able 'to throw some light on the vexed native question' in the Provincial Council and his list of priorities was African-orientated.

The first point in his programme was the readjustment of taxation, 'so that the burden might not fall so heavily on the poor but on the rich who were able to afford it'. He favoured changes in the educational system: free elementary education for those who could not afford it, the extension of the principle of compulsory education to African schools, mother-tongue instruction in the lower classes and the introduction of hygiene, agriculture and handicrafts in the schools to improve the quality and productivity of African life. He wanted to see public institutions such as hospitals managed by 'representative Boards' drawn from all sections of the community. He favoured the training of African nurses to look after their own people. On the local level, he wished to see municipalities vested with powers to sell or let sites to Africans in the vicinity of the towns instead of forcing respectable and industrious people to live in overcrowded townships under unfavourable conditions. He wanted the government to take over from municipalities in policing these townships.

Returning to more general matters, he said more roads, bridges and railway services should be provided to increase the productivity and accessibility of the region. The Transkei was poorly served in this regard and, if elected, he would be ever ready to make representations. Before ending his statement, he once again affirmed his faith in the Cape franchise, called for adequate remuneration for onerous tasks of headmanship, supported existing liquor restrictions for Africans, and spoke in favour of the more beneficial use of land 'locked up' by speculators, the appointment of government agricultural experts to go out and instruct the African people and a solution to the African labour question which would not be beneficial to the mines alone but to the Africans as well.

This was a typical election speech, full of promises and lofty intentions, but it also reflects very well Rubusana's determination to promote African interests and his confidence that the Provincial Council would provide an effective vehicle for him to do so. His decision to stand as an Independent also showed that he did not intend subjecting himself to party constraints in this matter.

The nomination of Dr Rubusana as a candidate in the election caused a stir. The local *Territorial News* newspaper described it as a 'political bombshell' that had created a 'demoralising and humiliating situation' for the constituency. (145) To prevent Rubusana from being elected, Gray proposed to the other white candidate, Clarke, that they should hold a plebiscite of white voters to decide which one of them should retire, but this was rejected by Clarke. (146)

It was obvious that Rubusana would probably emerge as the winner if voting took place along racial lines. Blacks comprised 49,5 per cent of the total vote in Tembuland. Under the new delimitation the Elliot district had been excluded from the constituency and the Glen Grey division, (147) with its 504 African voters, had been incorporated into it. The number of black voters was 1 399 out of a total of 2 846 electors. There were only forty-eight more white than black voters. The black voters were subdivided into 898 'Kafirs', 396 Mfengu, 103 other (people of mixed descent) and 2 'Hottentots'. (148)

The *Territorial News* now tried to divide the black voters. It warned blacks that Rubusana's election would lead to the closing of the 'open door' and declared that they had an absolute duty to themselves and the rest of the black voters in the Cape to prevent this from happening. (149) The pro-Unionist *Daily Dispatch*, the largest newspaper in the eastern Cape, pursued a similar line. (150) Neither did Rubusana get help from Jabavu, whose *Imvo* was the only African newspaper in the region.

The *Imvo* did not report Rubusana's candidature until early September, and then Jabavu used the editorials on the issue to take a swipe at the Unionist press for criticising an 'old devotee of the Prog cult' for standing, as well as implicitly to hit at Rubusana himself. (151) It said that Rubusana should not have sprung his nomination on the constituency, thereby 'forcing them to vote in panic'. The voters should have been given time to weigh up the issue. What had also been conspicuously absent was a strong call from the Tembuland electorate for him to stand. (152) It suggested that the attitude of the black voters in Tembuland towards Rubusana should be 'to criticise his case as if he were no black, for if they give him any advantage over the other candidates because of his colour then they run the risk of being classed with those who insist on the colour bar against them. . . . Let voters consider his qualifications and qualities apart from colour.' It made no attempt to list any positive qualifications and qualities that Rubusana might have had. (153) While this was a sound non-racial argument, the *Imvo*'s whole attitude to the matter lacked form, particularly in view of the fact that Rubusana had only recently tried to help Jabavu get a seat as well. And even though Jabavu had finally decided not to stand, he had at first been genuinely interested in the prospect of doing so.

Dr Abdurahman's APO newspaper did not share the *Imvo*'s reservations about supporting Rubusana. It commented that Rubusana would doubtless get the unanimous support of every African and coloured voter, and the six APO branches in the Tembuland constituency gave Rubusana their full support. (154) It is unclear whether or not the African voters took any premeditated decision to support Rubusana as a group. The *Territorial News* reported that a congress of African voters from several districts was held in Cala early in September to discuss the coming election but no details had come to hand. (155)

Dr Rubusana was duly elected as the MPC in the Tembuland seat. He gained 766 (42 per cent) of the 1 766 votes cast, beating Gray into second place by only 25 votes. William Clarke gained 235 votes. There were 24 spoilt papers. (56)

Rubusana was the only candidate present when the election returns were announced. In a short speech, he thanked the electors for having put him at the head of the poll. He said the policy of the constituency was clearly not the policy of the *Daily Dispatch* or the *Territorial News*. He promised to do his best for Tembuland. (157)

The *Ilanga lase Natal* greeted Dr Rubusana's victory in true African fashion by placing in the Zulu columns a poem lauding his achievement. (158) The *Ilanga* also published a long profile of Dr Rubusana. It said his election was 'a happy sign to the fatherland and one which should calm many a troubled breast, proving as it does that white men can and will recognise ability in a black man'. Further, it had given hope to those who envisaged a great South Africa in which 'the white man and the black man, though different, shall both work, respect and help one another'. (159)

The *Tsala ea Becoana* and the APO newspaper also responded with delight. The latter said that every coloured man in South Africa would watch with pride and interest Rubusana's career; there were MPCs who would look askance at Dr Rubusana, but he had nothing to fear as he was infinitely superior in intellectual capacity, educational qualifications, eloquence, common sense and manners to many of them. Dr Rubusana used the *A.P.O.* to publish a letter of thanks to his 'numerous friends' in Britain and South Africa who had sent him cables and letters of congratulation. (161)

The *A.P.O.* also took Jabavu to task for not supporting Rubusana's candidature and trying to 'damn his cause by faint praise'. (162) Even after Rubusana's victory, the *Imvo* maintained a lukewarm attitude. While offering its congratulations, the newspaper said Rubusana had the South African Party to thank for not taking issue with him. Rubusana was now between the 'Devil and the Deep Blue Sea'. The South African Party 'if they know him at all', would regard him as an 'old and implacable enemy' and the Progressives had shown they did not want him. Would he continue to lick the boot that kicked him? Nevertheless, the *Imvo* conceded, Rubusana 'has put himself and the natives in with his *coup d'état*', but then again, 'his success is perhaps preferable to his failure' because now some unsophisticated people, who would have thought they had been saved from some dire disaster if he had failed, would be able to see that he was not the cannibal they feared. (163)

Another sour response to Rubusana's victory came from his former close political ally, A. K. Soga. They had split because of Dr Rubusana's 'self-appointment' as a delegate to Britain the previous year. Soga said this alleged unilateral action was something he would always protest against. He now accused Rubusana of disloyalty to the South African Native Congress and of promoting his own self-interest by 'running in advance of his race'. Soga declared that it had been a blunder for Rubusana to stand in the first place. If he had failed it would have been a 'disgrace' for Africans and next time around the whites would make sure he did not repeat his victory. (164)

There is no doubt, however, that Dr Rubusana's win in the Tembuland election came as a powerful psychological boost for Africans. He also immediately began to make use of his newly-earned privilege of unlimited first-class rail travel and a handsome salary. (165) He had no sooner returned to East London than he travelled to Natal where he met, amongst others, Charles Dube, the acting editor of the *Ilanga lase Natal* in the continued absence of his brother overseas. (166) Indeed, since his return from Britain with the Coloured and Native Delegation in September 1909, Rubusana had in more ways than one covered much ground.

### The 'Native Senators'

All that remained to complete the composition of the South African parliament after the general election was the announcement of the names of the eight senators nominated by the Cabinet. Thirty-two members of the Senate of forty had already been chosen by the colonial parliaments in their final sessions. Four of the nominated senators (the 'native senators') were to be chosen 'on the ground mainly of their thorough acquaintance . . . with the reasonable wants and wishes of the coloured races of South Africa'. (167) In the hope of influencing the nominations, several black interest groups put forward the names of people they considered would best represent black interests to the government.

The ball was set rolling by the South African Native Convention. At its annual congress in March, the SANC decided to ask the authorities to appoint Sir Bisset Berry (Cape), Dewdney Drew (Orange Free State), William Hosken (Transvaal) and Sir David Hunter (Natal). In forwarding these names to the Colonial Office in London, Rubusana said that these men had shown themselves to be consistent friends of the African people. (168) The APO annual congress held a few days later in Port Elizabeth ratified the SANC's decision. (169) The two bodies were clearly co-operating in this matter. The SANC and APO delegates had already discussed with Lord Selborne their preferences for the senatorships in an interview on their return from Britain, (170) Dr Rubusana had attended the APO conference (171) and, shortly after the arrival of the Governor-General in May, Dr Rubusana requested an interview between him and a joint SANC/APO deputation to discuss the senate appointments. (172)

When it became known that W. P. Schreiner had decided not to seek a seat in the House of Assembly, the two bodies immediately substituted his name for that of Sir Bisset Berry on their list of favoured candidates. (173) Instead of making himself available for the Assembly, or for a place on the bench, (174) Schreiner had decided his services would be more useful in the Senate where he would speak for all blacks, enfranchised and unenfranchised, and thus have for his constituency not merely the Cape Province but the whole of the Union. (175) Having announced his wish to be considered a senator, Schreiner was an obvious favourite with the black people. The APO newspaper declared that it would be a national calamity if 'our W. P.' were not nominated (176) and the *Imvo* echoed these views. (177)

In a joint representation to the Governor-General, the Orange Free State Native Congress and the Bloemfontein branch of the APO supported the decisions of the national bodies to request the appointment of Dewdney Drew to represent blacks in the province. (178) However, Drew's nomination did not meet with the approval of all parts of the OFSNC. Henry Poho of the Winburg Native Vigilance Society claimed that the delegates from all the areas outside Bloemfontein at the OFSNC annual congress at Winburg on 16 February had disagreed with Mapikela and the Bloemfontein people about their suggestion that Drew should be the choice of the Congress, and that Drew's case had been forced through with the help of delegates from the other colonies at the SANC meeting in March. Poho said nine of the ten districts represented at the OFSNC conference, all in the northern Orange Free State, wished to see A. M. Baumann of Winburg appointed. (179)

Here was a clear clash of local versus national interests. While people like Rubusana and Mapikela probably realised that Drew with his experience as a newspaper editor and parliamentarian stood a far greater chance of being elected as a senator than the unknown Baumann, the local groups were insistent about proposing a local man who would help Africans in the northern districts of the province in the 'great difficulties' they were experiencing.

There were also other representations in which a national perspective on the matter was subordinated to local preferences which had little chance of success. A meeting of the Africans in the Kamastone and Oxkraal reserve in the Queenstown district recommended to the Governor-General H. J. Greeff, a farmer on an adjoining farm who had twice failed in elections for the Cape parliament, (180) and the coloured people in Campbell in Griqualand West proposed a local man, H. J. le Riche, who was the chief inspector of sheep in the region. (181)

However, the virtually identical petitions of the Griqualand West branch of the APO, the African chiefs and headmen of British Bechuanaland and the chiefs and councillors of the Batlapin in the Taungs Reserve for a senator to represent the blacks in the northern Cape were a somewhat different matter. There were approximately 144 000 blacks in the northern Cape and, as the petitioners pointed out, they had no representative among the eight senators already elected by the Cape parliament. Accordingly they recommended J. D. Duncan of Kimberley. (182) In addition

to the four people nominated by the SANC, the Transvaal Native
Organisation drew up a long list of preferred candidates, which
included William Windham, Howard Pim, Vere Stent, W. A. King,
E. H. Schlaeffi, E. Creux, J. S. Marwick and Melt Marais (Trans-
vaal), Colonel Stanford and Sir Bisset Berry (Cape), Colonel
Royston (Natal), ex-President Steyn (Orange Free State) and H.
C. Sloley (Basutoland). (183)

John Tengo Jabavu's group, now calling itself the Cape Native
Vigilance Association, asked the Governor-General-in-Council to
consider the merits of W. P. Schreiner, Colonel Stanford, William
Hay (an ex-Cape parliamentarian and editor of the *Cape Mercury*)
and William Hosken. (184) Later Jabavu requested that Hosken's
name be replaced by that of Thomas Searle, the defeated Nationalist candidate in the general election in the Queenstown constituency. (185)

The names of the eight nominated senators were announced on
13 October. The four chosen to represent black interests were W.
P. Schreiner, Colonel Walter Stanford, J. C. Krogh and F. R.
Moor. (186) The choice of Schreiner was universally approved by
blacks. (187) Dinizulu spoke for many Africans when he told
Schreiner, 'All my trust is in you. ... May the Lord keep you
and give you power fearlessly to advocate the just and equitable
treatment of the Natives of South Africa.' (188)

Although some sections of the black political élite had reservations about Stanford's suitability, (189) his appointment was
generally popular. (190) Those of Krogh, a resident magistrate
and Native Commissioner in Nylstroom in the Transvaal, who
had been a member of the South African Native Affairs Commission in 1903–1905, and Moor, Natal's last Prime Minister and
Minister of Native Affairs, who had been defeated in the recent
general election, were a different matter. The reaction of blacks
to their appointments was unfavourable. Neither of them had
been recommended in any of the representations made by black
interest groups to the Governor-General or mentioned as suitable
candidates in the black press.

Moor's appointment, particularly, came in for tremendous criticism. The APO newspaper described it as a scandalous party job
and added, 'He has been a hopeless failure in politics, is discredited and rejected by the whole white people of Natal, and distrus-
ted and detested by the Natives of South Africa. ... Of course,
anything that is rejected by Europeans is good enough for the
blacks; so we shall have to put up with Senator Moor.' (191) The

*Imvo Zabantsundu* reacted in a similar way. It commented that no one seemed more out of sympathy with African aspirations than Moor. How he would represent African interests was a mystery. (192) Newspapers such as the *Bloemfontein Post* and the *Natal Mercury* also described Moor's appointment as unacceptable both to Africans and to whites. (193)

But 'our W. P.' was in the Senate and Africans had no doubts that he would do his best to protect their interests. Moreover, two other men who had been suggested by Africans, William Hosken (Transvaal) and Marshall Campbell (Natal), were in the Senate as ordinary members.

With the appointment of the nominated senators in mid-October the composition of the Legislature was finalised. South Africa now had its own national Executive, Legislature and Judiciary. South African Union had finally been consummated.

# 11  African union

Union did not bring the 'fresh start' that politicised Africans had hoped for. The northern colonies predominated in the new state: it was essentially their interests and traditions rather than those of the Cape that prevailed. In the white political arena, a vigorous segregationist movement developed around the key figure of J. B. M. Hertzog, calling for a South African 'native policy' based on former republican policies, and during the first year or so of the Union, parliament passed several discriminatory statutes which indicated a shift in this direction. Statutes promulgated during 1911 included the Native Labour Regulation Act, which made breaches of labour contracts by Africans a criminal offence; the Mines and Works Act which had the effect of restricting certain skilled jobs in the mining and engineering fields to whites; the Defence Act, which established a European permanent force and citizen force; and the Dutch Reformed Church Act, which excluded black members of that church in the Cape from becoming members in the Transvaal and Orange Free State. (1)

In the same year, as a consequence of parliamentary select committee investigations and lively public discussions on the crucial issues of land and labour, the Native Settlement and Squatters Registration Bill was introduced. This aimed to increase the availability of labour on white farms by placing onerous taxes on semi-independent African squatters on farms, while entirely exempting farm labourers in fixed employment from taxation. In addition, a clause in the Bill debarred African syndicates from buying land. (2)

Africans in the Civil Service also found themselves affected by the segregationist movement. Increasingly African interpreters were replaced by whites, and in some areas African workers on the railways were retrenched to provide job opportunities for poor whites. (3) These measures were all motivated by the broad principles of restricting social integration, ensuring an adequate supply of disciplined and inexpensive black labour for white enterprise, and hampering African access to skills, organisation and land. All were resented by the African public.

Thus it was that African political leaders intensified their efforts to ensure an effective African voice in the new state. Denied full political representation, they tried to compensate by consolidating political organisation on a local and national level; by establishing more newspapers to express African opinion more forcefully; by forming economic, social and religious bodies to promote the general advancement of the African people; by enlisting the support of sympathetic white groups and individuals; and by using all constitutional channels open to Africans, including petitioning and lobbying local authorities, the Native Affairs Department, the 'native senators' and the government. In the Cape, African voters could also still use their electoral influence to exert pressure on the members of the Provincial Council and parliament. The number of Africans on the voters roll at the time of the last Cape general election in 1907 was 8 418. The total rose to 14 282 in 1921. (4)

Represented in the Senate and the Cape Provincial Council by the 'native senators' and Dr Rubusana respectively, many Africans had at first hoped that these bodies could be used as effective instruments to voice African interests. However, the so-called native problem was not to be resolved in the Senate or Provincial Councils, but in the House of Assembly, where effective power lay and from which blacks were barred. W. P. Schreiner had accepted nomination as a senator in optimistic mood, declaring that his constituency was now the black people of the whole of the Union, not merely the enfranchised voters in the Cape. One parliamentary session was enough to disillusion him. At the end of it he foresaw that the Senate, which had in essence acted as a rubber stamp for the House of Assembly, would become a 'useless body unless it carries out its proper function of deliberation'. (5)

Rubusana was faced with similar constraints in the Provincial Council, where the focus was more on provincial and local, non-political matters. The brief minutes of his first session, which started towards the end of January 1911, show that he occupied himself with such matters as telegraph communications in his constituency, relief for a sick ex-serviceman, the creation of a bridge across the Bashee River, East Coast fever, the stoppage of ox transport from Umtata, teachers' salaries and colour distinctions in new regulations for examinations for teachers' certificates. (6) Only one or two of these issues related specifically to the protection of African interests. Nevertheless, despite the limitations of the institutions in which they served, both Rubusana and Schreiner (and to a less conspicuous extent the other three 'native senators') were able to use their offices to promote African interests generally. They had access to the authorities. They could act as channels between Africans and the government. They were able to use their positions to highlight and articulate African concerns. And they could exert pressure on behalf of Africans. (7)

### Attempts to consolidate African political unity

In the absence of direct political representation in the new Union, African leaders saw that a strong national organisation to represent African opinion and open up channels of communication with the government was urgently required. The people at the head of the South African Native Convention continued with their attempts to consolidate the SANC into an effective, representative organisation in the post-Union period. In moves designed to make its presence felt, the SANC wrote to Prime Minister Botha urging him to govern in a way which would satisfy all the inhabitants of the country regardless of colour, class and creed; it attempted to influence the appointment of the 'native senators'; it forwarded the resolutions of the annual conference in March 1910 to the government when the South African parliament assembled for the first time in October; (8) it placed notices in newspapers to publicise its existence; (9) its office bearers wrote to the press in support of African interests; (10) and it arranged for its third annual meeting in Johannsburg on 5 May 1911. (11)

The proceedings of the 1911 SANC meeting were not reported in the press, a comment in itself on the struggling nature of the aspirant national movement. However, contemporary newspaper sources show that its affiliated branches at this time were the Transvaal Native Union, the Orange Free State Native Congress and the Natal Native Congress. (12) Dr Rubusana remained its president, but at least one new face, that of Cleophas Kunene (Secretary), appeared on the executive. (13) Another newcomer to the scene was Pixley Ka Isaka Seme, who had recently returned to the country after completing his legal studies in Britain. He appears directly to have assumed a leadership role. A few weeks after the annual meeting, a meeting of the SANC executive was held in Seme's office in Johannesburg (14) and reports of another meeting described the presence of 'Mr Attorney Seme, B.A., Transvaal, S.A.N. Convention (Johannesburg)'. (15) Seme's entry to the political arena was to have far-reaching consequences.

It is clear that by the middle of the 1911 ambitious new plans, inspired by Seme, were afoot to strengthen the national movement so that it could function more effectively than before. An important part of these plans was that the organisation should accommodate not only the educated élite, but also the traditional leaders with their mass followings, their symbolic importance— and their financial sufficiency. The primary business at the SANC executive meeting in Seme's office on 17 June was 'to draw out the Constitution of the South African Native Convention'. The other business was to consider the 'resolution passed at the last session of the Convention', and to hear the government's reply to the resolutions submitted the previous year. (16)

In the next development a second meeting of the SANC executive was held on 7 August. (17) There Seme tabled a draft constitution, which was most likely the outcome of the discussions at the June meeting. The proposed constitution had a preamble and three articles dealing with membership, office bearers and meetings of the 'Congress'. The preamble emphasised the need for a federation of existing organisations so that 'a well digested and accepted native opinion should be easily ascertainable by the government with respect to the great native problem in its various ramifications'. (18) The meeting resolved that the constitution should be printed and referred to the SANC branches for scrutiny before the next annual meeting.

The meeting was attended by representatives of all the affiliated areas. The Orange Free State Native Congress was represented by its President and Secretary, John Mocher and Thomas Mtobi Mapikela. Their counterparts in the Transvaal Native Union, William Letseleba and J. Mopela, were also present. Pixley Ka Isaka Seme and Cleophas Kunene, both Johannesburg-based Zulus, represented Natal. From British Bechuanaland were S. J. Molema (on behalf of Paramount Chief Lekoko) and Chief Silas Molema. Local leaders included Z. J. Makgothi (Winburg), J. T. Moloi (Harrismith), J. S. Noah (Krugersdorp), Thomas Fakazi (Johannesburg), J. K. Sephaphathi (Randfontein) and S. Gompo (Nancefield). In addition to the official delegates, H. R. Ngcayiya, L. T. Mvabaza (editor of the *Umlomo wa Bantu* newspaper), J. G. Mahlamvu, William Wauchope and several others attended. They were allowed to participate in the discussions, but not to vote. Letters of support were read from Sol Plaatje and Chief Mamogale and nine other South African chiefs. (19)

The meeting discussed the launching of a newspaper to serve as an organ for the national organisation. In reply to a question by the editor of the *Umlomo wa Bantu* whether yet another newspaper would not lead to the closure of existing ones, the delegates replied that additional newspapers would rather heighten political awareness and lead to greater enlightenment. The executive also appointed an unnamed arbitrator to try to resolve a dispute which had arisen between the Transvaal Native Union and the Transvaal Native Organisation under S. M. Makgatho. Both the TNU (January 1909) and the TNO (May 1910) had been formed with the aim of uniting the various bodies that existed in the Transvaal, but organisational unity had still to be realised. The meeting ended with the executive entrusting the SANC President, Dr Rubusana, with the task of calling the next meeting, preferably sometime in November. (20) The delegates then returned home to report back to their members. (21)

Seme's next move was to send a circular to African leaders, societies and newspapers outlining the need for unity and for a South African Native Congress to put this into effect. (22) He stated that 'Native Union' under a South African Native Congress was essential. Co-operation was the key and watchword which opened the door to progress and national success. The aim of the Congress would be to get

... all the dark races of this subcontinent to come together, once or twice a year, in order to review the past and reject therein all those things which have retarded our progress, the things that poision our national life and virtue; to label and distinguish the sins of civilisation, and as members of one household to talk and think loudly on our home problems and the solution of them.

Such national conferences would provide Africans with an effective platform to publicise their views on matters that affected them, enable the 'native senators' to remain in close touch with the people whose interests they were supposed to represent, provide a direct and independent channel of information to the government itself, and make it easier for the government to have a uniform 'native policy' for the whole of South Africa. Only through such a Congress could Africans influence public opinion and the legislative process.

Seme said that the Congress should be convened as a matter of urgency. He therefore appealed to African leaders to cast aside personal differences and selfishness:

The demon of racialism, the aberrations of the Xhosa-Fingo feud, the animosity that exists between the Zulus and the Tongaas, between Basothos and every native, must be buried up and forgotten; it has shed among us sufficient blood. We are one people. These divisions, these jealousies are the cause of all our woes and all our backwardness and ignorance today.

He claimed that the organising Executive Committee, 'which is simply a committee elected by a part of the people', had been greatly encouraged by the support it had received throughout the country. He said the movement was known and 'in a great measure openly supported by nearly all leaders and greater chiefs of at least three colonies and all the protectorates'. He called on African leaders, societies and editors to explain the news to the people at large so that they could arrange to send delegates to the first meeting of the Congress, scheduled for December. The circular ended with a programme for the proposed meeting.

A caucus was held in Johannesburg on 13 November to set a date for the first Congress meeting, and to consider once again the draft constitution Seme had presented to the committee in August, before it in turn was sent out for consideration to the various organisations so that they could discuss it at the Congress meeting. (23) Because it was convened at short notice, the caucus was attended mainly by delegates from the Transvaal, but several other organisations and leaders had sent in letters of support. Amongst those present were Seme, S. M. Makgatho, Sol Plaatje, J. H. Mahlamvu, Edward Tsewu, H. R. Ngcayiya, D. D. Tyakwadi and Chief Maama Letsie and other supporters from Basutoland. (24) The caucus decided to summon the South African Native Congress to meet in Bloemfontein on 8 January 1912, a month later than originally planned. It then approved a programme for the meeting which was sent out to interested parties and publicised in the African press, together with the draft constitution. (25) It is clear that by now Seme and his colleagues had decided that in expanding the functions and structure of the national organisation they should drop the title of the South African Native Convention and form a new organisation altogether. This course of action was probably motivated by the need to make a fresh start and the desire to involve interest groups, such as the Jabavu camp in the eastern Cape, who had withheld their support from the Convention.

In order to iron out existing differences in the Transvaal, it was also decided at the caucus that the organisations in that province should hold a meeting early in December to confer on common policy towards the forthcoming national congress. A committee was appointed to prepare a report in this regard. The committee was composed of Seme (convener), the Revds Tsewu, Ngcayiya, Tyakwadi and Nochula and Messrs Makgatho, Mvabaza, Makhothe, Kawa, Letseleba and Sokopo. (26) All the bodies in the Transvaal were represented. The province would now be able to speak with one voice. As the change of venue of SANC meetings to Johannesburg and the initiatives for the new organisation demonstrated, the Transvaal had become the driving force behind the African national movement. The programme for the impending congress also reflected this. The three British-trained laywers—Seme, Mangena and Montsioa—who were to introduce the resolutions to constitute the new organisation, and seven of the eleven people assigned to lead the various discussion topics, were based in the Transvaal.

One vital area where Seme and his colleagues lacked support for their nationalist plans was in the eastern Cape. The enfranchised group there still saw their future salvation in terms of participation in the Cape electoral system rather than in involvement in an African national movement removed from the (white) mainstream of political life. Even Dr Rubusana, the one notable link between the eastern Cape and the rest of the country in the two years since the first moves towards national unity, was not actively involved in the initiatives. Scarcely a fortnight after presiding at the annual meeting of the SANC early in May, Rubusana accompanied Paramount Chief Dalindyebo of the Thembus on a three-month trip to Europe. (27) Dalindyebo had been advised to go to Europe for medical reasons. He also wished to attend the coronation of King Edward VII. Rubusana was thus absent from the domestic political arena at an important stage. According to Seme, he was nevertheless 'in complete sympathy' with the movement (28) and he subsequently attended the Bloemfontein congress.

While abroad, Rubusana and Dalindyebo also attended the Universal Races Congress in London, along with John Tengo Jabavu, his son D. D. T., who was studying in London at the time, Palmer Mgwetyana, W. P. Schreiner and a number of other white South Africans. (29) Held at the end of July, the Congress was the culmination of five years of planning. Its objective was to encourage international understanding and co-operation, particularly among the so-called white and so-called black nations. Close on one thousand people attended. Among those represented were a large

# Index